D1548184

Decades of Doubt: The John McCabe Murder Saga

This book is inspired by a CBS *48 Hours* Murder Mystery

by Eric Wilson

with John Turner

WALDORF PUBLISHING

Published by Waldorf Publishing
2140 Hall Johnson Road
#102-345
Grapevine, Texas 76051
www.WaldorfPublishing.com

Decades of Doubt: The John McCabe Murder Saga

ISBN: 978-1-94327-536-6
Library of Congress Control Number: 2015957004

This book is inspired by a CBS *48 Hours* Murder Mystery.
Book Cover Photo Credit: Stacy Davis

Printed in Canada

Preface

Fact: sometime between 11:00 p.m. on September 26 and the early morning hours of September 27, 1969, John McCabe was murdered.

Fact: John Joseph McCabe was a fifteen-year-old high school freshman in Tewksbury, Mass., who attended a dance at the Knights of Columbus in Tewksbury on September 26, and multiple witnesses remember him leaving the dance at about 11:00 p.m. John's body was found in a field in the nearby town of Lowell the next morning.

But the *facts* about how John McCabe ended up in that field, and the *facts* about who put him there, have not been proven, and may never be.

Like old-school Southern lawyers are apt to say, this case has more twists and turns than a snake in a hurry. Following the 1969 murder, multiple police agencies launched a massive investigation, interviewing scores of Lowell and Tewksbury residents. Over the next two years, despite the authorities' numerous leads—many with bizarre connections—the case produced no solid suspects, and the investigators had little forensic evidence with which to work. Then two years stretched into three, then five…and finally into four decades. It wasn't until Lowell Detective Linda Coughlin took over the investigation in January 2011 that the cold case began to thaw.

And within weeks, the investigation turned white-hot. Sometime during their four-decade probe, authorities had learned that three local teens, Walter Shelley, Michael Ferreira, and Edward Allen Brown, had allegedly picked John up shortly after the dance as he was hitchhiking home. Coughlin chose to zero in on that evidence, even though indications also pointed elsewhere. When Coughlin repeatedly questioned Brown in March 2011, he finally admitted, after being fed information, to being present that night. He, Shelley, and Ferreira had taken John to the vacant field, he said, then roughed him up, bound him with rope, and put tape over his eyes and mouth—*allegedly* because Shelley suspected that John had been flirting with his girlfriend. According to Brown, the three left him there, and when they returned to the field a short while later, John was dead.

In exchange for a reduced sentence—one that included no jail time—Edward Allen Brown became the prosecution's key witness in the subsequent trials of Ferreira and Shelley. But in numerous rounds of questioning, and later at trial, Brown gave conflicting accounts, telling as many as six varying versions of what should have been the same story.

What follows is an account of the entire ordeal, from the 1969 murder, to an investigation that lasted forty-three years, and finally to the complexities of two murder trials. But even though the final verdicts of those trials have been rendered, questions remain: was Ed Brown telling the truth, or did he, in fear and desperation, simply tell the police what they wanted to hear? Were any of the three teens involved, or was the murder committed by someone else entirely?

The most important question of all: Who *really* killed John McCabe?

Table of Contents

Part Three: The Mike Ferreira Trial

Part One:

1969-2002

1. Friday, September 26, 1969

In the fall of that year, Tewksbury, Mass., was enjoying the remnants of some warm summer weather, and preparing to button itself up ahead of another harsh New England winter. PTA meetings and Pop Warner football were in full swing. The town of about 22,000, located about twenty miles northwest of Boston, enjoyed its stereotypical small-town pace, and seemed to be a place where a teenager could safely wriggle his or her way into adulthood.

Each Friday, those teenagers would descend upon the Tewksbury Knights of Columbus Hall on Main Street to shake what their mama gave 'em, and dance to hits like "Sugar Sugar," the Stones' "Honky Tonk Women," and R&B hits by the Isley Brothers and Aretha Franklin. And on September 26, fifteen-year-old John McCabe attended his second such shindig. A freshman at Tewksbury High School, John was an auburn-haired, freckle-faced busybody who, like other boys his age, liked riding his bike and getting his hands dirty.

John, along with his sisters Debbie and Roberta, seventeen and six at the time, lived with their parents Bill and Evelyn on Pocahontas Road. The house was in a subdivision off Chandler Street, and a little less than three miles from the K of C—an easy distance for John to cover (especially if he was lucky enough to be picked up while thumbing a ride).

That Friday, John showered, dressed himself in his favorite ensemble of a red shirt, green pants, and a corduroy jacket, then headed to the kitchen, where his mother gave him her blessing. Just as he was leaving, she reminded him to wear his belt (as he sometimes forgot to do so), and John assured her that he had one on—though she recalled later that he never actually showed it to her.

Not long after he started up Chandler Street, his thumb cocked out, John actually *did* score a ride. Nancy Williams, an older teen, stopped to pick him up as John was passing the Catholic church's novitiate; in the car with Nancy was her friend, an older boy named Mike Ferreira, and Nancy's sister Sandy in the back seat. Nancy told John that they were headed to Sandy's house in Lowell, so they wouldn't be going in the direction of the K of C, but they could give him a ride up to the corner of Chandler and Main.

Apparently, after the trio dropped him off John either thumbed another ride or walked the rest of the way to the dance, because multiple witnesses testified at trial that he was in fact there. One such witness was Carol Ann (McFrederies) Roberts, who was fourteen in 1969. During her testimony, she explained that she and John danced together often that night—John had a crush on her, she speculated—and after the shindig was over, her father drove her home.

Little did she know at the time, but that was the last time Carol Ann would see John alive.

2. Saturday, September 27

Six miles away as the crow flies, in Lowell—known amongst locals as "The Gritty City"—two young boys were walking through a rocky, brush-filled lot off Maple Street at 8:30 a.m., on their way to a nearby swamp where they hoped to catch some frogs. After passing through the long shadow of the railroad tower that stood just north of the lot, they rounded a thick bramble of bushes...and about thirty feet away, on the slope of a shallow mound of dirt, was a teen boy lying on his stomach. As they approached him, they could see rope around his ankles, and his wrists were tied behind his back. Another piece of rope was loosely knotted around his neck, and his skin was an odd purplish color. They glanced at each other, fearing the worst. Nine-year-old Bobby, the elder of the two, tentatively called to him in a near-whisper.

"Hey." No response, no movement. "Hey! You okay?"

"Is he...? Go see if he's all right," said Dennis, two years younger. His eyes were saucer-wide.

Bobby crept toward the prone boy—though it was only a few feet, it seemed like crossing a football field—and stopped a foot away. Closer now, he could see adhesive tape covering the boy's eyes and mouth, and the edges of a green corduroy jacket that was under him. "Hey!" he said again, almost yelling. Still nothing. He reached out with his right foot and prodded the boy's rib cage with his toe. "Hey!" The body moved, but only a little; instead of a malleable give, the entire body shifted an inch or so, as if it were a department store mannequin.

Glancing back at Dennis, his own eyes saucer-wide, Bobby knelt and touched the boy's hand, which was tight against his back. Cold department-store-mannequin plastic.

"Uh…" Bobby involuntarily murmured. He stood and stumbled backwards. "He's…he…c'mon, we gotta find somebody!" He grabbed Dennis's arm, and the two sprinted toward Maple Street. Dennis, who was only seven, began wailing as they ran.

* * * *

An hour later, the field was crawling with cops. The boys had run to Bobby's house a block away, on Lincoln Street, and when they told his mother what they'd seen, she dashed next door to a neighbor's to call the police. As she was doing so, she spotted three Lowell PD officers in a cruiser up at the corner of Lincoln and Gorham Streets, and flagged them down in a panic. She had the two boys repeat their story to the officers, who put the boys in their cruiser and drove over to the field.

The cruiser stopped at the edge of the clearing, and as they'd been trained to do, the men sent only one officer— the senior one, Lieutenant Broderick—up the path to investigate. The lieutenant, treading lightly so as not to disturb any evidence like footprints or tire tracks, reached the body, felt for a pulse, and found none. There was a white rope—about two feet long, Broderick calculated, maybe a little less—around the boy's neck, and Broderick used his thumb and forefinger to loosen it. Then he returned to the cruiser using the same path.

Broderick radioed his commander at the station, Captain McGuane, and gave an initial report, then returned to the body and covered it with a gray blanket. McGuane in turn radioed all available officers to report to the field off

Maple Street, then spent the next fifteen minutes on the phone with detectives from the Lowell Criminal Bureau and with the Massachusetts State Police. Within minutes, several detectives arrived and cordoned off the area surrounding the body, then dispatched officers to start a neighborhood canvass. While the detectives stood in a silent sentry, Dr. Karbowniczak, the medical examiner, lifted the blanket, and after a quick examination, declared the boy deceased. The unofficial cause of death: ligature strangulation.

An officer from the Tewksbury PD arrived with a photo of John J. McCabe, who'd gone missing the night before, and the ME quickly determined that the body was that of McCabe. Time of death, he speculated, was between 10 p.m. and midnight the previous evening. After the body was removed and placed in the hearse belonging to O'Donnell Funeral Home, where the autopsy would be performed, detectives began a thorough inspection of the lot. One keen-eyed detective, a Lieutenant Conlon, spotted a fresh set of tire tracks in the dirt along the path, and these were photographed for possible identification; other officers, meanwhile, collected trash and debris from the area, paying particular attention to an old concrete building foundation a few yards away from where the body had been discovered. A police dog arrived, along with several state troopers, and the search—both human and canine now, and led by Lieutenant Conlon and others from the Lowell Criminal Bureau—continued.

One of the younger Lowell detectives was tall, mustachioed Gerry St. Peter, who after being promoted to the criminal bureau the previous year, had just been told he would be the lead investigator—even though this was his first homicide case. Fresh from six months' training with the Massachusetts State Police at its Boston facility, St. Peter was already developing a reputation as a solid, dexterous investigator, with the ability to morph from an easy-going, fun-loving jokester to a hardened, forceful inquisitor in an instant. His breezy disposition served him well as a detective; behind the kind eyes his brain was constantly on the move.

St. Peter knew that railroad employees occupied the tower adjacent to the lot on a twenty-four-hour basis, so he walked over and spoke to the switch operator on duty. The employee, who'd been on duty since 7:00, said he'd seen nothing, and gave the detective the names of the two men who'd worked the previous shifts.

As he was walking back to the lot, St. Peter was approached by a young man—late teens or early twenties, the detective guessed—who identified himself as Barry Moran.

"Sir, I have some information you might wanna hear," Moran told him.

"All right," St. Peter said. He pulled the boy a few feet off the trail, away from the other cops and assorted personnel bustling through the area. "What is it?"

"Well…me and a coupla buddies were up by the switching station last night, we went up there to take a pi— uh, to relieve ourselves. And we saw a car in the field next to the dirt road, right about there." He pointed to an area adjacent to the gravel road leading from Maple Street to the railroad tower.

The detective's ears pricked. "A car, huh? Can you describe it? Like make or model, or what color it was?"

Moran glanced briefly to the right—a sign that he was remembering, and thus being truthful, St. Peter surmised, using the interrogation techniques that were by now second nature for him. "It was a Chevy, probably a '64 or '65. I think like…maroon? Some kinda dark purple color. Or maybe even black."

St. Peter scribbled in his notepad. "Okay…and what time was this, you think?"

Another brief glance to the right. "Maybe 11:00, 11:30? And…I think we saw someone sitting in the car, on the driver's side."

More scribbling. "Okay. Anything else, Barry?"

"Um…" Long downward look to the left. "No…I think that's it."

"You sure?"

"Um…yeah."

"Thanks for your help." The detective turned to go, mentally adding Barry Moran to his "persons of interest" list.

"Oh, wait." St. Peter faced him again. "On our way out, we passed by the car, and we saw the license plate. It was real quick, and we were pretty far away, but…it might have started with the letter P."

St. Peter added this to his notes. "Anything else?"

"No sir."

"Thank you." And Moran was gone.

Kid must have some kinda great vision, St. Peter thought as he ambled back over to the crime scene. *From the road to where he said the car was, gotta be…a hundred feet. At least. For him—for* any *of 'em—to see a license plate from that far? Hm.*

7

Back at the clearing, he got word that the initial canvass of the neighborhood was complete, and other than a dog barking at about 7:30 that morning, no one reported anything the least bit suspicious.

* * * *

At the McCabe residence on Pocahontas Road, Bill and Evelyn were practically frozen with fear. What had only been slight unease when John hadn't yet come home after the dance at 11:30 the previous night had elevated to true worry when Evelyn and Debbie jumped in the family car a little after midnight and drove along the route between their house and the K of C, searching for him. When they returned home—alone—Bill called the police. The Tewksbury PD had sent a cruiser by, and Bill and Officer Walter Jamieson prowled the streets in an ever-widening arc, hunting for John. Evelyn, with a normally nervy disposition, couldn't remain still as she sat in a chair by the front window, peeking through the curtains every thirty seconds looking for either John or Bill—or hopefully both!—to come walking up the driveway.

At 1:30, the cruiser dropped Bill off, and he alone shuffled up the walk beneath a misty rain. *God, I'm begging you…help me find my son,* Evelyn thought as her husband came through the door, slapping his hat against his leg to remove the light coating of raindrops.

"I need a photo of Johnny," Bill said in his thick New England accent. "Walt wants one so they know who they're looking for."

Evelyn grabbed John's 8x10 school photo off the hall wall, and Bill took it out to the cruiser. The couple then sat at the dining room table until 3, Bill staring grimly at nothing while he held Evelyn's hand, both of them glancing intermittently at the front door in hopes that John would suddenly open it. After forcing themselves to go to bed, they both tossed and turned until what had become panic drove them back to the kitchen table about 6. John still hadn't come home.

And now, at 11:00 a.m., panic instantly morphed into terror as they saw two police officers mounting the front steps. Evelyn sent six-year-old Roberta, who was playing listlessly with dolls on the floor, to her room.

"Go sit at the table," Bill commanded as he went to the door. He greeted the officers, and after a bit of hushed conversation, they walked to the door leading down to the basement. "Stay here," Bill added as he led the two men downstairs.

Evelyn knew from previous experience that she could hear everything that went on in the basement through the heater vent in the first-floor bathroom. She raced down the hall into the bathroom, then laid on the floor next to the toilet with her ear against the vent.

She couldn't hear the officers word for word, as they seemed to be talking rather softly, but what she did hear drifting up through the duct was enough: *Found…Maple Street…Lowell…rope…tape over…and mouth. Sorry to…is deceased.* She heard Bill whimper. *Funeral home in…the body.*

At the word *deceased*, a wave of nerve endings seemed to simultaneously electrify and numb Evelyn's entire body. Resting her head against the cool metal of the heating vent, she began sobbing. "I shouldn't've…I shouldn't've…" *Let him go* was the rest of the sentence her grief prevented her from uttering.

The next thing she heard were the men's footsteps ascending the stairs. She went out to meet them, and collapsed into Bill's arms. He gently pushed her away. "Going over to see Johnny," he said, holding her at arm's length. His face was stone, his eyes red-rimmed.

"Where? Take me with you! I need to see…I…oh, my Johnny…" Evelyn collapsed onto the couch, face buried in her hands.

"Stay…*here*," Bill instructed, then the three were out the door.

Evelyn jumped up and began pacing, her mind zooming in every direction. *Not possible. Not possible. He just…he went away. He did talk about New York City a lot. That's where he is. He* has *to be.* Each time her mind began to focus on an image of John lying in that field, the thought would be violently shoved aside by her brain's survival mechanism in horrible cases like this one: hope. The hope that her husband would come home and say it was a horrible mistake, they had the wrong boy. Or that John would call from the bus station in Boston, saying sorry I didn't tell you, but I came down here with some friends. Most of all, she hoped he would just walk through the door, smiling as if nothing had happened.

But the phone didn't ring, and the door remained shut. So she continued pacing and crying in the stillness of the house. At some point little Roberta wandered in to see why her mommy was sad, and when Evelyn failed to respond to her daughter's repeated inquiries, Roberta began bawling too.

A few minutes later—Evelyn was sitting on the couch again, by now, with Roberta in her arms—the front door actually *did* open.

"*Johnny!?*" Evelyn cried, spilling Roberta off her lap as she jumped up. Debbie, her oldest daughter, swooped into the room.

"Ma? Ma, what happened? The cops picked me up, said I had to come home right away—"

"It's Johnny! The police came and said they found him in a field; he was tied up…your father went with them to the funeral home…" She grabbed her daughter in a bear hug and wailed.

"Wait. Funer—" Debbie shrugged out of Evelyn's grip. "You mean—*Ma!*" Evelyn quieted a bit. "He's…John's…dead?"

Evelyn could do no more than nod, her lips pursed as the tears streamed. And in her soundless acknowledgment, the first seed of acceptance of the horrible fact planted itself in her brain: her son, John Joseph McCabe, fifteen years, six months, and two weeks old, was gone.

* * * *

At 1:00 p.m., every available seat in the McCabe living room was occupied. Evelyn and Debbie were on the couch, along with Bill, who had returned a few minutes before from identifying his son's body; he was quite shaken, but attempting to remain steady for the family. With Bill were Detective St. Peter and another investigator from the Lowell Criminal Bureau, Detective John Clarke, both of whom had met up with Bill at the funeral home. On their way back to the McCabe house they'd picked up Father Heinz from St. William's Catholic Church, where the McCabes had been parishioners for years. The priest had pulled up a chair next to Evelyn on the couch, and every few minutes he whispered comforting words to her, to ill effect; Evelyn seemed destroyed.

11

"Bevvie had something to do with it. It was Bevvie; I know it!" Debbie said, her voice shaking with anger.

"Now, who's 'Bevvie'?" The question came from Detective Clarke, a thirty-year LPD veteran who'd recently been relegated to desk duty until his pension kicked in and he could retire. And as usual, Clarke had about as much tact as a lawn mower.

"Kevin Bevilacqua, you're talking about, right?" St. Peter intervened. "He and John were running buddies?"

"He's an asshole, is what he is!"

"Deborah…" Bill warned her, but only weakly; his anguish seemed to have made him smaller, somehow, as if John's death had simply lessened his existence.

"Well, Dad, he is," Debbie answered. "I heard he hasn't been home for three days. Sometimes he sleeps in the Serafinis' shed because he just doesn't wanna stay at home…I also heard he and John were planning to borrow money for train tickets."

"*What*!??" Evelyn moaned. "Where was—"

"Evelyn…" Bill warned again.

St. Peter waited for Evelyn to calm herself. Then: "Debbie, tell me how you know John wanted train tickets." Debbie hesitated, her eyes darting around the room. He could tell she was uncomfortable and needed time to think about her response—and how the others would perceive it. "Debbie?"

"Um…Nancy told me. Nancy Williams."

"What exactly did she say? Tell me everything you can."

"She said…she gave Johnny a ride. He told her he was gonna hitchhike to Lowell. A couple of my girlfriends were at the dance too…they said he told them the same thing."

12

She paused again, staring at nothing while she either recalled the memory or fabricated it. Then she jerked her head to her father, eyes wide, her words erupting: "Johnny was looking for Bevvie, and they were gonna buy tickets to New York and he needed twenty-four dollars for it, and then Bevvie killed him, and NOW HE'S GONE!" She wailed as she buried her face in Bill's chest.

St. Peter scribbled in his notepad, his face blank. The only sound in the room was Debbie's sobbing; eventually, Evelyn joined her.

* * * *

"We're gonna go find this Bevilacqua kid, I take it," Clarke said from the passenger seat as he and St. Peter pulled away from the McCabe home. "Sounds to me like he may be our guy."

"Maybe," St. Peter said after some consideration. "It's…I think it's too early to make any snap decisions. We need to ask a lot more questions, to a lot more people. But I think we need to have a conversation with him. And the sooner the better."

Clarke radioed in a request for the Bevilacqua address, and a couple of minutes later they parked in front of the Leary Drive home. St. Peter got out, and as Clarke opened the passenger door to join him, St. Peter leaned down into the open driver's side doorway.

"I'll handle this, John."

Clarke's expression clouded. "But—"

"He's probably not here, like Debbie said. So it'll only take a minute. And if he *is* here, I'll let you know, and you can take the lead on the questioning." He was lying, and he knew that Clarke probably knew it was a lie, too, but they both let it go.

13

"Whatever." Clarke shut his door again.

How long till his papers go through? St. Peter mused as he walked to the door. But it didn't matter. No one answered his repeated knocking, and a quick glance through a gap in the curtains over the front window revealed a dark, still living room.

"Hey, you'll find him," Clarke said when he returned to the driver's seat. (St. Peter almost laughed aloud at Clarke not including himself in his comment.)

Driving back to the Tewksbury police station, St. Peter let his mind wander through the facts he had so far. *John McCabe was left tied up in a field. By whom? Bevilacqua? If so, why? If not Bevvie, then who? And he was fifteen. He wanted to go to New York. Why? His family seemed to think of him as some kind of choir boy...but I wonder if he wasn't starting to sow his wild oats.*

As if reading his mind, Clarke asked, "So what's your next step?"

"We need to find out what kind of kid McCabe really was. Bill and Evelyn must've seen him through their parental filter. That's normal. But who was he *really?* What—or where—was his dark side? We figure that out, we're off and running. So we need to talk to people who knew him—people besides the family. And besides Bevvie."

"And who would those people be, oh great detective? Who should we bring in for interviews?" Those were questions St. Peter couldn't answer—at least, not yet.

"Everybody."

3. Saturday, September 27, Part Two

Though many of its guests were reluctant visitors, by that evening the Tewksbury police station had become the most popular joint in town. St. Peter's comment in the car had been a forecast of what was to come; when he and Clarke had gotten back to the station, they learned that Captain McGuane, who'd been given a temporary office at TPD, had ordered every available officer to start working the phones setting up interviews.

And an hour later, they got lucky: Tewksbury High School had defeated its archrival, neighboring Billerica, in a football game earlier that day. So at about 4:30 p.m., Sergeant Bradanick, a senior TPD officer, spotted a "victory caravan" of at least thirty carloads of teenagers snaking its way through town. Bradanick used his cruiser's P.A. to order the cars to the high school parking lot; there, he again used the P.A. to ask anyone with information on John's whereabouts the previous evening to come forward. But that was where their luck ran dry: of the four teens they spoke to, none had any relevant information other than that they saw him at the dance. Nor did any of them know anything about his movements afterward.

As the evening wore on, additional personnel arrived, including other members of the Lowell Criminal Bureau; St. Peter was glad to see that Inspector Farley, a senior LCB detective (and his favorite colleague) was among their number. The Lowell PD now outnumbered the Tewksbury officers, in TPD's own station. Also present were State Police detectives and stenographer Linda King, who would transcribe interviews in shorthand when needed.

As the inquiries commenced—either by phone or in person—and word spread requesting relevant info about what had happened, St. Peter's suspicions had begun to be confirmed: young John McCabe hadn't been as saintly as his freckle-faced persona projected. A Tewksbury resident named Richard Greter was one of the first to call, and he reported that his son Brad—a mature-looking seventeen-year-old, St. Peter knew—had been given money by John and his friends "to buy beer for their party Friday night." Not long afterward, an anonymous caller cast even more light on John's delinquent nature.

"According to this person, John was 'a bastard and a cheat,' and was always yelling at his parents," St. Peter wrote in his report detailing the call. "He sold copper at one of the junkyards, and when it was weighed, he wanted two checks so he could cheat the boy he was partners with. His mother was present and knew of this, and did not seem a bit concerned.

"According to this person, Evelyn protects Debbie at all costs."

St. Peter was sitting at his makeshift desk in the squad room, ruminating on this last bit of information and its place in the larger scheme of the investigation when a teenage girl appeared from the seating area.

"They…are you the detective?" she asked, her voice barely above a whisper.

"I'm Detective St. Peter. What can I do for you?"

"My name is Judy Montague. I'm a friend of Debbie's. I have…my dad told me I should come talk to you."

St. Peter gave her his warmest smile and gestured to a chair next to the desk. "Have a seat."

Over the next ten minutes, Judy relayed information she'd recalled Debbie telling her over the last several months—and its message to St. Peter, at least on a subconscious level, was that the McCabe family had its share of dysfunction. Debbie had experimented with drugs, she said, and Evelyn knew of Debbie's drug use, but kept it a secret. This was just one of many pieces of info they hid from her father, Bill. They would routinely change Debbie's report card, Judy said, and show Bill the altered copy. And Bill was completely unaware that Debbie skipped school often.

"And she would—and this is really what I came here to tell you—she always calls John a 'brat.' She says he's really mean and sarcastic to everybody else, but not to his parents. Especially Mr. McCabe. She says they—Mr. McCabe and John—they're really close because he's their only son. And Mr. McCabe doesn't really—*didn't* really know him." Her eyes pooled with tears.

St. Peter scribbled, averting his gaze to give her space to work through her grief.

"It's not fair," she said after a moment. "Even if he was a brat…nobody deserves *that*. Do you…you have any ideas yet? About who did it?"

St. Peter looked up. "It's still early, Judy. We—"

"Detective?"

He turned and saw Captain McGuane standing near his temporary desk. Which meant it was urgent because McGuane only left the chair behind his own desk for urgent matters.

"The Bevilacqua boy is here."

On his way down the hall, St. Peter saw Farley getting ready to enter the interview room where Bevvie waited and stopped him. They conferred while various personnel scurried through the hall around them.

"I want you to take the lead on this kid, Farley," St. Peter said. "I just wanna watch. I'm afraid if I go at him, I might spoo—"

"McGuane already talked to me," Farley said. "He says it's Bradanick's show." Sergeant Philip Bradanick was with Tewksbury PD, and in St. Peter's estimation the only TPD officer capable of handling a weighty interrogation like this one. "But he did say I could jump in if Bradanick doesn't get anywhere."

"That's good, that's good. You do that. And sooner rather than later. Ready?"

Apparently, St. Peter was not alone in his need to observe. When the two men entered, they saw a half-dozen others, all from the Lowell bureau, seated around the room. Linda King, the stenographer, was at a desk in the corner, notebook and pencil at the ready. Bevvie was at the eight-foot-long table in the room's center, his face a perpetual smirk; his father sat next to him looking both angry and scared. St. Peter and Farley took seats at either end of the table.

For a time, nobody moved. The only sound was the steady *tick...tick* of the clock on the wall.

"Well, this is fun," Bevvie finally said. "We just gonna sit around and—"

"Enough, Kevin," his father cautioned.

Another moment passed, then Bradanick breezed in carrying a thick file in a manila folder. He sat opposite Bevvie, and with a nod to Linda King, began the questioning with no prelude. He first had Bevvie give his full name and address, then Bradanick immediately conveyed the gravity of the situation.

"We want you to understand that we're trying to find the truth to this matter. We are getting some of it from you, some from other people. Did you see or talk to John yesterday?"

"No." Bevvie's answer was immediate, his eyes locked on Bradanick.

"Did you have a conversation with anyone in his home?"

"Yes."

"Who was that?"

"His mother."

"Is that all?"

"Yes."

This was news to St. Peter. *Why didn't Evelyn mention this?* he wondered as he listened.

"What did you say to her?"

"I don't know—I just said hello. She wanted me to go home. She told me to go see a priest and talk to him—that a priest would help me take care of my problems. That's about it."

"I see." Bradanick paused to examine the file. From his seat at the end of the table, St. Peter analyzed what he was seeing. *The kid stares at Bradanick. No pauses, no averting his eyes to think. He's either a liar or a complete weirdo. Or both. Either way, something's off here.*

Bradanick continued, shifting gears a bit. "Did you ride in Nancy Williams's car?"

"No."

"You never rode in her car yesterday?"

"No."

19

"You didn't go to the K of C dance last night?"

A brief pause and glance to the left. "No."

"Okay." Bradanick marked something in the file. "Were you at the Oaks?" (The Oaks was a burger joint just down the block from the hall where the dance had been held.)

"Yes."

"Who were you with?"

"Larry Bruce, Richie Gildart, Richie...I don't know his last name. And Walter Serafini."

"Okay. Now Kevin: between Wednesday and Friday, did you make plans to...did you ask him—John—to run away with you?"

"I called him when I ran away from my house—Wednesday, at 8:00 p.m. I talked to him for a second, but he said he was busy. I told him I'd call him back at 9:00, but when I did, his number was busy. So I just left."

"You never mentioned anything about twenty-four dollars to run away with? John never asked if you wanted to run away with him?"

"No."

"Okay. Is there anything that's maybe come back to you insofar as seeing John yesterday? Anything at all?"

He's losing him, St. Peter thought.

"Nope."

"Where were you between 7:00 and 11:00 p.m.?"

Bevvie sighed. "I already told you, at the Oaks. We split up, me and Richie Gildart, and Larry and the other kid." He continued, but the info was consistent with what they already knew. Bradanick began asking for details about the other boys—info that was irrelevant, St. Peter thought. *Yeah, he lost him.* He gave Farley a pointed look and cocked his head as if to say, *Get in there, man.*

"These are the actual events from last night?" Bradanick was asking.

"Yes, they are."

"You didn't meet or take a ride with Nancy Williams?"

Bevvie sighed again. "No, I *didn't.*"

Farley finally interjected: "Did you make a call to the McCabe home today, Kevin?"

Bevvie turned to him, looking unnerved for the first time. "I...not this morning. Yesterday morning I did. I didn't talk to anyone today."

"Did you talk to Debbie McCabe?"

"I think my mother did. Yeah, she did—I'd told her about Nancy Williams."

"What about Nancy Williams?"

"Just that she gave John a ride."

Farley paused, seeming to gather his thoughts. *Here comes the big play,* St. Peter thought.

"Okay, Kevin, think about this: Debbie McCabe is a girl whose brother has been murdered, and she is trying to help us. I've kept an open mind on this matter, and I feel like this could be a case where it started off as a prank to scare John McCabe, and ended up as a tragedy. If it started off as a prank, or if there is anyone involved that you know of—or you yourself—then now is the time to tell us. Not tomorrow, not a week or two weeks from now. *Now* is the time. This is not gonna end until we come up with some answers. If it was an accident that started off as a prank, tell us *now.* If you know anything about this, you need to tell us, Kevin."

Silence in the room. Bevvie looked around, thinking. St. Peter tried to read his thoughts, but found it impossible. Finally, he gazed at Farley again and reapplied his requisite smirk.

"I don't know of anyone who could have done this."

"You didn't contact John?"

"No."

"You weren't with him at all?"

"*No.*"

Farley was relentless. "How was John dressed last time you saw him?"

"I don't know! That was four days ago!"

Mr. Bevilacqua had had enough. "All right, Detective, stop. That's enough questions."

But Farley wasn't giving up. "We're not done yet, sir. Not by a—"

"Are you gonna arrest him? No? Then we're leaving." He stood and grabbed Bevvie's arm, and marched him around the table and out the door. As they left, Bevvie turned and gave them all another smirk.

The detectives filed silently out of the room, each man lost in thought. Only St. Peter remained; he put his feet up on the table and reflected on what had just happened. Which, looking at the bigger picture, wasn't much. *There's definitely something off about that boy. But I don't think he did this. He's a smartass little punk, but that doesn't make him a murderer. But if not him…then who?*

Back out in the station's main room, St. Peter knew he was in for a long night. He counted seven people waiting to give statements, so he conferred with McGuane, who said he was going home, then he and the others got to work. First up was Carol Ann McFrederies, fourteen, who basically told the detectives what they already knew: that she'd danced with John often the previous night at the K of C, and that he said he planned to go to New York. She saw him as they were leaving the dance, and nothing else unusual occurred.

The evening plodded on, witnesses were talked to and dismissed, and nothing new was learned. At least, not until St. Peter spoke to Nancy Williams. His main purpose during her interview was simply to discover a correct timeline of John's movements prior to the discovery of his body (which had only been twelve hours before, but seemed like twelve days).

"I'd like to go over the facts again, just to verify things," he told her after they sat down. "Last night you picked John up, right? Can you tell me about that?"

"We picked him up by the novitiate on Chandler Street," she said. "We let him out at the corner of Chandler and Main."

"And you turned left and went to Lowell, right?" She nodded. "What did John do?"

"Got out and started walking toward the K of C, thumbing."

"Okay. You said, '*We* picked him up.' Who was with you?"

"It was me, my sister Sandy, and Mike Ferreira."

"What happened next? You went into Lowell?"

"Yeah. I dropped my sister off on Pond Street, then we came back to Tewksbury, back to my house."

At that point, St. Peter had pretty much gotten what he needed; he asked a few more questions simply as a matter of course. "What'd you do then?"

"Mike left with Walter Shelley and Bob Ryan."

"Did they leave in a car?"

"Yeah. Walter's."

"And what kind of car does he have?"

"A 1965 Chevy."

St. Peter's pulse quickened. "What color is it?"

"Maroon."

St. Peter mentally replayed what Barry Moran had told him that morning: *It was a Chevy, probably a '64 or '65. I think like…maroon.*

He asked Nancy a few more questions, but later he realized he had no memory of them. From the time she described Walter's car until the end of the interview, his thoughts were focused on two things: finding Walter Shelley, and getting to the funeral home for John McCabe's autopsy.

* * * *

John McCabe's naked body lay on a metal table in the prep room of the funeral home. His skin was a sickly combination of lavender and yellow, lips almost black, eyes closed, face frozen in misery. Around his neck was a circular mark that appeared to have been made by a thin rope. The time was 8:15 p.m.

Standing over the body was Dr. Michael Luongo, a pathologist from Boston who'd been summoned by Dr. Karbowniczak, Associate Medical Examiner of the Fifth Middlesex District. Karbowniczak had never performed an autopsy on an alleged murder victim before, so he'd called Luongo, a friend he'd known since medical school, to ask if Luongo could make the forty-five-minute drive up. Luongo, Karbowniczak knew, could do the autopsy with more expertise and speed than he possessed—and the detectives had told him they needed the findings posthaste.

24

St. Peter had just hurried in, and now he sat in a chair a few feet away to observe; he wanted to be on hand in case the autopsy revealed anything that needed immediate follow-up.

While Luongo prepared by scrubbing down and hanging a portable tape recorder around his neck, Karbowniczak took numerous photos of the body, from every possible angle, position, and state of undress. After he'd taken more than eighty shots, he summoned his assistant responsible for developing photos and told him to get busy. "They said they'd be by at 10:00 to get these. So…make it snappy," he said, both of them laughing a bit at Karbowniczak's attempt at a pun.

"Ready to begin?" Luongo asked. Karbowniczak nodded. So with Karbowniczak assisting by moving the body when required or fetching various instruments, Luongo turned on the recorder.

"The body is that of a healthy, lean white male, approximately fifteen. Sixty-five inches in length…weight a hundred and fifteen pounds. Hair is blonde with a reddish tint." Luongo moved closer to the table and started his examination of John's head and face, continuing around the table inches at a time.

"Conjunctivae"—medical-speak for the inner lining of the eyelids—"suffused with blood. Petechial hemorrhages in the facial skin…slightly depressed ligature injury encircling the neck…" Luongo continued the external exam. After nearly an hour, the findings that he thought would be of interest, and which he relayed to St. Peter, were "double ligature marks encircling both legs," and "similar marks about both wrists." Also of note: "an area of purplish-red ecchymosis"—a small bruise—".25 inches in greatest diameter in the skin of the shaft of the penis." Later Luongo also examined the adhesive tape over John's mouth under a microscope, and found black cotton fibers in the glue, which he speculated was material transferred from gloves the assailant had worn.

Luongo also noticed signs of lividity (the postmortem settling of blood due to gravity) on both the front and rear portions of John's body. This meant that in all likelihood, the body had spent some amount of time—*after* death—lying both face-up and face-down, in two contrasting positions.

After the external exam was completed, the pair conducted an internal one, examining John's brain, heart, and major organs; the only noteworthy finding was that John had a .02 blood alcohol content when he died. Given his size, Luongo speculated that he'd had one drink—or even a part of one—within an hour of his death.

When Bradanick arrived at 10:15 p.m.—St. Peter had already left by this time—they were dissecting John's spleen.

"Got the pictures. Anything else you can tell us?" the detective asked.

"Well, it'll be tomorrow before I can type up my report, but I can give you an official cause of death," Luongo told him. The same information was at the top of the report Luongo composed the next morning on an ancient Olivetti in Karbowniczak's office:

"It is our opinion that John J. McCabe came to his death as a result of asphyxia due to strangulation by ligature. Homicide."

* * * *

Just after midnight, Walter Shelley walked into the station looking anxious. After rushing back from the funeral home, St. Peter had done some quick pre-interview investigating and had learned that Shelley was eighteen, had poor school marks, and was quite a safe distance from genius. St. Peter had dispatched a patrol car to Shelley's home to let him know his presence was requested at the station, and surprisingly, he'd come right away.

St. Peter had asked Farley to assist him in the interview, and as the three of them sat down to begin, St. Peter tried to make a quick mental appraisal of Walter's temperament, with no success; behind his thick glasses, Walter's expression was unbelievably dull, as if his few remaining brain cells were having trouble locating each other. His thick glasses made his eyes look enormous, as if he were constantly astonished by something.

"Did you go to work last night, Walter?"

"Yes sir."

"And where do you work?"

"Professional Services. Out of Waltham."

"What time was your shift?"

"Last night? From 6:00 to 8:30."

"What'd you do after you got off?"

"I met up with Mike Ferreira, then we just kind of…messed around. Nothing special."

Mike Ferreira again. That name keeps popping up, St. Peter thought. Aloud he said, "You said you 'messed around.' Can you be more specific? Did you go to the K of C dance?"

"No sir. I met Mike at Nancy Williams's house, then we went over to Lowell."

"What time was that?"

27

"About 11:00."

"Where'd you go in Lowell?"

"To South Lowell, to a store that was open. We got some cigarettes."

"Whose car did you go in?"

"Mine."

"It's a maroon '65 Chevy, right?"

"Yes sir."

"Just you and Michael in the car?"

"Yes sir."

Start easing in. "Did you meet a boy by the name of McCabe?"

"No sir. I never heard of him. I went to school with his sister Debbie, but I don't know him."

"Would you know him if you saw his picture?"

"No sir."

St. Peter showed him John's school photo. "Are you sure you don't know him?"

"Yes sir." St. Peter put the photo back in the file.

"Okay. After you went to South Lowell, where did you go?"

"Home."

"Did you get in any fights last night, Walter?"

"No sir."

"Any arguments?"

"No sir."

Make your play. But be careful. "Do you know what murder is?"

A single bead of sweat rolled down Walter's brow. "It's when someone gets killed."

"Do you know how serious a crime this is?"

"Yes sir."

"Did you see that boy last night?"

"No sir." He said it quietly. St. Peter guessed he was either scared to death, or lying. *Maybe both? Either way, it's big-play time.*

"Did you go to a vacant lot off Maple Street?"

"No sir." Practically a whisper.

"You weren't in a vacant lot in Lowell at 11:00 last night?"

"No sir." Behind the glasses, tears shone in his big eyes.

St. Peter gently placed a photo in front of him. The shot, taken at the autopsy, showed a naked John McCabe from the waist up. The pallid skin and charcoal lips were enough to rattle both men.

"Do you know what happened to this boy?"

"I know he got strangled."

"How do you know he was strangled, Walter? You said you didn't see him."

Walter was silent. He just stared at the photo, eyes huge.

"How do you know this, Walter?"

"Everybody's talking about it."

St. Peter switched gears. "What grade are you in?"

Walter huffed a sigh of relief. "In school? I'm a junior."

"Who's your girlfriend?"

"My—? I…I don't have one." *That's bullshit*, St. Peter thought. And as the interview ended, and Walter was leaving looking both relieved and shaken, St. Peter's focus shifted once again. And now it was on finding Mike Ferreira.

4. Sunday, September 28

"State your full name for the record."

"Michael Francis Ferreira."

"Your address?"

"3 Erland Avenue, Tewksbury, Massachusetts."

"Your date of birth?"

"July 25, 1953."

"So you're sixteen. Mrs. Ferreira, do you have any objection to us talking to your son?"

"Not as long as he isn't being charged."

"Do you object, Michael?"

"No."

Mike and his mother sat facing St. Peter and Farley. Linda King was in her usual place in the corner, dutifully transcribing the interrogation in her notebook. St. Peter hoped he didn't look as exhausted as he felt; after finishing up with Walter Shelley the night before, he'd gotten home at 2:00 a.m., slept hard until 7:00 or so, and was back at the station by 8:00. And though he wasn't yet sure there was any connection between Shelley, Ferreira, and John McCabe, his instincts told him to keep looking. *The Moran kid reported seeing a car fitting the description of Shelley's Chevy. I have to cover all the bases.*

So he'd driven to Ferreira's residence that morning. Mr. Ferreira had said that his wife and son were attending Mass, but would come by the station as soon as he could tell them. And surprisingly enough, they'd come by a little after 2:00 p.m.

"Nobody's being charged, Mrs. Ferreira," he said now. "We're just trying to piece everything together. Michael, starting Friday at about 5:00 p.m., give us a complete list of your activities."

"Um, okay." Mike squinted his blue eyes. He was on the shorter side, St. Peter surmised, and stocky, with a mustache typical of sixteen-year-olds. *But...when I look at him, I get the feeling he's hiding something. Sooner or later I'll find out what it is.*

"We were down at Nancy Williams's house until 6:00 or 7:00, then we left."

"Who's 'we'?"

"Me, Nancy, McGovern."

"And who's McGovern?"

"I don't know his first name. He lives off of Pine Street. We went to Lowell to pick Nancy's sister up."

"Whose car were you in?"

"Nancy's. A 1963 Ford Galaxie. Purple."

"Go on."

Mike continued the play-by-play of his evening, which was uneventful until he met up with Walter Shelley a little after 9:00 at Nancy's house. The two went to another friend's to watch TV for an hour or so, then went back over to Nancy Williams's. Also present, he recalled, were two friends of theirs named Jane Thompson and Bobby Brown. At one point during the interview, they all took a short break, and when they were all gathered again, St. Peter had Mike start over with his retelling of what he did the night of the murder. Mike's story, this time, was essentially the same—except this time, he added the detail of picking up John McCabe on Chandler Street, then dropping him off at Main. *Wonder why he didn't tell that part before?* St. Peter thought as Mike talked. And as Mike went on this time, his version of events began to diverge even further from the version Walter had given the night before.

"When we went over to Nancy's, she was just pulling out of the driveway, so we followed her over to where Mary Ann Richard was babysitting. We stayed there till midnight or something, then went over to Lowell to get some cigarettes."

"Okay, back up. First you went where to watch TV?"

"Over to Mary Ann's. We left a little before 11:00. Then…we were gonna go get Carol Ann McFrederies from the K of C dance, but we figured it was too late, that her father had already picked her up. So we went back over to Nancy's, but she was just leaving. We followed her back to Mary Ann's, left there about 12:15, and went to Lowell."

St. Peter chuckled, trying to keep the conversation light, and keep Mike off-guard…all the while gauging the best time to pounce. "Okay, I think that makes sense. What'd you do in Lowell?"

"Aw…rode around for a while. We went through the center of town and saw a kid I knew, Paul Bishop—they call him Jughead—so we stopped and talked to him." Mike seemed totally relaxed, his story flowing. "We only talked to him for a minute because there was traffic behind u—"

"Michael!" St. Peter slapped the table with his palm. "Do you understand why you're here tonight?"

Mike looked dazed for a moment. "I…yes."

"Do you understand that a boy has been murdered?"

"Yes."

"Do you know what murder is?"

"Of course I do."

"Do you know what we are looking for?"

"I do."

"We need a straight and honest story from you."

Mike gripped the edges of the table, head bowed. When he looked up again, he spoke each word plainly: "I'm telling…you…the truth."

St. Peter slid a photo of John McCabe's body—the same one he'd shown Walter Shelley—over to Mike. "Look at this boy, John. You know what happened to him, don't you?"

"*No.*"

"This family needs—and *we* need—some answers. Did you read the paper? Did you read about what Bill McCabe said? This man is hurting, Michael. He needs to know what happened to his boy."

"I didn't d—"

"Detective, please." It was Mrs. Ferreira, who until this point had only been a quiet (albeit frightened) spectator. "Can we take a break? I'd like to speak to Mike outside."

St. Peter wasn't sure why she needed to speak with him privately, but let them go. "Sure. Only for a minute, though. We need to continue. We need to get to the bottom of this matter."

"Thank you." She and Mike exited.

Mike and Walter's stories don't jibe, he thought after they were gone. *Walter didn't give me much, but…he damn sure didn't say anything about trying to find Carol Ann. There's something here. Has to be.*

They came back in a moment later, Mike looking more uneasy than ever. They sat back down, and Mrs. Ferreira said: "Well, go ahead."

"Ma—"

"*Now, son.*"

33

"Well…I didn't wanna tell you this before…but me and Walter was…we were trying to get some beer. That's why we went over to Lowell. To get beer and cigarettes."

Wonder what else he isn't telling me? "All right. Tell me exactly what you did."

"It's just like I told you. We took the ride to Lowell 'bout 12:15. We went down the square. Me and Walter."

"Just the two of you?"

"Yes. We went looking for Tommy Mahr. He lives over in South Lowell, and he buys us beer. But we couldn't find him. That's when I saw my buddy Jughead, like I told you."

Damn. He's not coming off his story. Damn! "Did you talk to him?"

"Yes. Asked him what he was doing, he said, 'Nothing,' so the traffic was coming and we went. We went over to Cunningham's store."

"Okay. Where's that?"

"Know where the old railroad bridge is?" *Of course I know. It's yards away from where McCabe was found.* "The store is right before the bridge. I went in and got two bags of chips and two packs of cigarettes."

"Okay. What did you do then?"

"We went home. Walter dropped me off at my house."

"What time was that?"

"Sheesh…" Mike blew out a breath. "Musta been 1:30 or 2:00."

"Was it raining then?"

"I don't think so."

"Did Walter have his wipers on?"

"I don't…I don't remember."

"Were they working at any time during the night?"

34

"Yes. For most of the night."

C'mon, Mike. You don't think it was raining, don't remember the wipers being on, but then say they're on most of the night? This is horseshit. He switched gears. "Do you know the area where John McCabe was found?"

"I know where the B&M Railroad is."

"Ever hung out in that area, in those fields?"

"No."

"Was Walter's car parked anywhere in those fields Friday night?"

"No. Not that I know of."

Dammit. "Michael, would you agree to a polygraph exam?"

"Ye—"

"Michael." Mrs. Ferreira again. "I'll need to check with my husband on that. And I think we've answered enough questions, sir. So unless you—"

"No, it's okay. We're done here."

* * * *

Evelyn McCabe wrapped Bill in the old sheet she always used when she gave him a haircut, both of them draped in the sad silence that accompanies shock. With practically no sleep in the past two nights, they were both exhausted; though it was midafternoon, they'd spoken only a handful of times since breakfast. They'd skipped Mass at St. William's for the first time since last year, when they'd both been laid up with the flu. As Evelyn began snipping, a low bass note of tension hung in the air.

"Not too much this time, dear," Bill muttered. As Evelyn cut, he just stared dismally at nothing, as if…well, as if he'd been told his son was murdered. At one point he heard Evelyn sobbing softly behind him, but he was simply too miserable to react.

Evelyn was finishing up when the stress finally boiled over. With her brain overrun by worry, she hastened a question about the investigation—even though Bill had earlier pronounced such talk as off-limits.

"I read that newspaper story. It was good, you asking people to come forward. Think it'll help?"

"Dunno." Barely a murmur.

"Have the detectives learned anything n—"

"Evelyn." He looked over his shoulder, his eyes shining. "I won't have it. You'll finish trimming my hair, we'll go to the funeral tomorrow, and that's that." Evelyn was crying again, and she sank into a kitchen chair.

"I'm sorry, dear," she managed. "I just—we can't—have they—"

"Enough, dear." Bill stood and turned to face his wife, and blew out a long, slow breath. "The detectives haven't told me anything. I don't think they *know* anything. I know this, though: we'll find out who killed Johnny. I don't care how long it takes." He walked over to gather Evelyn in his arms. They stood embracing for a few moments, and soon tears were coursing down Bill's cheeks, too.

"Johnny drank," she nearly whispered, the words muffled by her husband's shoulder.

Bill pulled her back to arm's length. "What…what'd you say?"

"He drank, Billy," she repeated, nodding her head in affirmation. "Other things too. He's not the boy you th—"

"Aw, I don't believe that." He walked into the living room, then stopped. "Not Johnny. He's a good boy." He turned to face Evelyn, who'd crept along behind him. "Why would you say something like that?"

"Because it's true, dear," she said. They both sat on the couch. Evelyn figured she might as well lay it all out. "He wasn't always honest. Remember the money he said he made selling all that copper? Half that money belonged to his friend Stuart Hersey, but he lied to Stuart about how much the copper was worth. Debbie said he's asked her to try to get beer for him and his friends." Tears were cascading down Bill's face, but Evelyn soldiered on. "She said he's...he acts like a brat to everybody else but you. And Billy, he's a brat to me, too. When you're not here he—"

"Stop it." Bill closed his eyes, trying to will away the pain. "He's a good boy."

"He *was* a good boy, dear," she said. "He was a beautiful boy." More tears were on her own face now. "But you need to realize that Johnny wasn't an angel. And...he might've been into things that got him in trouble."

"Pahhh..." Bill waved a hand at her. He tried to dismiss the idea that his only son was a bit of a delinquent, but found that he couldn't; the part of his brain in charge of logic knew that it was most likely true. *He* was *fifteen, after all,* he thought.

They both sat silent. Eventually Evelyn laid her head on Bill's shoulder, and the two of them dove into their memories of their son.

"Remember when he brought home that Canadian goose?" Evelyn asked, and they both laughed. "He wanted to keep it as a pet...and name it Rory." They giggled again. "I could never figure out why he picked that name. 'Rory.'"

"I'll never understand why he liked to put all those grasshoppers in the closet," Bill said. "And why he would spend all that time collecting them."

"To scare his sisters. Why else? And Debbie would get *so* mad at him. She—"

As if summoned by the mention of her name, Debbie came in the front door carrying a garment bag covering the black dress she'd bought for the funeral. "Hey," she said softly. Evelyn went to her, holding her arms out for a hug, but Debbie dodged the embrace—"Not now, Ma"—and went to her room.

"Hope you didn't spend too much on that dress, Deb," Evelyn called to her.

"I didn't," Debbie recited. It was a conversation Bill had heard them have many times. Deb came back into the living room. "I stopped by the police station. They said th—"

But Bill wasn't having it. "Your mother told me Johnny asked you to get booze for him," he said from the couch. In an instant, the tender moment he and Evelyn had shared was over.

Debbie looked as if she'd been gut-punched. "What? I—Ma! Why would you—"

"Enough, Deborah," Evelyn said. "I told your father about Johnny. About how—"

"*He was a good boy!*" Bill repeated with even more passion. "So he took a drink a time or two. He cheated his friends. So what if he was a brat? He was fifteen! *Every* kid his age is a brat!" He went to the table and got his hat, then went to the door.

Evelyn was beside herself. "Where are you going?"

"I've had enough," Bill said. "I'll be back later." He slammed the door. A few seconds later, Debbie likewise slammed her bedroom door. Evelyn burst into tears yet again as she watched Bill squeal the tires of his Plymouth when he drove away.

* * * *

Richie Gildart was a pudgy, good-natured kid that St. Peter liked—and trusted—immediately. Since Richie was one of the boys Bevvie had testified to being with that Friday night, the detectives requested that he come to the station to answer questions. And now, as Richie sat at the interview table with his father—an even pudgier, better-natured version of his son—St. Peter relaxed for what seemed like the first time in two days.

"Richie, I want you to know that you're not in any trouble," St. Peter began. "We just need to ask you some things about Friday night—we're talking to a whole lot of people."

"Uh...okay," Richie answered, glancing at Mr. Gildart, who nodded and smiled.

"Tell me what you did that evening, starting with when you got out of school."

"Okay. Well, first I went home. I messed around there until about 6:30, then I called my friend Larry. Then I went—"

"Larry Bruce, right?"

"Yes sir. I called him, then met up with him a few minutes later at the light at Shawsheen and Main—that's our usual meeting-up spot."

"Okay. Was Larry by himself?"

"No." St. Peter noticed Richie throw a furtive glimpse at his father. "Bevvie was with him. Larry didn't say anything about Bevvie coming."

"Then what happened?"

"We messed around, walked down to the bridge and skipped rocks. At 8:30 we met up with Jimmy Croucher. And..." Richie paused and looked at his father.

"Go on, Richie," Mr. Gildart said.

"Well...Bevvie was talking about trying to get some beer. I didn't want to. I thought we'd get in trouble. And then..." He seemed to steel himself, then turned to St. Peter. "I don't like Bevvie, sir. He makes trouble. He's a bully, too...but I don't want him to be mad at me, or beat me up. So I'm nice to him."

St. Peter just smiled. "I understand, son. Now...what happened after you met Jimmy?"

"It was getting chilly, so I came back home to get my jacket. Bevvie said he'd come with me. I don't know why he wanted to—he's never been to my house. But we went. We were there about ten minutes. Then we went back and met Larry and Jimmy on Main Street. But..." He stopped and stared at his father, afraid to go on.

Mr. Gildart continued the narration. "It seems that while Richie was getting his jacket, the Bevvie kid stole some beer from our fridge. Ten of them."

St. Peter recalled the autopsy report he'd read shortly before the Gildarts had arrived: *Victim's blood alcohol content was .02.*

"Bevvie showed them to me when we left my house," Richie said. "I was mad, but I didn't say anything."

"Okay. Thank you for being honest about this, Richie. What happened next?"

"Well…me, Jimmy, and Larry wanted to go to McDonald's. But Bevvie didn't want to. He said he had to go."

St. Peter's internal radar was pinging. "Where did he go?"

"I don't know. He just took off down the street. But he said that if anyone asked, to tell them he was with us."

Ping. "What do you think he meant by that?"

"I don't know."

"What were his exact words? Do you remember?"

"Yes sir. 'If anyone asks, I was with you all night.'"

Ping ping ping ping ping… "What happened next?"

"We went to McDonald's, then we went to the bowling alley. At 11:00 I called my dad, and he came and picked me up. Then we went home."

"Did you see Bevvie again after he left the first time?"

"No sir."

"What happened to the beer?"

"He took them all with him."

St. Peter had a hunch about where Bevvie had gone. "Do you know if he went over to the K of C?"

"I don't know."

"Okay. Anything else you remember about that night?"

"No sir."

The detective paused to consider this new info. Then: "Richie, you've done a good thing, telling me about this. Now: what you said before, about Bevvie causing trouble. I want you to know that everything that's been said here *stays* here." He leaned in close and put his hand on Richie's shoulder. "Son, do you think Bevvie had anything to do with what happened to John McCabe?"

"Well…" He looked at Mr. Gildart again, as if to steel his courage once more. "He might've."

"What makes you think so?"

"Well…it's just a feeling I have. I don't know anything but what I already told you, but…Bevvie's no good. I heard he and John wanted to go to New York City, so maybe it was about that. I just know I don't trust him. Nobody does."

St. Peter thought for a moment. "Thank you, Richie. You've been a big help."

* * * *

Two hours later, St. Peter was ordering Bevvie into a seat at the same table. After the Gildarts had left, they'd lucked out: a kid named Frank Stout had come by to report that Bevvie *had* in fact been at the K of C dance, and that he'd seen Bevvie and John talking outside.

"Would you mind sticking around for a bit? Reason being, we're trying to locate Bevvie now and bring him in to…have another conversation," St. Peter had asked Frank. "We might need your testimony to compare with Bevvie's statement."

And Frank had agreed. "Anything I can do to help," he'd said, a little too happily, in St. Peter's opinion.

And now, Bevvie and his father both seemed anxious when St. Peter handed them each a sheet of paper with the words MIRANDA WARNING printed across the top in bold, threatening letters.

"What's this?" Mr. Bevilacqua asked.

"This is routine, nothing to worry about," St. Peter said. "I'd like both of you to read it. Basically, it says that you have the right not to talk to us. I will say it would be in your best interests if you do, Bevvie, but you don't have to."

Bevvie shrugged. "I don't have anything to hide." Beneath the perpetual smirk, though, St. Peter thought he detected the briefest glimpse of fear in Bevvie's eyes.

"It also says you can have an attorney here if you so desire. Do you need one?" Bevvie shook his head. "Good. Do you understand these rights?"

"Yes," they answered simultaneously. Then Bevvie asked: "Am I under arrest?"

St. Peter stepped onto the legal tightrope. "Not yet. Ready?"

Bevvie smiled. "What do you want to know?"

"Did you take some beer from the Gildarts' fridge?"

"Nope."

"Why would Mr. Gildart say you did?"

"I don't know. Maybe he just doesn't like me. Or maybe he's an alkie. Maybe he drank them all himself."

"Okay." St. Peter moved on. "Maybe this is true and maybe it's false, but…we have a fellow who says you arrived at the dance at approximately 10:30. And because of the way you were dressed, you weren't allowed inside, but you *did* have a conversation with John McCabe shortly thereafter. True or false?"

"False."

Why would a fellow you know say he saw you there?"

"I don't know. I would call this 'fellow' a liar."

St. Peter took a few steps on the tightrope. "Then I'll let you do that." He nodded to the officer by the door, who exited, then momentarily reappeared with Frank Stout. The two boys exchanged cold glares.

"Bevvie, do you know this gentleman?"

"Of course I do. That's Frankie Stout."

"Okay, I'll ask you again: were you at the K of C dance Friday night?"

"Nope."

St. Peter turned to Frank. "Was Bevvie at the dance?"

"Yes sir. Outside."

"Frank, what time did you arrive at the dance?"

"About 7:30."

"Tell me about when you saw Bevvie there."

"Yes sir. I was sitting at a table next to the door. I saw John McCabe walk out. When he got outside I could see Bevvie out there. They were standing at the bottom of the steps, talking. When I looked again I didn't see them anymore."

"And what time was this?"

'It was right before the dance was over. About 10:45."

"Did you see either of them again?"

"I didn't see Bevvie anymore, but I saw Johnny. I got in the car with Al Castro, and we saw him thumbing."

"Thank you." St. Peter turned to face Bevvie. "So: what do you say to that?"

Bevvie glanced around at the others, eyebrows raised. Finally he said with artificial drama: "I would say…that that's false."

Can't believe the balls on this kid, St. Peter thought. "Bevvie, would you be willing to take a lie detector test?"

"Absolutely."

"Okay." St. Peter paused to consider his next move. *Either he's really confident in his skills of deception, or he's just stupid…or maybe he didn't do this after all.* He asked Frank: "Have you and Bevvie ever had any arguments?"

44

"Yes sir, a few."

He looked at both boys. "Are the two of you friends?"

"Yes," Bevvie said.

"Not really," Frank answered at the same time.

"Bevvie, can you think of a reason Frankie would lie about this?"

"I have no idea. But he's lying, sir. I wasn't there."

Frank immediately responded, stepping toward Bevvie and pointing his finger: "You were! You were right outside!"

But Bevvie wouldn't back down. He jumped up and faced Frank. Their noses were inches apart. "No...I...*wasn't.*" The boys stood like that for a few moments, neither willing to budge.

"Gentlemen." St. Peter diffused the situation by delicately pushing them apart and guiding them back to their seats.

"Frankie, thanks for your help," St. Peter said. "You can go with the officer." Frank exited, scowling at Bevvie the entire time.

"Bevvie, you need to stay here while we check some th—"

"No sir." It was Mr. Bevilacqua, who at this point had been sitting silently at the end of the table. "We've answered all your questions. Kevin even volunteered to take your polygraph. He didn't commit this crime. I'll ask you like I did before: do you plan to arrest him?" St. Peter was silent. "Well? *Do* you?"

The detective sighed. "No."

"Then we're leaving. Call us when you need Kevin to take that lie detector test." And they walked to the door. No smirk on Bevvie's face this time, only a mixture of fear and relief.

* * * *

At 2:30 a.m., the phone in the Tewksbury PD squad room rang. The room was mostly dark, and completely quiet; the only person currently in the station was Lieutenant Walter Jop, who'd volunteered for the overnight desk duty. Aside from the handful of officers out on patrol, everyone else had gone home for some much-needed rest ahead of the funeral, which every available man would attend both to pay their respects and to perform reconnaissance on the other attendees.

The jangling of the phone startled the lieutenant out of a half-snooze. He listlessly lifted the receiver. "Tewksbury PD."

"Um…I wanna talk to somebody about Johnny McCabe."

Jop was instantly fully awake. The voice, he estimated, was that of a teenage boy, one possibly the same age as John himself. "I can help you, sir. Do you have some information?"

"Um…well…yes. I did it."

A wave of nerve impulses jolted Jop's entire body. "Well, you need to turn yourself in, son. Where are you now? I'll send a—"

"I don't wanna do that. I'm afraid—" The boy's voice was interrupted by a *ding*. Jop thought it sounded like the noise of a bell when a car rolled over the black hose next to a gas pump. "—That they'll beat me."

"You're worried that you'll be beaten, you said?"

"Yes sir."

"Son, I can assure you, nobody will beat you up. But you need to turn yourself in. Right away."

"I'll think about it." The boy paused. "I read what Mr. McCabe said in the paper. I think…I want—" *Ding!* "—To do the right thing, but…the cops beat me one time before. I don't wanna get beaten again."

"I promise you, you won't be beaten this time," Jop said. "I'll even come get you myself, right now. But son, you need to *turn yourself in.* Where are you?" *Ding!*

"Ah…I'll think about it." Then he hung up.

The lieutenant immediately radioed a cruiser to proceed forthwith to the Texaco station at Main and Chandler, the location of Tewksbury's only twenty-four-hour gas station. He likewise called the Lowell PD and asked them to do the same at the three all-night stations there. Officers responding to the four locations found no one suspicious.

5. Monday, September 29

St. Peter and Farley left the Tewksbury PD a little after noon, heading (in a roundabout way) to St. William's Church for John's funeral. First they planned to stop by the Texaco to get the name of the overnight attendant, who they would question later that evening. They also wanted to be the first to arrive at the church, so they could do some casual (yet covert) observing of the guests as they arrived.

After Jop told them about the anonymous caller, they'd spent the morning reviewing arrest records for teenage boys, keeping an eye out for any incidents of violence or resisting arrest (meaning a possible tune-up by officers); their search included records for their main "persons of interest"—primarily Bevvie, Walter Shelley, and Mike Ferreira. No records matched their search criteria. So St. Peter had requested that they leave early and just ride the roads for a while. For some reason, St. Peter found he could clear his head and think best with a steady motor humming and some peaceful countryside rolling by.

They left the Texaco by way of Main Street, then veered right onto North Street Road, which offered plenty of the pastoral landscape for which St. Peter was yearning. As Farley drove, St. Peter rested his head against the passenger window, staring at the unfurling scenery, and lost himself in thought. Eventually, he closed his eyes.

At some point—St. Peter couldn't tell if seconds or minutes had passed—Farley interrupted his musing. "Hey, you awake?"

St. Peter opened his eyes, a little dazed and a little frustrated, too. "Yeah. Just…going over things in my head."

"Okay. So where are we?"

He chuckled. "Where are we? Well, we're on North Street," he teased. "Look over there, we're passing Ames Pond—"

"Very funny, asshole. I mean where are we with the case?"

St. Peter paused, searching for the answer. Finally, he let out a dry laugh. "Honestly? We're pretty much nowhere. The solid evidence: we have a witness who reports seeing a mid-sixties, dark-colored car in the field around the supposed time of the murder. We have an anonymous phone call from a boy who says he did it, that he wants to turn himself in, but he's afraid of getting beaten. And that's it. No fingerprints. No forensic evidence—none that we've found, anyway. All the stuff we sent to the State Crime Lab—the rope, the adhesive tape, John's clothes—will take weeks to be analyzed. All the rest is just speculation at this point."

They drove in silence. After a few moments, Farley asked: "What about Bevvie? Or those other two boys— Shelley and Ferreira?"

"Circumstantial. Bevvie? Sure, the general consensus is that he's an asshole. And if we find out that he's the doer, I won't be surprised. But nothing solid ties him to it. Same with the other two. They've both said they were in that area around the time of death…and Shelley's car matches Moran's description. But again, it's circumstantial. Nothing really pops. So until something *does* pop, until we get some kinda break…like I said: We're nowhere."

"Well…maybe something will pop at the funeral. Should be a lot of people there."

"Maybe." But St. Peter doubted whether that would happen.

* * * *

The church parking lot was already half-full when the detectives pulled into it nearly a full hour before the Funeral Mass began at 2:00. As they crossed the parking lot toward the front of the church, they could see a handful of people standing in small groups, talking in hushed tones. Among their number were various officers of both the Tewksbury and Lowell police, outfitted in their dress blues to mark the occasion. And one of the knotted groups consisted of members of the press, who'd been forbidden by the police from speaking with any of the guests until after the service.

Photography, though, was not part of the press moratorium (though they had both the common sense and the respect to only capture images from outside the sanctuary). Two cameramen from Boston TV stations had set up their tripods across the street and were already filming the proceedings. Several still photographers were darting about with their cameras, one of which was Boston PD officer Dan DeForrest, who was working undercover.

The idea to use an undercover officer to pose as a photojournalist had, surprisingly enough, been the brainchild of soon-to-retire Detective Clarke. A photographer, he reasoned—even a fake one—could take photos of guests as they arrived, without seeming out of place. Their plan was to use DeForrest's photos to identify unknown guests, soliciting help from the school administration, Father Heinz, and other assorted townsfolk. So Captain McGuane, with the intention of finding a cop from another jurisdiction (and therefore unknown to the funeral guests), had placed a call to the Boston PD. They'd in turn recruited DeForrest, who was a skilled photographer in his spare time; he'd made the drive up that morning with a *Boston Globe* reporter, acting as the reporter's assistant. The only reason they'd allowed photography at all at such a solemn event was to allow DeForrest to do his thing.

So, with DeForrest and the other photogs clicking away, the guests grew in number. St. Peter joined the growing gaggle of officers, positioning himself so that he could observe the guests without being too conspicuous. He recognized numerous friends and schoolmates of John's— many of whom he'd already seen at the station when they were there to give statements—along with people he assumed were members of the McCabes's extended family. He was also not surprised that no members of the Bevilacqua family, Bevvie himself included, were in attendance.

About 1:45, with the sanctuary already filling up, a group of high-schoolers made their way to the church door; two of them were Walter Shelley and Mike Ferreira. St. Peter quickly made eye contact with DeForrest, then nodded his head toward the group of teens, as if to say, *Make sure you get photos of these people.* DeForrest immediately obliged. One by one, the teens disappeared into the church vestibule.

Just before 2:00, as St. Peter and the others were wondering when the McCabe family would arrive, they saw Bill's Plymouth turn into the parking lot. One of the TPD officers ran over and moved his car from the prime parking spot next to the church, then waved the McCabes into it. (He'd parked there in hopes of doing that very thing.) The family emerged from the car and into the arms of several kinfolk, and tearful hugs and sad greetings were exchanged. The group slowly made its way toward the church, with Evelyn in the lead; she was flanked by two men St. Peter assumed were her brothers (or cousins, maybe). Her face was devastating to even look at: quivering mouth, puffy, glazed eyes, and an overall vacant expression. *She looks...defeated*, St. Peter thought.

Bill brought up the rear of the clan, but his face was chiseled in granite. St. Peter jogged over to offer his condolences.

"Mr. McCa—"

"We'll talk after," Bill snapped, not even sparing the detective a glance.

St. Peter waited until the McCabes had all left the vestibule and were proceeding down the aisle before he entered the sanctuary. Once inside, he saw nearly every pew filled. Many had lowered their kneelers and were praying silently, using the pew in front of them as an altar. Some were crying softly, and St. Peter would've been able to hear them if it weren't for Evelyn McCabe.

She, too, was on her knees, but it was in front of her son's casket just below the pulpit. Numerous flower arrangements stretched in a sad sentry on either side of the coffin. The upper portion of the casket's lid was propped open, revealing a billowy white lining. John McCabe's body was dressed in his finest suit—a green one, since that was his favorite color—with a white shirt and a dainty peach-colored tie. Maury O'Donnell from the funeral home had done an excellent job covering the angry purple ligature marks on John's neck with cosmetics; unfortunately, the rouge and light powder he'd applied to John's cheeks covered up the freckles that were the fifteen-year-old's signature. In death, the expression on John's face was that of boredom mixed with puzzlement.

Evelyn, in her place of dismal worship, was bellowing her anguish; the sound reverberated such that even the late-comers still outside the sanctuary were alarmed. Even after several minutes, her cries showed no signs of diminishing, so as Father Heinz prepared to begin the funeral liturgy, Bill went to her and gently coaxed her to her place in the front pew.

While the organist played softly underneath him, Father Heinz performed the Introductory Rites—the sprinkling of John's body with Holy Water, a prayer for his ascension into Heaven—then the congregation joined in for the traditional funeral hymn "Be Not Afraid." Tears dripped onto many of the hymnals from which the guests sang. After Father Heinz said a long prayer, Bill McCabe took the pulpit.

He surveyed the congregation for a moment, locking eyes with various members of the congregation. Out amongst the crowd, Mike Ferreira and Walter Shelley averted their own eyes, and Mike grabbed the nearest hand he could find—that of Elaine Callahan, one of his circle of friends who happened to be sitting next to him. Elaine was startled, but when she looked at Mike—head down, eyes brimming with tears—she understood.

At the pulpit, Bill looked down at a Bible: "A reading from the letter of Paul to the Romans." He recited the verses in a choked but clear voice, pausing occasionally to gaze upon the crowd.

"Why do you pass judgment on your brother or sister? Or you—why do you despise your brother or sister?" When Bill spoke those verses, Elaine felt Mike's hand tighten on hers, and she heard a soft sob escape him. And the final verse: "So then, each of us will be accountable to God." At that, Mike squeezed Elaine's hand so hard that his ring dug into her fingers, leaving a welt that remained for a couple of days.

"The Word of the Lord," Bill finished.

"Thanks be to God," responded the congregation.

Then Father Heinz took the pulpit to deliver his message to his grieving flock.

"'He was taken too soon.' That's a common response one might hear when a child passes on from this world," the priest began. "John Joseph McCabe was fifteen years, six months, and two weeks old—to be sure, too early to be taken into the arms of God. And many of us, myself included, are angry. Angry that the life of this young man ended so soon. Angry that it happened in such a horrific manner. And we're angriest of all—at least *I* am—that the perpetrators have not confessed their terrible acts. Not to the police, and most importantly, not to God.

"But it is in God's word that I find solace—and I hope you, my brethren, can find some peace in it, too. The second chapter of Luke tells the story of the boy Jesus at the Temple." Father Heinz went on to summarize the fable of Mary and Joseph losing Jesus as they were returning to Nazareth from Jerusalem; days later they found Jesus sitting amongst the teachers at the Temple. The priest used the last verses to drive his point home.

"His mother said to him, 'Son, why have you treated us like this? Your father and I have been anxiously searching for you.' Then verse forty-nine explains it: 'Why were you searching for me?' he asked. 'Didn't you know I had to be in my Father's house?'

"We can equate Mary's confusion with our own. Why would God allow young John McCabe to be 'taken too soon'? Jesus answers that very question: 'Didn't you know I had to be in my Father's house?' John is no longer with us, and that is a tragedy…but let us pray to God that we can rejoice, because like Jesus, John is in God's house now."

Father Heinz then encouraged the congregation to celebrate John's life, rather than mourn his death; he related the stories, told to him by Bill and Evelyn the previous evening, of the goose and the grasshoppers. He closed his message with an earnest plea.

"The police are working nonstop to bring those responsible for this terrible crime to justice," he said. "And whoever those people are, may God show them mercy." He paused and swept his gaze across the crowd. "It may be that they're sitting here today. They may be here—*in God's house*—with us at this moment. If so, the time is now to show courage. Stand and speak. Atone for your sins. Let this family"—he gestured to the McCabes in the front pew—"and this community put this terrible matter to rest."

No one moved. The sanctuary was silent.

After a few moments, the priest looked down at his Bible. "First John, chapter one, verse nine: 'If we confess our sins, He is faithful and just to forgive us our sins and to cleanse us from all unrighteousness.'" He closed the Bible and returned to his seat.

* * * *

Ninety minutes later, John's casket was lowered into the freshly dug grave at the back corner of Tewksbury Cemetery on East Street, which was barely a ten-minute drive from St. William's. During the funeral Mass, a sad, steady rain had begun, and the graveside service had transpired under a canvas tent, which only covered the grave itself and the surrounding rows of chairs—where family and close friends huddled—dozens of others stood under umbrellas around the site.

And now, Bill sat with Evelyn and Debbie, who both bawled as a gravedigger shoveled dirt onto the casket. (Roberta, while being too young to fully understand the gravity of the situation, knew her family was sad; she played listlessly with a doll in the adjacent row.) Out at the small drive which wound its way through the cemetery, the press corps had cornered Detective St. Peter; though they'd shown respect throughout the Mass and the burial, and knew not to approach the family until they were ready to speak, the reporters were grilling St. Peter hard.

Of course, the detective knew from experience that it was a game: the press guys had to appear as though they were doing their utmost to learn new information (which they were); likewise, St. Peter needed to give the impression that the investigation was progressing (even though it really wasn't), and that the police were doing everything in their power to solve the crime (which they *absolutely* were). So St. Peter did the dance, deflecting real questions with the usual "following all leads" answers, along with the standard request that "anyone with any information should report it immediately."

Just as it seemed the reporters were running out of questions, St. Peter felt a tap on his shoulder. He turned to see Bill McCabe standing there as stone-faced as ever...but there seemed to be a glimmer of hope somewhere beneath his stern demeanor. He had a spiral notebook in his hand.

"Mr. McCabe." St. Peter nodded respectfully. "If you'll give me a m—"

"I'd like to say something to them," Bill said. "I won't answer any questions…but I want to make a statement."

"Um…okay." St. Peter glanced over his shoulder at the reporters. "Are you sure?"

"Yes, I am."

"All right." St. Peter took Bill's arm and nudged him forward. "Gentlemen, Mr. McCabe wants to give a brief statement. No questions, please." He gestured to the reporters as if to say, *They're all yours.* The cameras and microphones shifted to Bill.

"I know that this detective"—he nodded toward St. Peter—"and the entire Tewksbury and Lowell departments are doing everything they can to find out who killed our Johnny. So far, they haven't figured out who done it." He looked at the detective. "I'm not criticizing you." To the press: "It seems like whoever did this is a coward, and they're afraid to come forth. So I want it known that I'll be assisting them." (At that, St. Peter groaned inwardly.) Bill held up the notebook. "I started writing in this last night. I wrote about what Johnny did the week before his death, and I wrote about my memories of my son. This book will be a way to keep his memory alive, and it'll have information that we may need in the investigation.

"Johnny was a good boy," he said after a moment. "He didn't deserve this. And I say to you, as a man: As long as I'm breathing, I won't stop looking until we find out who committed this crime. Thank you." And he was gone.

Every reporter present, it seemed, instantly shouted a question: "Who do you believe killed your son!?" "Will the notebook be made public?" "Is it true John was drunk at the time of the murder!?" But Bill was already striding back toward his family. St. Peter trotted after him, wondering how in the *hell* the press could have known about John's alcohol consumption. *They probably just heard the rumor,* he thought. *Let 'em keep thinking that's* all *it is—rumor.*

As Bill reached the gravesite, he saw Ted and Emily Ward, along with their twelve-year-old son Jack, talking quietly to Evelyn and Debbie. The Wards had moved into the neighborhood the year before, and little Jackie, though two and a half years younger, had been John's friend (a fact that, for some reason, hadn't been relayed to St. Peter and the other investigators). While Bill greeted them, St. Peter stood back a few feet to show some respect. After they all exchanged a few "sorry for your loss" and "we'll be praying for you" comments, Ted motioned for Bill and Jackie to step away with him. *Time for some "man talk,"* St. Peter observed.

"Bill, we heard what you were telling the reporters," Ted said. "And I want you to know that Jack and I will be keeping our eyes and our ears open, for as long as we need to. Right, son?" He looked down at Jack and put his hand on his shoulder.

"Yes sir." Jack's eyes were focused on the ground. He was a slight, meek boy, making him a perfect foil for John's boisterousness. And at this moment, he seemed more sheepish than ever.

"Actually, I've been wanting to talk to you, Jackie," Bill said, pulling up a chair. He sat down so he could be at eye level with the boy. "Is it okay if this detective talks with us too?" He gestured to St. Peter.

"Um…sure." Bill waved St. Peter over. The detective took a seat next to them.

Bill put his hands on Jack's shoulders. "I want you to tell us everything you remember about last Friday. Can you do that?" Jack paused, then nodded. His eyes shone with tears, Bill saw. "Don't be scared, son."

"Well…me and Johnny were supposed to hang out that night. But he…he never showed up. So I just hung around the house, watching TV and stuff. He told me he wanted to go to the dance. But I'm not old enough to go…so he said he wasn't gonna go either." Jack purposefully left out a crucial part of his story: that actually, their plan had been to meet at 7:30 at Sullivan Parkway, a subdivision on the south side of town that was still under construction (and therefore mostly empty of houses) to have a party. John had collected money from several people, Jack included, to try and get beer for the party. Out of both fear of his father and respect for his friend's memory, Jack kept that information to himself. "He never showed up," he repeated, his bottom lip now quivering. "I went to bed about 11:00, I guess…and the next day Mom told me—told me they found Johnny…and…" He dove into his father's arms, crying; he suddenly seemed to regress from twelve years of age to about five.

Bill looked away, teary-eyed himself. St. Peter sat still, giving Jack time to grieve. When Jack had regained some composure, the detective finally spoke: "Thank you, Jack. You're a brave young man. Now: you said you didn't know John was going to go to the dance?"

Jack sniffed and wiped his face with one arm. "No sir. I didn't know he went till I talked to Carol Ann a couple days later."

"Okay. And did he…never mind. Is there anything else you can tell us?"

59

Jack thought for a moment...while looking down and to the left. "Uh...no sir." *A lie,* St. Peter thought. *But that's okay. He's twelve. Don't think it'd be relevant.*

"Okay. Thank you, young man. You've been a big help." He turned to Bill. "A quick word before I go?"

"Sure," Bill said. He ruffled Jack's hair. "Remember, Jackie: ears open, right?"

"You bet, Mr. McCabe." He even smiled a little as he echoed his father's statement. "For as long as you need me to."

Bill returned the smile and lightly punched Jack's arm. "That's my boy." He and St. Peter stepped away, then turned to face each other.

"I'll be frank, sir. Regarding what you told the press: normally, we hardass cops can't *stand* it when people— especially family members—insert themselves into an investigation. Usually they just get in the way, and end up doing more harm than good. But—" Bill opened his mouth to protest, but St. Peter held up a hand to stop him. "*But:* I and the others will let you help us. God knows, it's the least we can do. And besides...at this point, we need all the help we can get. We're following all the leads, but...honestly? Nothing looks promising. Not so far."

"Well...I'm glad you're being honest, Gerry." Bill's face clouded over. "But...*nothing*? What about the Bevvie kid? He—"

St. Peter stopped him once more. "Mr. McCabe, listen to me: we are following every lead. I guarantee you that. Is Bevvie a piece of crap? He is. Did he kill your son? I don't know. The circumstantial evidence keeps leading us back to him...but that's all it is. Circumstantial. We don't have anything solid yet. But we'll find it. I promise you we will. It's like Jackie Ward said: *as long as it takes*."

Bill's face was still hard. "Gonna hold you to that, Gerry."

"Absolutely. Just promise me this, Bill: that you won't take any action on the case—of any kind—without talking to us first. And you'll share any information you put in that notebook with us. *Anything.* Got it?"

"I got it."

"Maybe you can give us updates every week or so?"

"I'm praying it won't last that long, but I will."

"I'm praying too, Bill." The detective offered his hand, and Bill shook it. "Thank you, sir."

* * * *

St. Peter spent the next few hours holed up at his cramped desk at TPD, going through the files that were already stacked nearly a foot high, trying to tie up any loose ends. *Somewhere in here, there's a murderer, dammit,* he chided himself as he eyed the rows of manila folders. He poured himself a huge mug of muddy coffee, then dove in.

He read through numerous reports of interviews with witnesses, few of which were helpful. Janice Houser, for example, was a schoolmate of John's who'd had a party Friday night that John was supposed to attend; according to Janice, John never showed up. Another report detailed the interview of nineteen-year-old Margaret Cogan, who said she heard through the grapevine that another teen, Edward Johnston, knew who the killers were. When Johnston was questioned immediately afterward, he said it was just a rumor, and that he knew nothing about the crime. Several other reports were nearly identical: interviews with teens who all said they saw John at the K of C dance, he left just before it was over, and that he was planning to take off for NYC with Bevvie.

Next St. Peter went over the crime scene inventory for about the fifth time, looking for something—*anything*—he'd missed. When he came to the list of the clothes John had been wearing, he conjured a mental image of John's outfit, envisioning each item being added to a department store mannequin: *maroon shirt…green pants…brown loafers…* When he finished the mental inventory, he noticed something odd: John hadn't been wearing a belt. *Or, at least, none was found when his body was discovered.* St. Peter added yet another item to his to-do list: *ask Evelyn McCabe if she noticed whether he was wearing a belt when he left for the dance.*

An hour or so after his mannequin imaginings, Farley and DeForrest (the *faux* photographer from the funeral) emerged from an interview room. Accompanying them was the vice principal of Tewksbury High School, an ancient woman everybody just called "Miz Gaines," who'd been working in the school district for decades; she seemed to know every student that had attended Tewksbury schools for the past thirty years, so the detectives had asked her to come down and help identify kids in the photographs whom the detectives didn't know. In a matter of minutes, she examined the freshly developed photos and named six unknown teens. The only one of interest to St. Peter was a petite brunette girl whom Miz Gaines said she'd seen with Walter Shelley more than once. Miz Gaines had identified the girl as a seventh-grader named Marla Shiner. She didn't know the particulars of Marla's and Walter's relationship, only that she'd seen them together a few times.

At about 8:00 p.m., as St. Peter noticed that his eyes were beginning to cross while reading yet another report, a tall, bearded man entered the station. He spent five minutes talking to St. Peter and Lieutenant Jop, and they learned four facts: he was Ralph Danner, a co-worker of Walter Shelley's; Walter had worked for their cleaning company, Professional Services, for about eighteen months; there had been recent complaints about Walter's shoddy work (even though he was previously known as an excellent employee); and earlier that day, Walter had quit to take another job at some place called Astro Circuits.

"So…whaddya think?" Jop asked as they watched Danner exit.

"Hm…what do I think? I think it's pretty odd timing," St. Peter mused. "Why would he suddenly be doing crappy work, then all of a sudden find another job? Something's not right."

"Roger that." The men stood in silence, the cogs in their brains whirling. Jop eventually spoke up: "What now?"

St. Peter blew out a long breath. "Boy…you up for an all-nighter? Whaddya say we go sit on Walter Shelley's house? See how the young man's living?"

Jop grinned. "Sounds good to me…I've been sleeping too much lately as it is."

* * * *

"Hand me that thermos, will ya?"

Jop reached down and grabbed St. Peter's thermos, a monstrous aluminum canister that served equal duty on his camping trips and his stakeouts. They'd filled it with an entire pot from the coffee maker at the station, then driven to Walter's Nelson Street home about 11:30. And now, though it was only 2:15, they were already halfway through the thermos's contents.

Their objectives for the stakeout were twofold: first, they wanted to get a sense of Walter's comings and goings (if there were any) and see whether or not he was a night owl. But more important, they wanted to get a sample of the paint on Walter's car, and if they were lucky and the car was unlocked, fibers from the car seat and floorboard carpet (all in case the State Police lab report, which was due back within the next week, documented samples of unknown paint and/or fabric material). And as they coasted to a stop across the street with the car lights off, they hoped no one would notice their arrival, meaning they could at some point sneak over and collect the samples from Walter's car, which was parked by the curb in front of the house.

They were out of luck—at first, anyway. A light was on in the large front window, and seconds after St. Peter killed the engine they saw a darkened face appear between the curtains, where it remained for several seconds.

"Dammit. They made us," Jop said from the passenger seat. And as the night oozed by, it seemed that the occupants had not only made them, but were deeply concerned about their presence, because the same face peeked through the curtains every ten minutes or so until they left at dawn. At one point, St. Peter happened to observe the curtain in one of the darkened rear windows ease back, and they saw one eye contemplate them for nearly a minute before the curtain eased back into place. Fortunately, at about 3:00 a.m., Jop found a window of opportunity and dashed over to Walter's car—which *did* happen to be unlocked—and collected the various samples, then scampered back to the stakeout car undetected.

The night continued its oozing. The men bided their time by having a long conversation about sports: first they debated the Red Sox's previous season, and whether the Sox would be able to catch the Baltimore Orioles, whom they'd finished the season twenty-two games behind, the next year. Eventually, talk turned to football, and the men pondered the fate of the Boston Patriots, who were an AFL team but would likely join the NFL East division if the rumors of an AFL-NFL merger turned out to be true.

Just as the eastern sky was beginning to lighten, Jop looked at St. Peter, who'd been silent for a while, and was staring out the car window at nothing. Save for the face at the window every few minutes, there seemed to be no activity in the Shelley house—but the living room light was still on. Jop asked the exact same question St. Peter had heard sixteen hours earlier: "So Gerry…where are we?"

St. Peter, who was too tired to be a smartass, just sighed. "With this case, you mean? I honestly don't know, Walter. We've got all sorts of little circumstantial stuff, but nothing solid."

"Have you thought about the sister?"

"Debbie? No way. She didn't do this."

"No, I know that, but…I mean as a lead. Rumor has it she's into drugs. Or was, at least. If she didn't do it, maybe somebody connected to her did."

St. Peter sighed again. "Well, it's worth looking into. What else have we got? Bevvie? He looks right…but damn, I just don't *feel* like he's the one. And these guys?" He gestured to Walter's house. "Shelley and Ferreira? They don't add up. They tell different stories about what they did

Friday night—even though they both said they were together. The Moran kid said he saw a car like Walter's in the area around the time of the murder. And...I don't know. I just get an odd feeling whenever I talk to either one of them about the whole thing. But that's all I've got—a *feeling*. And we can't arrest anybody based on a feeling."

Both men stared at the house. After a few moments, Jop said, "I just wish something would happen. We need for something to break."

"Me too, Walter. Me too. But...we might need to prepare ourselves for the long haul with this one."

The last sentences of St. Peter's report detailing the stakeout, which he wrote upon arriving at the station early the next afternoon, summarized the entire evening: "We collected the needed evidence from Walter Shelley's car, but were otherwise unsuccessful. This night was a standoff."

6. Wednesday, October 1

St. Peter took the rest of the day off after writing the stakeout report, and he came to the station the next morning feeling refreshed after fourteen glorious hours of sleep. And apparently, he didn't miss much during his time off. Farley told him upon his arrival that the only newsworthy information was that they'd gotten a call the previous afternoon from a kid named Larry Dover, who was fifteen. Dover explained that he'd overheard some boys at school— he didn't know their names—saying Debbie McCabe was on drugs and that, according to Dover, "John was going to squeal on the guy (or guys) selling to her."

So Jop was right, St. Peter thought. "And?"

"I called her right after the kid called us," Farley said. "When I told her that we'd…'gotten some information' about her taking drugs, she got pissed, emphatically denied it, then she hung up on me."

St. Peter grunted. "Sounds like a junkie to me." At that both men gave an ironic chuckle.

"So what do you wanna do with it?"

"Let's just sit on it for now. If more comes out about it, we'll look at the drugs angle more closely. Meantime, let's focus on other things." He grunted again. "That is, if there's other things to focus *on*."

* * * *

Later that morning, something else indeed drew their attention entirely. St. Peter and Farley were traveling from store to store in Tewksbury and Lowell, stopping at each one that sold rope, trying to find a possible match for the rope used to tie up John McCabe. They were in downtown

Lowell, on their way to Woolworth's after leaving King's Department Store, when their CB radio crackled.

"TPD dispatch to LPD alpha."

"LPD alpha, go ahead," Farley said into the handheld mike.

"Need you to 10-19"—return to station—"immediately, regarding new info in the McCabe homicide."

The detectives glanced at each other, eyebrows raised. "Copy that. LPD alpha, 10-19, forthwith."

Forthwith was an understatement. While Farley slammed the blue bubble onto the dash and activated its switch, St. Peter pulled a quick U-turn, narrowly missing a lumbering semi traveling in the opposite direction. Though the call wasn't a Code 3—"use lights and siren"—the dispatcher's use of the word "immediately" told the detectives the information would undoubtedly be important. The unmarked skidded to a halt in front of the station five minutes later.

The detectives trotted inside, where the scene was somehow frenetic and focused at the same time. The dispatcher, Denise Tomlin, was seated at the squad room's main desk, where she took any of TPD's incoming calls during the day shift. Standing on either side of her were Captain McGuane and Sergeant Bradanick, who were conferring and referring to Tomlin's daily call log. St. Peter was all business as he approached the desk.

"Whadda we got?"

McGuane spoke first. "Denise got a call from a Father Walsh over at St. Margaret's, in Lowell. He said—here, read the notes." He thrust the call log forward.

St. Peter scanned the log. He had to force himself to read slowly because Denise's handwriting, in her rush to transcribe the call, was barely legible. But St. Peter got the gist of the report. "Jesus."

Father Walsh, Denise had summarized, had received a call from a man who said he'd killed John McCabe, and that he wanted to talk to a priest about it. He wanted to turn himself in, Walsh reported, but Denise wrote that "Lowell police beat him up before—didn't want it to happen again."

St. Peter thought about the late-night caller—who'd Jop guessed was a teenager—from two days before. "Any idea how old this man was? Did Walsh say? Did *he* say?" Denise shook her head.

The man had finished the call by telling Walsh that he'd call back later in the day "and let Fr. know when/if he'd come see him."

"We need a tap on Walsh's phone," St. Peter said. "The rectory at St. Marg—"

"Lowell PD is already on it," McGuane interrupted him.

"Okay, good. Then Farley and I'll head over there. St. Margaret's—Stevens Street, right?"

"That's it. I'll ride over with you," McGuane said, already heading to his office to grab his jacket and holster.

* * * *

A little before 1:30 p.m., the rectory phone rang again. St. Peter and McGuane were on the couch, listening to Father Walsh talk about "troubled parishioners." (Though he was skirting the idea, the priest couldn't quite bring himself to admit that a member of his congregation would be capable of a crime like murder.) An LPD technician was sitting quietly in the corner next to the phone and the trace

69

equipment attached to it, ready to spring into action should the man call again. Farley had just returned from fetching lunch for everybody when the phone jangled.

The men all froze momentarily, then got moving. McGuane snapped his fingers and pointed at the phone tech, who was already preparing the machine to start the trace. Father Walsh raced to the phone, but before he could answer, St. Peter stopped him. The two men stared at each other; St. Peter held up a hand and breathed deep, then mouthed a one-word admonition: *Easy.* The priest nodded, then picked up the receiver and brought it to his ear. "Hello?"

He listened for a moment, then nodded emphatically. The tech switched on the trace equipment, which he'd said would need between thirty and sixty seconds to determine the location of the call.

Though the detectives could only hear Walsh's half of the conversation, they had no problem guessing what the man was saying. They'd coached the priest to try and find out anything he could about the man but above all else, to *keep him on the line* until the trace went through. And Father Walsh was playing his role to the hilt.

"Uh huh…yes. No, I understand. No cops…you have my word, sir." The technician, his eyes glued to the equipment, spun his index finger. *Keep talking,* the gesture said.

"I'm Father Thomas Walsh. And your name is…? Okay. No, it's all right." Walsh listened for a few seconds. "I understand that. But sir, you need to confess your sins. To God, and to—no…well, I'll be here at whatever time you want me to be." The tech gave him a thumbs-up. *Got it.* "8:00 p.m.? I'll be waiting for you. I understand. No, I won't call them. Okay. Goodbye." He hung up. "He'll be here at 8:00. He specifically said, 'No police.'"

"Yeah we got that," St. Peter snapped. "What else?"

"Not much, really. He said he's afraid of getting beaten again. Hm…he also said you won't find any fingerprints at the crime scene, 'cause he was wearing gloves. I guess that was about it."

St. Peter's mind again flashed back to Jop's late-night anonymous caller. "Any idea how old he was?"

"Just from his voice? I…no idea."

St. Peter gritted his teeth. "Take a guess."

"Hmm…it was sort of high-pitched, I guess…but he didn't talk like a little boy. Could be anywhere from mid-teens to mid-twenties. Sorry."

The tech, meanwhile, had been on the phone with the Tewksbury switchboard and information operator, finding out the address for the exchange from which the man called. Now he hung up. "Payphone at Middlesex and South streets!"

The detectives wasted no time, screeching to a stop in front of the booth less than two minutes later. Though the pay phone was only four blocks from the rectory, by the time they arrived the booth was empty. St. Peter scanned the streets in all directions, but saw nothing—or no one—out of the ordinary.

"Dammit," he muttered. "Dammit! We had him!"

"Relax, Gerry," McGuane told him. "We'll get him. Sounds like he's feeling pretty remorseful. He'll show up at the rectory. Don't worry."

"Speak for yourself," St. Peter said, then started for the car.

The others followed. Farley said, "I'll drive." He held out his hand for the keys, but St. Peter breezed past him without a word, got in on the driver's side, and slammed the door.

On the short drive back to the station—fifteen minutes or so—St. Peter was like a caged lion, both in his personal manner and his maneuvering of the vehicle: he tailgated every car he got behind, honked the horn repeatedly, and even passed numerous cars on the right. And he was muttering to himself the entire time.

Just after they crossed the Tewksbury town line, St. Peter nearly rear-ended a car that braked suddenly. He laid on the horn: "Let's go!!!"

"*Enough,* Gerry," McGuane said from the back seat, slapping his hand on St. Peter's right shoulder. "Christ. What's eating you?"

"Aaah…" St. Peter jerked the car over to the shoulder and stopped. He swore and slapped the top of the steering wheel with both hands. "This *case* is eating me, Cap. We had him! Par for the course. Seems like every time we get close, whatever we're chasing just slips away."

He calmed himself some, then turned to face McGuane. "This is getting old, Cap. It's like the priest said at the funeral: it's time this was put to rest. It needs to end. The McCabes deserve answers. The community too. *I* need answers. How long will this go on? This isn't Boston, or New York City…it's Tewksbury. It's a small town. We don't *have* cold cases here!" The car was silent. "Ah…screw it." He pulled back onto the street.

McGuane finally responded as they were pulling into the station. "Why don't you take the rest of the day off, Gerry? We'll handle the St. Margaret's situation."

"I'm okay, Cap," St. Peter said evenly. "I wanna be there to cuff this guy myself."

* * * *

The detectives arrived at the rectory a little after 7:00, plenty of time to be in place out of sight from the man when he arrived. They were discussing their hiding places, and the technician was at his post next to the bugging equipment (which they'd left in place) when the phone jangled once more. Father Walsh trotted over to answer it.

"Hello?" He listened momentarily, then his eyes grew wide. He pointed at the receiver and nodded his head: *It's him.* The tech immediately began the trace. "No. It's just me here. I didn't…but those were…okay. Sir…I think—" He pulled the receiver from his ear. "He hung up."

"Dammit!" St. Peter said.

The tech looked up from the equipment. "Not enough. Couldn't get a number."

"He said he saw you come in," Father Walsh said. McGuane ran to the window and started scanning the street while the priest continued. "I tried to tell him you weren't cops, but he said he knows who you are." Father Walsh looked at each of them. "He said he *might* call me back another time. That was it."

"He had to have called from close by," St. Peter said as he headed for the door. "Let's go see if…" His voice trailed off as he exited, and the others hurried after him.

While St. Peter, McGuane, and Father Walsh performed a frantic investigation of the block surrounding the rectory, Farley jumped in the car and sped over to the same phone booth the man had called from that afternoon. And once again, their combined search was fruitless.

"Well, that's it. We lost him," St. Peter said to Farley. They were in the car returning to the TPD station to fill out their incident report before calling it quits for the night. This time St. Peter relinquished the driving duties to his unofficial partner; he was instead staring dejectedly out the open passenger window.

Farley let out a small laugh. "C'mon, man. You don't know that. Have a little faith, will ya?"

St. Peter just continued to stare out at the passing neighborhoods. Finally, he turned to Farley. "My faith's about run dry. We had him again. And *again,* he slipped away. How many more times is this gonna happen? How long do we have to keep doing this?"

Farley answered with words St. Peter had himself spoken to Bill McCabe just two days before: "As long as it takes."

That sentence, spoken with such simple, honest conviction, somehow changed St. Peter's entire outlook on the case (though he'd actually uttered the same words himself). It was as if his ego—the part of him that needed the crime solved *now,* for no other reason than to make himself feel like he knew how to do his job—suddenly loosened its grip. He realized, probably for the first time in his career, that he needed to solve crimes because it was the right thing to do. He realized that being a good detective was not something he did, it was *who he was.* And this abrupt epiphany made him start laughing.

Farley looked at him with both amusement and concern. "What's so funny? You okay?"

St. Peter's giggling subsided. "Yeah, I'm all right. I just…you were right. 'As long as it takes,' right? And…with all these hissy-fits I've been throwing I keep forgetting that this murder only happened five days ago. Seems like weeks." They pulled into the station and exited the car.

"I was gonna say months," Farley joked as they walked to the door.

"Haha," St. Peter added. "Ye—"

"Detectives?" It was Jop, who was working the evening dispatch shift. He was standing in the open station door. "Another priest called. Said the same man just called him. C'mon, I'll tell you the details."

St. Peter looked at Farley with a wry smile. "See? Farley, you need to have some faith."

They hurried inside. Jop was headed to an interview room, where McGuane and several others were waiting. "What was it Yogi Berra said?" Farley quipped as they went. "It's like déjà vu all over again?" To which St. Peter gave a smirk.

"All right, here it is," Jop said once they were all settled. He had the call log in front of him, but told them directly from memory. "About"—he checked his watch— "twenty minutes ago I took a call from Father Cahill, of St. Peter's Parish over in Lowell. He—"

"That's a Catholic church too, right?" St. Peter asked. "You can bet this guy is Catholic. He calls two different Catholic priests on the same day? He's gotta be."

"And the McCabes are Catholic too," Farley added. "I wonder if this guy—"

"Fellas," McGuane interrupted, "later. Let Walter talk."

"Anyway," Jop continued. "Cahill said a man had just called him and told him he was the one who killed the McCabe boy. He told Cahill he was twenty-three, lived in

Lowell. Said he'd called another priest, but that priest called us. He s—"

"He must've called Cahill right after Walsh!" St. Peter interjected. "He—"

"Gerry, *please,*" McGuane said. "Later. Okay?" He gestured to Jop to continue.

Jop cleared his throat. "Cahill said he actually talked to the man for a couple of minutes. I asked him if he knew where the man was calling from, or if he said where he was. Cahill said he didn't, but he—Cahill—could hear cars going by in the background, so he figured the guy was at a pay phone. Cahill said he told the man he would absolutely not call us." Jop paused and looked around the room with a goofy grin, soaking in the irony of his last statement. "And then…here's the good part." The others leaned in. Jop referenced the log for a moment, then continued.

"Cahill asked the man if he could prove he had anything to do with the murder. So the man said—here, I wrote this part down." He read from the log: "The man said to call the boy's parents and ask if they have the belt that was missing when the boy was found. They'll say no…because he said he still has the belt."

St. Peter slammed his fist on the table. "I *knew* it!" McGuane threw him a dirty look. "Sorry."

"Cahill asked him what color the belt is, and he said the man said, 'Black,'" Jop said. "And that's it. That was everything the priest said." And before Jop was even finished, St. Peter headed for the door.

"Where you going?" McGuane asked.

"Gonna call Evelyn McCabe," he answered, and was gone.

The others remained, trying to figure out how they could find the mysterious caller. Farley asked the question on everyone's mind: "So…did Cahill say anything about meeting the guy?"

"Nope," Jop said. "Nothing like that at all. I told you everything he told me."

"Great. So…what do we do now?"

"We wait," McGuane answered. "We just hope the guy's conscience keeps eating at him like it's been doing already, and maybe he'll reach out again. I don't know what else we *can* do."

"I say we go talk to this Father Cahill," Farley said. "No offense to you, Walter—I'm sure you told us everything he said—but maybe a face-to-face interview will help him remember. Especially if Gerry's there. He—"

"You talking about me behind my back?" St. Peter came in looking a bit conflicted. He collapsed into a chair. "I called the McCabes, and Bill answered, said Evelyn was already in bed. Asked him if he knew whether John had on a belt when he left the house. Said he didn't know, but his wife might. Then—I didn't tell him details of why I was asking—he wanted to know why *I* wanted to know about the belt. Asked me all sorts of questions. I guess he really meant what he told the press."

"What do you mean, 'what he told the press'?" The question was from McGuane.

"Oh," St. Peter said, and uttered a nervous little laugh. "You don't know about that, huh?" He then summarized what Bill had told reporters after John's funeral—"said he would be 'assisting us in the investigation,'" St. Peter told the others, to which they all vocally opposed—and he explained the notebook in which Bill had started keeping notes, and how he asked Bill to share its contents with them. This brought more protests from the others.

"Bad move, Detective," McGuane said. "You *know* we can't let him in on where the—"

"I know, I know," St. Peter said. "But the way I see it, how can it hurt? He may be able to find out things we can't. Listen: I know it's a fine line to walk. But my plan is to keep him out of the loop on most of what we know or find out. Just let him know enough to keep him on our side—to make him think he's helping us, even if he really isn't. Make sense?"

Everyone pondered this for a moment. McGuane finally spoke up: "Okay, Gerry. But I'm sure you know this is against policy, and it's a *huge* gamble. So it's gonna be your responsibility. And the minute Bill starts getting in the way, he's out. Period. Understood?"

"Understood," St. Peter acknowledged. "And I know it's a gamble. But at this point, what else do we have to go on? What do we have to lose?" He looked around the room. No one spoke.

7. Friday, October 3

St. Peter finished his lunch and sat at his temporary desk, arms behind his head, staring into space. He was once again mentally reviewing and organizing the case information—something he did whenever he had some downtime during an investigation.

And after his umpteenth reassessment of the evidence—what relatively little of it there was, anyway—one thought was starting to replay itself in his head: *This one's gonna take a while.*

The unknown caller to Fathers Walsh and Cahill was turning out to be a dead end. They'd gone to St. Peter's the day before to speak with Cahill personally, but he said the caller had mentioned nothing about a possible meeting, and he hadn't heard from the man since the first call. Cahill promised to notify them immediately if the man contacted him again.

Evelyn McCabe had nothing to offer either, other than worry and interference (unintentional though they may have been). St. Peter had called her the previous morning to ask whether she remembered if John had a belt on when he left for the dance.

"Why? Did you find out something about it?"

"Just part of the investigation, Mrs. McCabe," St. Peter said, struggling to keep his voice even. "Do you remember?"

"Well, Johnny would forget to wear one, so that night I reminded him. He said he had one on…but now that I think about it, he never showed it to me. He just walked out the door! Why are you asking? Have you learned someth—"

"Just routine questions, ma'am."

"I see. Well, Bill told me you want us to help you," she said. *Correction: we want* him *to help us,* St. Peter thought. *And I'm starting to wonder about even that.*

"We'll let you know when" (*and if,* he thought but didn't say) "we need you. Until then, don't do anything, or talk to anyone, without checking with us first. Okay?"

"We'll do everything we can to help you find out who killed our Johnny," she said, her voice breaking.

Unfortunately, that's what I'm worried about, he thought. "Do you know how many belts John had? Did he wear more than one?"

"Far as I know, he just had one he wore—if he wore one at all. A black one."

A slight chill ran through St. Peter's body. "Black, you say? Okay."

"Was he wearing one when…when you found him?"

"I…I don't have that information in front of me," he lied. "Listen: could you do me a favor and go check in his room, and see if there are any belts in there? Then call me back?"

I'll do that right now!" She hung up. While he waited, St. Peter reflected on the current situation. Although he knew it helped the McCabes to be involved in finding John's killer, and while St. Peter rarely regretted his actions, he was starting to have *enormous* misgivings about letting Bill (and by proxy, Evelyn too) in on the investigation at all.

The phone rang less than ten minutes later; Evelyn said that the only belt she found was a brown one buried in his sock drawer. She hadn't seen him wear that one "in forevah," she said in her New England brogue, and she guessed it was by now too small for him.

St. Peter thanked her, and told her that if it was okay with her, they'd send someone by to search John's room for that and for any other clues. When Evelyn launched into a barrage of more questions, he begged off, saying he had things he just *had* to do.

"Okay, I'll call back later, when you're not so busy," she said.

"Um…I'll call you when I have more questions, all right? 'Bye now." And he hung up before she could respond.

Apparently, Evelyn either didn't hear St. Peter's last statement, or she chose to ignore it, because she called back that afternoon. St. Peter was meeting with McGuane and Farley, talking about where the investigation should go next, when Denise stuck her head through the doorway.

"Detective St. Peter, Evelyn McCabe is on the line? She says it's urgent."

St. Peter growled. "Boy. It *better* be urgent," he said as he went to the phone. And of course, there was nothing urgent about it; Evelyn simply wanted to ask more questions.

"With all due respect, Miss McCabe, I'm very busy right now," he said, mustering every ounce of self-control he possessed. "I'll say again: we'll call you if we have questions." When he returned to McGuane's office, the captain asked him what had been so important.

"Oh…it wasn't anything," he answered, color rising to his cheeks. McGuane was silent, but his raised eyebrows and pursed lips said plenty: *See what you've gotten yourself into?*

And now, as he sat at his desk the next day pondering the McCabes's meddling, St. Peter knew he needed to put an end to it. A round-table meeting with numerous personnel from both the Tewksbury and Lowell departments was set to take place that afternoon; the group planned to compare notes and discuss their findings in the case. St. Peter figured the meeting would be a good place to explain why he'd let the McCabes be involved—and shut down any future involvement once and for all.

An hour later, members of the two departments sat crowded around the table in TPD's back interview room, the station's most spacious one (and the only interview room with a two-way glass mirror, behind which one could watch a session without being detected). Lieutenant Jop and Sergeant Bradanick represented the Tewksbury contingent; the Lowell faction consisted of Captain McGuane, Detectives St. Peter and Clarke (the latter simply present for appearance's sake), Inspector Farley, Lieutenant Conlon, and Inspector Tim Donaghue, another member of the Lowell Criminal Bureau who'd joined the investigation earlier in the week. Linda King occupied her normal stenographer's chair behind them all.

McGuane knocked on the table to quiet the chatter. "All right, gentlemen: what's first?"

"I have something to say," St. Peter began. He then explained his *faux pas* of inviting the McCabes into the case, and why he'd done so. "Bill is starting a diary, if you will, about John. I thought it would be useful to us, being able to get information we wouldn't be privy to and the like. I had no idea they'd be so nosy like this. If it's caused anybody trouble, I apologize."

Donaghue spoke up. "'Nosy' is right. Clarke and I went to the McCabes's this morning to search the boy's room. Mrs. McCabe started in with the questions as soon as she opened the door…she tried to 'help out' with the search, and we had to tell her to stay out so we could work. And then we were sitting at the kitchen table with her and Debbie, and Debbie was showing us the telephone book. John had circled some numbers in it, and she said she'd already called some of them to find out why they were important to John, and she was planning to call more of them. I told her to stop doing it, as she was going to make those people worry for nothing. She just smiled and nodded. I wouldn't be surprised if she's still calling them."

"Sounds to me like she's conducting her own investigation," McGuane said. "From now on, I think we need to keep them out of it. We only share information with them if it's absolutely necessary. Agreed?"

The others nodded. McGuane moved on, and St. Peter breathed a sigh of relief. "Okay, what's next?"

Farley said that he and Clarke planned to go to the K of C dance that night to try and find witnesses whom they'd missed, and maybe get information they didn't yet have. "It's a long shot," Farley said, "but I figure it can't hurt."

"Long shots can solve the case. Do it," McGuane said. "What else?"

Donaghue then gave a report that pricked St. Peter's ears—for the first time in days. "Yesterday we talked to a"—he referenced a file in front of him—"Thomas Belben, age fifteen, of 150 Pine St. We saw him on Indian Hill Road, and he said he'd been wanting to talk to the police."

McGuane asked, "Did he say why?"

"I'm getting to that. He said he was at The Oaks Friday night about 6:30, and he saw Walter Shelley go by in his car. There was somebody else in the car too, but he couldn't see who it was. But he knows for sure he saw

83

Shelley. And then this: he knows Shelley because he had a fight with Shelley and Mike Ferreira. Said he's afraid of Shelley, and when Shelley has offered him rides, he refused.

"He also told us that earlier yesterday, he saw Kevin Bevilacqua and Mike Ferreira in the car with Shelley. Said those three have been together a lot the past few days. He said that all these boys are extremely close: Bevilacqua, Shelley, Ferreira, Bob Ryan, and Bob Brown."

"Those last two," St. Peter said. "Bob Ryan and Bob Brown. We haven't really looked at them yet, have we?"

"Hmmm…I don't think so," Farley offered. "Think their names have come up…" He leafed through a stack of files, then pulled one out, opened it, and scanned its contents. "Yeah. Ferreira said in his interview that he saw Bob Brown Friday night."

"See what you can find out about these two," McGuane said. "All right. Anything else?" He looked around the room, and the others shook their heads. McGuane knocked on the table again. "Have a good one."

The men (and woman) trickled out, discussing their plans for the weekend and other trivialities—and for the first time since the body was found the previous Saturday, no one included the John McCabe murder case in his small talk. Farley and Jop remained at the station, and headed over to the K of C dance a little before 8:00. Farley's self-described "long shot" was a complete miss: no one they spoke with at the dance provided any useful information.

8. Monday, October 20

St. Peter loved sitting with his feet up on his own desk. *His* desk, in his own office at Lowell PD. He'd moved back to it from the Tewksbury station over the weekend; in the two weeks following the joint meeting with the LPD and TPD members working the McCabe case, there was precious little new information to investigate, so St. Peter thought he could work better from his own office in Lowell.

New leads, though promising, had gone nowhere. The most encouraging one was that a kid named Walter Serafini, one of McCabe's (and Bevvie's) friends, had reported the previous week that a man had attempted to abduct him while Serafini was hitchhiking. The man, driving a '61 red Ford Thunderbird, picked Serafini up and tried to handcuff him, but Serafini had managed to escape. In the ensuing investigation, they found a teenager named Homer Hileman, a Tewsksburian who said he'd been given a ride by a man in a '61 T-Bird sometime in late September. (He couldn't remember the exact date, but he did remember it being a Friday night—possibly the 26th, the same night of the McCabe murder.) According to the interview report, the man, whom Homer didn't know, "asked him (Homer) if there was any action around town," then started talking to him about sex. At one point, the report stated, the man showed Homer a gun. He finally let Homer get out of the car at the bowling alley in Tewksbury. And though several other people—mainly teenagers— reported seeing a '61 red T-Bird driven by an unknown man in town, nothing more developed.

Likewise, a deeper probe of Debbie McCabe and her involvement with drugs proved useless. St. Peter and Farley had spoken with Paul Gauthier, Debbie's boyfriend, whom the detectives deemed to be on the up-and-up. Gauthier said that yes, Debbie had "dabbled in drugs, but she only liked a toke from time to time"; there was absolutely no way, Gauthier asserted, that Debbie's drug use, or the guys she bought pot from (who they were, Gauthier had no idea) had any connection to the murder.

Further investigation of Bob Ryan and Bob Brown was also discouraging; the only info detectives found that was at all relevant (if it could even be called that) was that Bob Brown had a brother, seventeen-year-old Edward Allen Brown, who was a member of the Shelley/Ferreira/Ryan/Bevvie circle of friends, and had a fairly shady reputation.

Another promising lead was supplied by Ralph Garland, owner of Garland's Greenhouses on Chandler Street in Tewksbury. In early October, Garland reported to police that a friend of his named Frank King—who, as it turned out, was the father of stenographer Linda King—stored a camping trailer at the rear of Ralph's property. On one of Frank's visits to the trailer, Garland said, he'd noticed a one-foot piece of rope on the ground next to the trailer's entrance; when he went inside the trailer he discovered it had been broken into, and a Johnson & Johnson first aid kit was missing. Among other items, the kit contained adhesive tape similar to that found covering John McCabe's eyes and mouth. The state police sent a chemist to the location to investigate, but again, nothing more developed.

And the forensics report, which had arrived from the state lab the day before, was of no help. The lab had been unable to specifically ID the tire tracks photographed at the scene; the only determination was that the tracks were "likely made by an early-1960's Michelin radial," which meant there were dozens of possibilities, since many car manufacturers installed Michelin radials on new vehicles. Soil samples taken from John McCabe's shoes were, in a nutshell, completely useless.

So here we are, St. Peter thought on that Monday morning, his feet propped in their usual position. *Nearly a month in, and we're nowhere.* He'd read through the case files again, then organized them into two boxes, hoping that he wouldn't have to eventually condense them into one so they could be in the correct order for the cold case files.

Cold case files. Three words that St. Peter had learned to detest. And he was just starting to wrap his brain around the fact that unfortunately, that was where the McCabe investigation was headed…when he found out something that stoked the case coals.

* * * *

St. Peter hurried into an interview room at the Tewksbury station, where he saw Bradanick sitting with a teenage boy who looked terrified. St. Peter had gotten a call from Bradanick twenty minutes before, and the TPD sergeant had told him to come to TPD immediately to "hear it for himself." Now St. Peter took a seat and looked expectantly at Bradanick. "Okay. What do you need me to hear?"

Bradanick looked at the boy. "Detective, this young man is Gerard. He has…an interesting story to tell us. Go ahead, son."

Gerard's eyes were wide, and he looked at both men and swallowed hard. *He looks familiar,* St. Peter thought. *And he looks nice enough...let's see where this goes.*

"Well...last night I took a ride with my brother," he began.

"Your brother is Lester? Lester Adair?" Bradanick asked.

"Yeah. And Mike Ferreira and Elaine Callahan were in the car too."

"Okay," St. Peter said. "What happened?"

"Well...they decided to go over to Pelham—you know, the State Line Market?—to get some beer. And I went with them. We went in my mom's car. Lester was driving and Elaine was in the front seat with him. Mike was behind her, and I sat behind Lester. We got to the State Line, and Lester got out to go in. Mike goes, 'Hurry up!' I think he'd already been drinking. So then Lester comes back with a *lot* of beer—like five six-packs or something— and we started to drive back."

Bradanick nudged St. Peter and nodded in Gerard's direction. "What happened on the way back, son?"

The boy swallowed hard again. "Well...we each cracked a beer...at some point, I brought up the McCabe murder. I asked Mike if the police were still hassling him about it. Then he goes, 'Not really!' Then he laughed. He goes, 'They're still after Walter, seems like, but they're leaving me *aaalllll* alone!' He said it like...I don't know...like he was getting away with something. I can't really explain it."

Kid must not know the word 'smug' yet, St. Peter thought. "Then what happened?"

"A little later, I just came out and asked him: 'Did you do it?' And he goes…'Yes, I did.' Then he goes, 'Here. I'll show you how.' And he reached over and put his hands around my throat. He goes, 'I choked him like *this*!' And he squeezed my throat real tight for a second. It scared me." His eyes pooled with tears.

Both men were quiet. Bradanick looked at St. Peter, eyebrows raised. St. Peter in a near-whisper: "What happened next?"

"They started talking about other stuff. But I didn't…I was shocked. I finally asked him what happened with John." A single tear ran down his cheek. "He…he said he saw John hitchhiking and gave him a ride. Said they rode around till about 2:00 in the morning…then he just…reached over and choked him."

No one spoke for a few moments. Gerard's face was wet with tears; he was staring at the table, apparently frightened by the memory. Bradanick finally opened his mouth to ask Gerard to continue, but St. Peter shot him a look and held up his hand: *Wait.* After a few seconds, the boy went on.

"I asked him why he did it…he looked at me all crazy-like, said: 'Cause I *hated* him!' Then he laughed. He…he just laughed. The others…I don't think they were paying attention. But I was scared. We stopped at the Howdy Beefburger in Lowell and got some food…while we were eating I asked him if he really did it. 'Did what?' he says. I says 'Killed John.' He goes, 'No, man…I was just kidding.' But…he didn't *look* like he was kidding. No sir, he didn't."

Another pause. After a bit, St. Peter asked: "Gerard? What happened after that?"

"Not much. We rode around a little more…Mike was pretty drunk by then. We dropped him off on Whipple Road, by the DPW, then we went home."

The detectives looked at each other, wondering who should speak, while Gerard collected himself. Finally St. Peter took the lead. He put a hand on the boy's shoulder.

"All right. This was a good thing you did, telling us about this. Now, let me ask you: what's your relationship like with Mike? Are you friends, would you say?"

Gerard shrugged. "I guess so. I just see him sometimes when he hangs out with Lester. He was always nice, I guess…till…till all this."

"What do you mean?"

He shrugged again. "I don't know. It just seems like…he's been…I don't know…*different* since John was killed. Maybe it's 'cause you guys are hassling him." He looked at St. Peter, seeming to expect a reprimand for that, but the detective just smiled and bowed his head. "He's always pretty nice to me, but lately, he's been acting…crazier, I guess. What he said last night sure was crazy, I know that much."

St. Peter asked him the million-dollar question: "Do you think he had anything to do with John being killed?"

Gerard scrunched up his face. "Hm. You know, I don't see how anybody could do something like that. But…after what Mike said last night—and the *way* he said it—I'm not so sure. I just…I don't know."

St. Peter patted him on the arm. "Thank you, son."

After Gerard left, the two men faced each other. St. Peter spoke first. "We need to get Mike Ferreira back in here. Immediately."

90

"That's an understatement. You want me to call Farley too?"

"Yep. And tell him to bring the polygraph expert. It's time for a little truth."

* * * *

Frank Joyce was a retired Lowell police officer who had made polygraph tests his personal hobby. And since he'd been a member of LPD for the better part of three decades, the criminal bureau put his expertise to use on the rare occasions they needed to administer polygraphs.

A bit before 8:00 p.m., St. Peter, Bradanick, and Farley waited while Joyce set up his equipment on one corner of the back interview room table. St. Peter had called the Ferreira home to ask Mike if he could come in—again—to "clear up some discrepancies." Mike wasn't home, his mother said, but she expected him back soon and would give him the message. And surprisingly, Mike had called less than an hour later to say he'd be there shortly.

Now, the four men watched coolly as an officer showed Mike into the room. St. Peter stood and thanked him for coming; he offered his hand, and Mike shook it. When he stepped past St. Peter to take a seat, the detective noticed a barely discernible odor of alcohol, but decided not to mention it, unless Mike showed visible signs of intoxication (which, so far, he hadn't).

Mike gestured to the polygraph machine. "What's this?"

"It's a lie detector test." St. Peter looked for evidence of nervousness on Mike's part when he said it, and saw none. "Your parents gave us permission."

Mike pondered this. "Well…shouldn't one of them be here?"

"Like I said, they gave us permission. So no. We're all set." St. Peter smiled. "Are you?"

Mike returned a grin. "Sure. I got nothing to hide."

"Okay. Frank, he's all yours." The three officers exited the room and went into the narrow viewing area behind the two-way glass.

Meanwhile, Joyce went to work. First he encircled Mike's chest with a canvas band, to be used to measure his rate of breathing (and changes in it). Then Joyce applied a blood pressure cuff to Mike's upper arm, for heart rate and blood pressure, then attached a pair of electrodes to Mike's temples. These last components were fairly new to polygraph machines at the time, and measured the amount of electrical activity in a person's sweat glands; the theory was that when a person was lying, even if he or she showed no signs of dishonesty in his or her voice or movements, the amount of activity in his or her sweat glands would skyrocket. Since the procedure was unfamiliar to Joyce, he didn't place much faith in it, but figured it was worth a shot.

The entire time Joyce was affixing the various components, mumbling to himself while he did so ("That's it…cuff…right there"), Mike stared at him with a look of maniacal glee. *This is so much fun!* the stare seemed to be saying. As St. Peter watched from behind the glass, his brain was at full gallop. *What's with the crazy look? This is gonna be interesting.*

Joyce finally sat back down. He looked over the equipment one more time, then nodded to himself. "Ready," he said to himself. To Mike: "All right, answer yes or no to the questions I ask you, okay?"

"No problem." The maniacal look never left his face.

92

"First question: Is your name Michael Ferreira?" The initial questions were control questions; most were meant to elicit a truthful response, establishing a baseline for the more important questions that would come later.

"Yes." The three styluses on the machine made a slight *scribble* sound on the graph paper that was feeding slowly through the viewing area.

"Are you sixteen years old?"

"Yes." *Scribble.*

"Do you live in Tewksbury, Massachusetts?"

"Yes." *Scribble SCRIBBLE. Scribble.* The elevated response to a truthful answer was puzzling, and Joyce glanced at the polygraph readout with a furrowed brow.

"Do you live at 33 Erland Avenue?" A trick question, as Mike's actual address was *3* Erland.

Mike chuckled. "No." But the machine registered its biggest response yet: *SCRIBBLE SCRIBBLE.* Joyce raised his eyebrows and just shrugged.

"Is today Monday?"

"Yes." *Scribble.*

Joyce asked a few more control questions, and though Mike answered truthfully to all of them, the machine registered responses that were all over the place. When asked if he attended Tewksbury High School, Mike answered "Yes"—the truth—but the styluses went *SCRIBBLE SCRIBBLE SCRIBBLE.* And when Joyce started with the important questions, the confusion continued.

"Did you know a boy named John McCabe?"

"Yes." *SCRIBBLE SCRIBBLE.*

"Did you give him a ride on Friday, September 26?"

"No." *Scribble.* "Wait—yes." *SCRIBBLE SCRIBBLE SCRIBBLE.*

"Did you ride in a car with Gerard Adair last night?"

Mike's crazy smile widened. *He knows where this is going*, St. Peter thought. "Yes." *Scribble.*

"Did you tell Gerard that you choked John McCabe?"

"Yes!" Mike seemed amused, as if laughing inwardly at his answer. *Scribble SCRIBBLE. Scribble.*

"*Did* you choke John McCabe?"

"No." *Scribble.*

Joyce pressed on. "Have you ever been in a vacant lot off Maple Street in Lowell?"

"Yes." *Scribble scribble.*

"Have you ever been in that lot with Walter Shelley?"

"Yes." *SCRIBBLE SCRIBBLE SCRIBBLE.*

"Have you ever been in that lot with John McCabe?"

"No." *Scribble. SCRIBBLE scribble.*

Joyce continued, but the remaining questions were perfunctory. None of the three officers knew what to make of Mike's erratic responses. When he finished, Joyce was removing the polygraph components when the other three filed into the room. The five of them just stared at each other for a moment.

"So...how'd I do?" Mike finally asked.

St. Peter was glum. "We'll let you know."

"So...I can go?"

"You can."

"Well...all right then." And still with the maniacal expression—it had never left his face, really—Mike virtually skipped out the door.

The three remaining men just sat quietly. Joyce examined the readout, trying to decipher what was basically undecipherable. "I don't…I've never seen anything like this," he finally said.

Farley looked at St. Peter. "Weird. So what say you, Gerry? Think he was pulling one over on us?"

St. Peter blew out a long, slow breath. "I don't know, fellas. I *do* know he'd been drinking. Smelled it on him." He turned to Joyce. "Would that alter the responses at all?"

"It shouldn't. I'd think if anything, he'd be *more* truthful under the influence. I just…" He looked at the readout again, and repeated: "Never seen anything like it."

"So what now?" Farley asked.

"I…I'm not sure." And for the first time, Detective St. Peter thought to himself: *We're not gonna solve this case.*

An hour later, St. Peter sat in the recliner in his darkened living room. A tumbler that had been full of scotch on the rocks now sat mostly empty next to the lamp on the table by the chair. The only light in the room was the tiny bit bleeding through the closed curtains from the streetlight outside. For some reason, St. Peter found he did his best thinking either in the car, or in the dark.

As the booze worked its way into his system, loosening his muscles (and his brain), St. Peter let his mind float. And of course, it didn't drift for long before it glided past the enormous cluster of facts surrounding the McCabe case; his mind hovered over them momentarily, then swooped down amongst them…and within milliseconds his brain was tangled in a synaptic orgy.

We got Bevvie. Also Shelley and Ferreira. We got a guy—a teenager, probably—who called us in the middle of the night and confessed. We got the guy who called the priests. Same caller as the late-night one? Good question.

Could one of the callers—or the caller—be Ferreira? Or Shelley? Bevvie? Somebody else?

He let his mind wander a little more, and now it settled on what he knew as the very basics of any crime—the detective's Holy Trinity: Means, Motive, and Opportunity. He'd learned in his training that another way to think of the three words was Ability, Reasons, and Opening. He added these synapses to the ongoing thought orgy.

Okay—Means. The ability to do the murder. Let's see...we got a sighting of a dark-colored mid-sixties Chevy in the area around the time of the murder. Shelley's car? Could be. If Shelley—which probably means Ferreira, too—was there, that's Means. Opportunity too. But Motive? Come back to that.

How 'bout Bevvie? If it's true that he saw McCabe at the K of C, and they left together—and if Bevvie had beer—that's Means and Opportunity. It's circumstantial, yes, but it's there.

Now his thoughts drifted over to the most challenging—and crucial—element of all: Motive. And try as he might, no matter how long the synapses of Reasons and Suspects engaged in their cognitive foreplay, St. Peter could not conjugate them. His mind went adrift again.

So: why would anyone want John McCabe dead? He was a teenager. Unless it was a random killing, it had to be somebody he knew. Somebody, he pissed off. And what pisses teenagers off?

He thought back to his own teenage years. He recalled the situations that charged him emotionally back then—and though those situations were practically innumerable, as any hormone-ravaged fifteen-year-old's would be, one thing was common to a lot of them.

Girls.

Maybe that's the key. Maybe this was all over a girl.

His mind floated once again, and hovered over the short list of suspects— and more specifically, who their girlfriends were, or if they even had one.

Bevvie? Don't know of any. Too much of a wild card to be tied down by one girl is my bet. Ferreira? Again, don't know of one. He probably considers himself a player, but…that doesn't mean he's got any girls played. So that leaves Walter Shelley. Hm. When I asked him about girlfriends, seems like he lied. Hm. What about that girl at the funeral Miz Gaines ID'd? Marla Shiner. She's…seventh grade? Yeah. Pretty young…but I wouldn't put it past a guy like Walter Shelley to have a "shine" on for a girl that age. (He smiled at his own pun.) *Plus, it would make sense for John McCabe to be interested in her too—she and John are only two grades apart. Hm. Think I'll look into that.*

When St. Peter went to bed a few minutes later, he slept hard. His last thought before he drifted off: *Girlfriends.*

9. Saturday, January 10, 1970

For as long as he could remember, St. Peter had absolutely hated snow. It made everything…just uncomfortable. Shoveling the walk, scraping it off the car, the treacherous driving—and, of course, it would chill a guy to his bones. Ever since he was a kid, when the first snow spit from the sky each November, he would start counting the weeks until the spring thaw—which, in New England, wasn't until late March or early April.

So, needless to say, on this Saturday St. Peter's level of comfort was near zero. The region had been pounded by a monstrous winter storm—a "Nor'eastah" to the locals—for the three days prior, and a good two feet of densely packed white powder covered every inch of…well, everything. The temperature only added to the misery: when St. Peter checked the somehow sad-looking thermometer on his porch that morning, it registered a miserable four degrees.

Now, as he waited in an interview room at the LPD station with Farley and Bradanick, St. Peter tried his best to shake off the customary winter funk. The reason for their meeting didn't help: they were waiting for Bill McCabe to make the slippery drive over from Tewksbury. Bill had been requesting this meeting for weeks, and after their decision to freeze the McCabes out of the investigation, St. Peter had put him off repeatedly. They only agreed to this meeting because Bill said he "had some new information," and because…hell, they needed the info.

For the past three months or so, St. Peter felt he had become a robot, almost. The days—and all info regarding the McCabe investigation, it seemed like—were becoming exactly the same: go to work, get a new lead, follow up on it, find out it went nowhere. They'd pulled out practically every stop with the investigation; they'd given a polygraph test to Bevvie, and he'd passed it easily. They'd given *two* to Walter Shelley, and he'd passed them both. (Not quite so easily, but St. Peter had attributed that to Walter's low IQ, which seemed to be about equal to that of a sixth-grader.)

Likewise, St. Peter's inspired hunch about jealousy over a girl as the motive for the murder was turning out to be only that—a hunch. Once again, what he'd considered a case-breaking clue turned out to be meaningless. He'd inquired at both the junior high and high school about Marla Shiner and the nature of her relationship with Walter Shelley, and was told by teachers, staff members, and schoolmates that they were only friends. He'd asked Walter Shelley about Marla during his second polygraph exam, and Walter had said the same thing—"we're just friends"— and the polygraph registered his answer as truthful. Investigators uncovered no relevant information about any girls Mike Ferreira or Bevvie might have been dating.

For a time in late November, St. Peter thought they had their man. Twenty-five-year-old Robert Morley, a man raised in Lowell, emerged as "a strong suspect," he wrote in an accumulative report. On November 29, Morley's brother Raymond reported to police that he suspected Robert of committing the murder. Robert was "a very promiscuous person with both sexes," Raymond told St. Peter, and he knew "all the prime suspects we've had in mind: Michael Ferreira, the Shelley boy, Robert Ryan, and Kevin Bevilacqua." Raymond also said that his brother was a heavy drug user. St. Peter contacted an attorney who'd represented Robert on a minor drug offense, and the attorney admitted that Robert had been a prime suspect in a murder case in the nearby town of Boxford. Unfortunately, St. Peter learned that Robert had recently gone to Florida after divorcing his second wife, and the trail ended there.

They'd also spoken to Nancy Williams again to try and clear up the confusion about Walter Shelley's and Mike Ferreira's whereabouts on September 26. Nancy corroborated what Mike had said during his first interview: that she'd been with Mike and Walter at the McCarthy residence, a home next door to Mary Ann Richard's, where Mary Ann was babysitting. They'd been there from approximately 11:30 p.m. until about midnight, she recalled, when Walter and Mike left to go to Lowell for cigarettes. And this was further supported by Mary Ann's brother Michael, who told police that he'd gone to bed at about 11:30 that night; when he heard car doors slamming a few minutes later, he looked out his window to see Walter and Mike driving away.

The only other development, for lack of a more accurate term, was that Debbie McCabe was having a tough time. She'd been present at a party in Lowell that was raided by LPD officers, who found drugs on several of the partygoers, including two of Debbie's friends. And during his questioning of pupils and staff at the high school, St. Peter had learned that Debbie ran with kids who were described as "questionable characters"; rumor was that Debbie was even selling drugs for them. Still, St. Peter and the others surmised, that type of behavior wasn't really out of the ordinary for a girl Debbie's age, and certainly not a motive for murder.

So the mood in the interview room was one of weary frustration as the three investigators watched Bill McCabe shuffle in and take a seat; St. Peter noted with some curiosity that Bill carried a thin manila folder under his arm. The four men exchanged pleasantries, then quickly got down to business.

St. Peter spoke first: "You said you have some new information for us, Bill?"

"You bet," Bill answered, opening the folder. "I've been—"

"We'll get to that," St. Peter gently interrupted him. *Gotta remind him of who's in charge here.* "First let's just talk. How's your family holding up?"

Bill's face darkened. "My…? They're fine." He gestured to the folder again. "But I think you'll wanna h—"

"We'll get to it," St. Peter repeated, more firmly this time. Bill closed the folder with a snap. "How's Debbie? She staying out of trouble?"

Bill said nothing, only stared at St. Peter. And as the seconds ticked by, his expression changed from one of cold, hard steel…to one of resignation and defeat. *That's it, Bill,* St. Peter thought. *Let that guard down. It's better for us if you do.*

"Guess you heard about what happened at that party over in Lowell," he finally told them. "Deborah is…she's hurting. We all are. She…I guess she's acting out 'cause she's angry. Well, hell, I am too! Problem is, I don't know how to do anything about it. Or *what* to do about it." His eyes pooled. "Her mother…hell. Ev and I are just trying to make it through the day. We never had to deal with something like your kid bein' on drugs."

St. Peter locked on Bill's watery gaze. He didn't have the heart to tell Bill that Debbie's "acting out" had started long before John's murder. "Listen, Bill: I've never lost my son. So I won't sit here and bullshit you and say I sympathize with you, or say 'I know what you're going through.' I don't. As far as Debbie goes…the only opinion I have"—not being a father himself, he was careful not to say *advice*—"is that if she were my daughter, I'd…well, I'd just let her know that I love her, and that I'm there for her. Then just let the chips fall where they may.

"About John's murder, let me tell you this: I'm frustrated, and I'm angry. Because there's somebody out there responsible for your son's death. We haven't found them yet. But we will. Believe me when I say: *We will find out who killed John.* Okay?"

Bill sighed. "Okay." He sounded utterly unconvinced.

"Now: let's talk some more about John…and about some things we've found out during this investigation." St. Peter knew he was taking a gamble revealing more info— vague though it may be—to Bill, but once again, he figured he had nothing to lose. And if Bill was doing detective work of his own—*true* detective work to find his son's killer, not just gathering hand-picked evidence in order to satisfy his own feelings of guilt or shame—then St. Peter suspected Bill already knew a lot of the info they were about to reveal.

And St. Peter's suspicion about Bill's knowledge of his son's true character turned out to be correct. As the men talked at length about what the detectives had learned— John's drinking and hustling, his "bratty" reputation amongst his peers—Bill slowly acknowledged that his son was not the angel he'd tried to make people believe he was.

"Look, fellas: I know Johnny was no choir boy," Bill said at one point. "He liked his booze, he knew how to con other kids outta money, apparently…and girls liked him. And he liked them too, I guess." St. Peter's quick mind momentarily flashed on the jealousy motive again while Bill continued. "But I don't think—well, I *wouldn'ta* thought—any of those things would give…give some guy a reason to kill him." His eyes misted again. "Was Johnny involved in something bad? Not drinkin', or hustling a few dollars, but something…I dunno. Something else, something bigger? He musta been. Why else would somebody want him dead?"

Bradanick spoke this time. "I—*we*—agree, Mr. McCabe. And like Gerry said, we're doing everything in our power to find out what that something was. We've followed every lead, every tip…but nothing's panning out. Not yet. But we *will* figure it out. We *will*." To St. Peter Bradanick sounded like he was trying to convince himself along with Bill McCabe.

And at that, Bill's cold-steel expression returned. "All right," he said, once more sounding unconvinced. "Thanks."

Bill left the manila folder with them. In it was a nine-page letter, written in longhand by Bill himself, offering numerous clues to the murder. Most of it was information the detectives already knew about, but one piece of intel, to which Bill referred repeatedly throughout the pages, concerned a group of teens that apparently evoked fear amongst the Tewksbury community. According to the rumors around town, Bill wrote, this group—or members of it, at least—was responsible for the murder. And two names amongst the six Bill wrote about caught St. Peter's attention: Walter Shelley and Mike Ferreira.

Even so, St. Peter thought, this info didn't help anything. Like Bradanick had said, they'd followed every lead, turned over every stone. Without more solid evidence, their hands were tied. The investigation was stalled. And St. Peter knew he was hoping against hope that it didn't conk out completely.

* * * *

"They're never gonna find out who did it."

Bill and Evelyn McCabe were lying in bed staring at the ceiling, both intermittently rolling their eyes down to the alarm clock on the dresser in the corner. (The last time Bill had checked, the glow-in-the-dark hands had read 2:20.) This nightly ritual—crawling into bed around midnight, glaring upwards while their thoughts raced, sometimes talking (but usually not) until blessed sleep overtook them near dawn—had become the norm for them in the months since John's murder.

And this particular night had been no different. After Bill had gotten home from Lowell, they'd eaten a silent dinner, sat lost in thought in the living room while "Bonanza" played on the TV, then wandered off to bed about 11:30. They'd heard Debbie come in an hour later, and though it was long past her eleven o'clock curfew—again—neither of them cared enough to get up and scold her.

At dinner, the only talk of Bill's meeting with the investigators was when Evelyn asked him how it had gone, and Bill had dismissed her with his usual "Paaahhh…" accompanied by a wave of his hand. And this latest bedtime statement about his doubts concerning the solving of the case had come at least thirty minutes after Evelyn had inquired once more about the meeting; when he didn't answer, she figured he'd either gone to sleep or just didn't care to explain. So his sudden declaration had made her jump a little. She analyzed his words for a moment before she asked him what he meant.

"They've done everything they can with the leads they have. The report I wrote out for 'em, they hardly looked at it. Think it was stuff they already knew anyway. This gang of kids—Shelley, Ferreira, Bevvie, Brown, the others—they've already looked at 'em all. Didn't find anything they can use. It's…there's gotta be something else. Some other reason we're not seeing."

Evelyn scooted over and laid her head on Bill's chest. They remained that way for several minutes; the only sound in the room was the steady, lonely ticking of the clock. Eventually, Bill heard his wife give a muffled sob, and he felt moisture from her tears soaking into his undershirt.

"*Why*?" Evelyn asked the question in a pitiful near-whisper. "Why would somebody wanna kill our sweet Johnny? Would it…was it because of a girl, ya think?"

"I dunno," Bill answered. "But *somebody* knows. Just wish they had the balls to say something."

As it turned out, eventually someone *did* speak up—but it was a year and a half later. And it was the investigators' duty to determine whether that someone was telling the truth.

10. Tuesday, August 24, 1971

Debbie McCabe blew a kiss to her boyfriend Paul, and watched him pull away after giving her a ride home from work. She checked the mail on her way into the house, and the mailbox contained a single letter-sized envelope. "Mr. and Mrs. McCabe" was scrawled across the front—no address, no stamp, no return address, nothing but the names.

"Mom?" Debbie called as she came through the door.

"In the kitchen." Debbie walked slowly through the living room, examining the mysterious envelope.

"This was in the mailbox. Did you see somebody drop it off?"

"No. What is it?" Debbie handed Evelyn the letter. She ripped it open and sat down to read the two-page hand-written note inside, composed in the same leaning scrawl as that on the envelope. A few seconds later, Evelyn let out a whimper.

Mr. and Mrs. McCabe:

After reading the articles in the newspaper, I feel it is my duty to tell you what I know about your son's murder. I know who killed your son, and I can no longer keep this on my conscience. I am sorry I didn't say anything sooner but I did not want to get involved (and I still don't). But I can, at least, tell you who done it. His name is Raymond Thibault and he lives at 75 Aberdeen Street in Lowell. I will now tell you what he told me.

Evelyn's whimpers had turned to moans, but she read on, with Debbie peering over her shoulder reading too. The letter's author explained that Thibault was a fifty-year-old married man who was also a sexual deviant "who likes young boys," the author wrote. Three nights previously, he and Thibault were out drinking, the author continued, when Thibault made a drunken confession: in the fall of 1969— "he said it was in September or October, he couldn't remember exactly"—he'd picked up a teenage boy. They'd shared a beer, then Thibault made a pass at the boy; he refused and "started to holler, so Ray picked up a piece of rope and put it around his neck to quiet him down." This excited Thibault, the author wrote, so he tied the boy up with more rope and put tape over his mouth. Not long afterward, Thibault noticed that "the boy was real quiet." Thibault panicked, thinking he was dead, so he dumped the boy's body in the first vacant lot he came to.

I wish I could be more help, the last paragraph read, *but as I said I don't want to get involved. If the police check into this man I am sure they will get the truth out of him.*

The author left no signature. Evelyn let out a long wail, then headed for the telephone. Debbie followed her and snatched up the phone directory. "Ma!? Who is that?" She started rifling through the pages. Who is Raymond Thi—"

"*Shush!*" Evelyn held up her hand. Into the phone: "This is Evelyn McCabe. I need Gerry St. Peter…yes. Tell him it's very urgent." There was a long pause, then: "Oh. No…tell him we just got a letter. It says, 'I know who killed your son.'"

* * * *

Ninety minutes later, St. Peter and Farley were burning their way up Main Street to Lowell, dashboard police light flashing, headed to the Aberdeen Street address named in the anonymous letter. After Evelyn's frantic call—which

St. Peter had luckily (if hesitantly) decided to take, since the John McCabe murder case was now officially a cold one—they'd first stopped by the McCabe residence in Tewksbury to obtain the letter and to speak briefly with Evelyn and Debbie.

C'mon, c'mon, St. Peter thought as they hurtled along. *Let this be the one. We* need *this.* And "need" was putting it lightly: no solid leads in eighteen months. And the clues they *had* found during that time had all died in the water. Walter Shelley had joined the Army just a couple of months before; St. Peter, upon hearing of this, wondered whether he was trying to run away (from the police, or his own guilt—or both). Various townsfolk had provided tips every now and then, but they were all info the investigators already had—with one notable exception. An anonymous caller had pointed the finger at a man named Frank Espinola, twenty-three, of Third Street in Lowell. The caller said Espinola was a member of the Hell's Angels; John McCabe had broken into his home and stolen drugs and money, according to the caller, and Espinola had killed him in retribution. Aside from Espinola's infrequent association with biker gangs, further investigation proved the tip to be of no use.

So as they knocked on the door of the small, shoddy house where Thibault reportedly lived, St. Peter was indeed hoping this was "the one." The man who answered the door seemed to fit the type: middle-aged, three days or so of beard stubble, and a stained white T-shirt.

"Yeah?" He said it like he'd just woken up, but St. Peter's trained senses knew better: *This man's drunk as a skunk.*

St. Peter ignored his intoxication—for the time being—as both men flashed their badges. "Are you Raymond Thibault?"

"Yeah, I'm Ray Thibault."

"May we speak with you?"

"Um…whass this about?"

"How 'bout we sit down and talk about it?" St. Peter took a step forward as if to enter the house, but Thibault didn't move.

"Well, my house…" He glanced over his shoulder at what appeared to be the living room. "The place is kin'a a mess." St. Peter saw he wasn't lying: every available surface—coffee table, end tables, even the TV—was covered with crumpled Pabst Blue Ribbon cans. Thibault gave a sheepish, half-hearted grin. "My wife, she's down t' Boston. Seein' her sister." He looked away momentarily. "Bitch…we can talk here." He gathered himself and stood straight. "Now whass this about?"

Farley took the lead. "Do you work, Mr. Thibault?"

"Nossir. I'm a mechanic…hurt my back a few years ago. Disability." He leaned against the doorjamb to hold himself upright.

"Okay. What do you like to do for fun?" Farley smiled, and Thibault gave a crooked, drunken grin of his own. "Besides lifting a cold one or three, I mean?"

"Wha…? Well…I like to take a ride now an' then." He lifted his chin toward the beat-up, ancient pickup in the driveway.

"Riding the roads, huh? You like to go alone? Ever take anybody with you?"

"Uh…" He thought for a moment. He hiccupped silently, then: "Sometimes I take a buddy, if he wants to go…" His face narrowed. "Why you askin' me these ques'ions?"

St. Peter took over. "Do you ever pick anybody up when you're on these rides, Ray?"

Thibault gave him a queer look. "Uh…I…I picked up somebody hitchhiking a time or two. Why—"

"Did you ever pick up a young man named John?"

"Wha…no…I never asked their name. Wha…?" He looked down, searching his memory. St. Peter noticed Thibault's eyes darting both left *and* right, as if visually scanning his own mind. Suddenly his eyes widened. He looked up at St. Peter. "You mean *McCabe*!? Oh, *hell* no! Nope! Din't have nothing to do with that! I—"

"You didn't pick up John McCabe in September of '69?"

"No. I. *Din't*! An' I can prove it to ya's!"

"How so, Ray?"

He barked a short laugh. "'Cause I was in *jail* when they killed 'im! Over t' County, in Billerica. 'Member readin' about in the paper. That was a Sunday mornin'…my wife was com—"

"Okay, Ray, we get you." St. Peter glanced at Farley with disgust. "What were you in for?"

Thibault's eyes blazed. "For somethin' I din't *do*! My wife's sister 'cused me of messin' 'round with her daughter. I was jus' helpin' her use the bathroom! I—"

"Ray. Ray!" St. Peter held up a hand. "That's enough. We get it."

"I din't have nothing to do with the McCabe boy," Thibault repeated. "Go check with the County, you'll see!"

"We're going to," Farley said. "In the meantime, don't go anywhere. Do we need a squad car to come babysit you while we check out your story?"

Thibault laughed. "Nope." He walked over to a cooler next to the couch and pulled out a dripping can of Pabst Blue Ribbon. "I'll jus' be right here enjoyin' a 'cold one.' Have fun!" He laughed again as Farley closed the door.

And Thibault was telling the truth. All it took was a quick phone call to the Middlesex County House of Corrections to learn that on September 26, 1969, Raymond Thibault, a fifty-one-year-old white male, was in his third week of a six-month stretch for child molestation. St. Peter figured whoever wrote the anonymous letter must be a relative out for revenge.

Both St. Peter and Farley went to bed that night dismayed, but determined to continue investigating the murder. Had they the ability to see into the future, though, they would've known to move on to other cases. Because no one would discover any new evidence directly tied to the John McCabe murder case for many years.

11. Wednesday, January 26, 1972

"Lemme show you this—it's cool."

Bevvie was sitting in the driver's seat of his car, parked at the curb in front of the North Street home of Marilyn and Laura Fraser. Jack Ward sat beside him, and John Shiner and Marilyn Fraser were in the back seat. The boys had stopped by the Fraser home an hour or so earlier to "hang out and listen to records," according to the subsequent police report. (Not included in the report was the fact that Bevvie had a pretty big crush on thirteen-year-old Laura.)

After a few minutes in the house, Laura had left with some friends, and Bevvie had gotten bored. "Hey guys, let's go out to my car," he'd told the others, the ever-present mischievous grin on his face even naughtier than usual. So the others, more out of curiosity than anything else, had followed him. On their way through the Fraser kitchen Bevvie had stopped to tear a paper towel off the roll hanging on the wall next to the sink.

Now Bevvie brandished one of the paper towels, then reached under the seat; he pawed around for a moment, then smiled as he retrieved a can of Pam cooking spray from the floorboard. He looked over at Jack with a look of pure lunacy.

Jack looked back at him, utterly confounded. "What...? What are you...?"

Bevvie put the paper towel over his mouth. "It's cool, man," he repeated, his speech muffled a bit. "Watch." He slowly exhaled, the bottom of the paper towel fluttering as he did so. Then, pressing the paper towel to his mouth with his index and middle fingers—they were spread apart over

112

the edges of his lips to look like a sort of ironic peace sign—Bevvie sprayed a generous amount of Pam onto the paper towel, then inhaled slowly.

The others all reacted instantly: "Hey!" "What the *hell*!?" "You're crazy, man!" Bevvie held the breath in for a few seconds, then exhaled slowly, the breath ending with a series of deep, dry coughs. Then he laughed.

"Whoooaaaaa…makes me light-headed." Bevvie stared into space. "Cooool."

Marilyn, who at eighteen was, at least, three years older than any of the others, pushed on Jack's seat. "This is nuts," she said. "Lemme *out.*" Jack opened his door and leaned forward, and Marilyn scrambled out of the back seat. Bevvie, meanwhile, had shifted the paper towel to a dry spot and was giving himself another blast. He followed this one with more coughing and even bigger laughter.

"Uhhhhhhh…" He collapsed back onto the headrest, a look of almost sexual ecstasy on his face. "Wowww…the colors…" He stared at nothing for a bit; then, shaking his head as if to clear it, he thrust the can at Jack. "Here—now you go."

Jack edged back into the space between the seat and the door, his palms out. "Um…that's okay." He looked confused and a little frightened.

"Well, okay then!" Bevvie put the paper towel up to his mouth again, using the only remaining corner that was still dry. He gave himself another blast, then collapsed back again, holding his breath.

John leaned forward from the back seat. "Does it…it really gets you high?" Bevvie nodded profusely, then expelled the breath in a wracking cough. Spittle flew onto the steering wheel. This time Bevvie didn't laugh; he only coughed for about thirty seconds. The other two boys glanced at each other, now visibly concerned.

"One more time," Bevvie managed once he stopped hacking. "Didn't get much that time." He held up the paper towel to examine it in the feeble light coming from the streetlamp above the car, but the entire thing was soaked through.

"C'mon, man," John said. "That's enough."

"Nope," Bevvie answered. "One more time." He put the wet paper towel to his mouth and depressed the can's nozzle. This time, he began inhaling simultaneously— which was a terrible mistake. After only a moment, the paper towel over his mouth split open, and he drew a good amount of cooking spray directly into his lungs.

Bevvie instantly dropped the can and the paper towel and coughed violently. After several more coughs, he groaned. The other two were staring at him, their faces pale.

"You okay?" Jack asked. Bevvie answered by spraying vomit all over the steering wheel.

"Shit!" Jack opened his door, then tore around the car, opened the driver's side door, and jerked Bevvie out and onto the street. Bevvie had begun to convulse. John, meanwhile, had exited the back seat and was running into the house to call for an ambulance. Bevvie struggled mightily for breath; his face was turning scarlet. Though he didn't know any life-saving techniques, Jack started pushing on Bevvie's midsection with both hands to see if he could force the cooking spray out of his lungs…but his efforts were useless. Every few seconds Bevvie's chest would hitch, and he would simply expel a yellow, foamy goop.

Lieutenant Walter Jop was the officer responding to the incident. "At 7:59 p.m. Sgt. Johnson told me to go to Lowell General Hospital to investigate a possible drug overdose," Jop wrote later in his report. "The following is from statements I took from three kids who were with the victim, Kevin Bevilacqua, at the time." The body of the report described the incident as told to Jop by Jack, John, and Marilyn. At the end of the report: "Bevilacqua arrived at the hospital by ambulance at approximately 8:15 p.m.

"At 8:51 p.m., Dr. Iovino pronounced him dead."

12. Wednesday, November 6, 1974

Just before 3:00 p.m., Lowell police arrested thirty-two-year-old Richard M. Santos, of 231 Cross St. in Lowell, and placed him in a cell at LPD. Under the supervision of Sergeant Bradanick, who was lead investigator on the case, and Walter Jamieson (the patrolman who'd driven Bill McCabe around looking for John on the night of the murder; he was now a detective), two officers searched Santos's apartment that evening. Among the items the officers found, listed later in the police inventory: handcuffs, over a dozen guns, four ski masks, a length of nylon rope, two rolls of white adhesive tape, and "approximately 200-300 murder/rape detective books."

In Santos's kitchen, the officers found what they were looking for: a green watch with a gold band. The previous Sunday, a man wearing exactly this watch had abducted a Tewksburian named Kathy (who, under Massachusetts law, may not have her full identity revealed) as she was walking along Route 38 just south of town. He'd forced Kathy into the car at gunpoint, bound and gagged her, then driven to the Tewksbury Holiday Inn. There, he'd held her in a room for over six hours, where he'd raped her repeatedly. At about 11:30 p.m., he tied her up again, drove her a few blocks to a vacant lot next to some railroad tracks, then used a rope to strangle her until she passed out.

An hour or so later, an off-duty police officer at a nearby restaurant heard Kathy screaming and came to her rescue. After calling the Tewksbury police, the officer rushed her to Lowell General. Bradanick briefly interviewed Kathy in the ER, then went straight to the

Holiday Inn, where the night clerk informed him that Santos had rented the room the previous day. Just after dawn, Bradanick obtained Santos's mug shot from LPD—he'd been arrested the previous year for burglary—and put it into a photo lineup with fifteen other mug shots.

Back at Lowell General, Bradanick re-interviewed Kathy, during which she told him about the green watch her attacker had worn. She picked Santos out of the photo lineup immediately. So Bradanick, assisted by two troopers from the Massachusetts State Police, finally located Santos at his place of employment three days later and arrested him on multiple charges: Rape, Kidnapping, and Assault with a Deadly Weapon.

When Bradanick questioned him that night, Santos admitted to being with Kathy, but denied raping her; he claimed that going to the hotel had been "her idea," and said he tied her up because "she liked it rough." He also admitted to having tied up people before. When Bradanick asked Santos about the variety of crime-related items found at his apartment, Santos had actually been honest and forthcoming.

"He claimed he used these items in his 'side job': robberies and hijackings," Bradanick wrote in his report. "He refused to give us any information on other crimes he had committed."

Shortly after the Santos questioning, Lieutenant Peter Agnis, investigator for the Middlesex District Attorney's Office, arrived at LPD. Agnis had learned of Santos's arrest, he told Bradanick, and was "extremely interested" because Santos's M.O. fit with several other open cases. Among them: Walter Serafini, kidnapping, Oct. 11, 1969; and John J. McCabe, murder, Sept. 26, 1969.

Agnis, Bradanick, and other members of the Tewksbury and Lowell departments investigated Santos for the next three months, but because Santos refused to cooperate, they were unable to obtain any more information connecting him to the McCabe murder.

13. Wednesday, August 14, 2002

"Evening, Gerry."

Lieutenant Tom Sullivan of the Massachusetts State Police came into the interview room at the Lowell Detective Bureau, then took a seat next to the detective. But the "Gerry" that Sullivan greeted wasn't Detective St. Peter; that Gerry had retired from the LCB in 2000 after nearly forty years on the job. *This* Gerry was Detective Gerald Wayne, a seven-year veteran of the Lowell Police Department. The day before, Wayne had called Sullivan to ask for his assistance in an interview. Wayne had told the lieutenant he'd just received a call from a Lowell resident named Jack Ward, who'd said he wanted to speak with Wayne about John McCabe.

Wayne, a hard-nosed, twist-your-balls-until-you-confess type of detective, was already familiar with the case. Not because he remembered the murder when it had originally happened—in 1969, he was a teenager living in Boston—but because he'd been assigned the cold case back in '99. And after discovering the mountain of evidence in the case file, he'd brought in Sullivan, a member of the detective unit of the Middlesex District Attorney's office, to help. In three years, they'd done some research on it, but had made zero progress in actually finding the killer(s).

Ward had told Wayne that he "knew about some things" that may help, and requested a sit-down with Wayne or another detective. So after Wayne set up the meeting, he'd contacted Sullivan, a burly trooper with years of experience and a near-genius IQ, requesting his presence for the meeting.

Ward arrived promptly at 6:00 p.m. Sullivan, no stranger to unconventional interviews like this one, got right to the point after Ward joined them at the table. "So what do you have for us, Jack?" Both officers picked up pens that were laying on yellow legal pads in front of them.

"Well, this is about something that happened five years ago," Ward began. "I'm just coming to you now because I didn't take it seriously at first…but it kept gnawing at me. I kept thinking about it, and as time went by I started feeling like I needed to come forward. So that's why I'm here."

"Okay," Wayne interjected. "Go on."

Ward explained that he and John McCabe had been best friends at the time of the murder, and the day of John's funeral he'd made a promise to John's father, Bill, that he would keep his eyes and ears open, and report anything he learned about the murder—no matter how long it had been since the crime occurred.

"Again, that's why I'm here. Anyway…in 1997 I went to a cookout—a 'pig roast'—at my friend Brian Gath's house, over on Marshall Street. Me and Brian work together at the Tewks Water Department; we've known each other since we were kids…anyway. One of the people at the pig roast was Mike Ferreira. He was—you know who that is? He was one—"

"One of the main suspects in the murder, we know that," Wayne said. Sullivan was scribbling furiously on his legal pad. "What happened next?"

"Well, we're all partying, drinking, having a good time…then out of nowhere, Mike comes up to me and says—I think he had a few beers in him, or maybe it was vodka—he says: 'I know why Walter murdered McCabe.'"

For a moment, no one moved. The officers glanced sideways at each other, eyebrows raised, before Sullivan scribbled some more on his pad. Then he looked up at Ward. "And then what?"

"Well…I was shocked. I says, 'What?' And he says it again: 'Walter Shelley murdered McCabe.' He…he had this funny look on his face, ya know? Almost like…like he was mad. Not *mad*, really, but…like he was…like he wanted revenge or something, I guess. Am I making sense?"

"Yes," both men answered in chorus. Sullivan was scribbling like mad.

"I just…just kinda walked away. I didn't know what to think. Was he kidding, or…? It freaked me out. I'm pretty sure my buddy Brian heard it too. And…suddenly it all made sense. It was because of Marla."

Sullivan looked up from his pad. "Marla? Who's that?"

"Marla Shiner. She was Walter Shelley's girlfriend." Ward went on to explain that Marla and Walter had begun dating shortly before the murder; even so, he said, Marla was one of two girls that John "had the hots for." (The other was Carol Ann McFrederies.) Marla and John had been much closer in age than she and Walter—he was nineteen to her thirteen—and upon discovering John's feelings for Marla, Walter flew into a jealous rage and killed him.

"Here's what I think: Walter, Mike, and maybe even Nancy Williams either committed the killing, or they know who did. Because after it happened, they all changed. Walter joined the service right away." He began using his fingers to check off items. "Nancy wasn't like she used to be—she became withdrawn, not like herself, she lost a lot of weight. And Mike was around, but he and Walter had a falling-out right before Walter went in the Army. I think Mike totaled Walter's car, I forget exactly."

Ward paused to catch his breath. Sullivan was still writing furiously. And Wayne was sitting in a daze, his face a scowl, trying unsuccessfully to process the sudden overload of info in his brain.

"Then there's this: a week or so before the murder, I was at the Wamesit Drive-In, seeing a movie. I think it was *The French Connection.* And I saw some of those guys there too—Walter and Mike. They were with some other guys—Derrick Stone, Butchie Cadell, I think John Shiner." He explained that a scene in the movie showed one of the characters tying another up "neck to feet. So I'm thinking that's where they got the idea to tie up John like they did." Sullivan's pen was racing across the pad to keep up.

The interview ended shortly thereafter. Jack Ward thanked the officers and got in his car to drive home. He didn't realize that he'd just breathed life into a case that, like his childhood friend John McCabe, had been dead for three decades.

John McCabe in early 1969

The field in Lowell, Mass., where John's body was found

John McCabe's body, as it was found by two young boys on the morning of Sept. 27, 1969

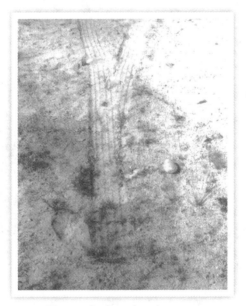

Tire tracks found at the scene

John's body, as it was found at the scene

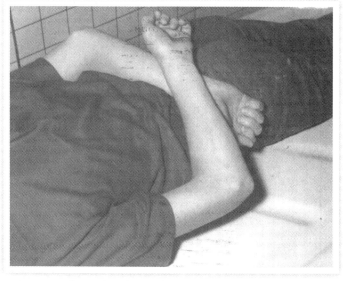

Autopsy photo detailing John's arms, which had been tied
behind his back before the onset of rigor mortis

Railroad tower in distance.

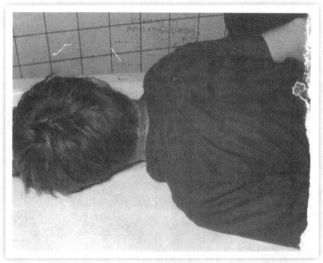

Autopsy photo showing the ligature mark made
from the rope around John's neck

Aerial photo of the vacant lot in
Lowell

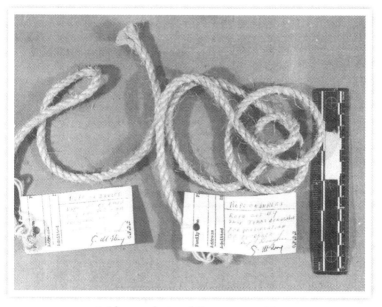

Evidence photo of the rope used to
tie John's hands and feet

Part Two:

2002-2013

1. August 2002-May 2003

The John McCabe murder investigation, though ice-cold, had remained active through the years because of one man. Not Detective Gerry St. Peter, who after working tirelessly on the case for two solid years, had moved on to other investigations. Nor was it Lieutenant Sullivan or Detective Wayne, who'd not even seen the case files until 1998.

The John McCabe murder case stayed alive through the work of a man who kept John's memory—and therefore, a part of John himself—fresh in his mind. And that man was Bill McCabe, John's father.

As the decades passed, Bill kept writing entries in the notebook he'd started transcribing in immediately after John's murder. In the beginning, the notes contained clues and rumors about the crime; after the first year or so, as the frequency of the entries decreased, the writings morphed into a sort of diary, a sentimental journal of Bill's favorite memories of his son. Starting in 1972, every March 13— John's birthday—the ever-dedicated Bill would call whichever detective was currently heading up the case to ask for an update. And most years, the responses were identical and sad: "Nothing new to report," "Still following leads," and similar empty talk. But Bill remained undeterred. Whenever he would hear tidbits of gossip or rumors about the crime, he would call the detectives and pass it along. And Bill did this regardless of the time; he would call Detective Wayne, with whom he eventually developed a personal, amicable relationship, at one in the morning so the two men could just chat about the latest developments in the case (of which there were usually very few).

But Bill's continued diligence finally paid off. In 2002, Bill had a flash of inspiration after his annual March 13 call. Bill's inspired thought: *Why not talk to Jackie Ward, see if he knows anything new?* Bill knew Jack still lived in Tewksbury—they'd in fact kept in touch through the years, and Bill had Jack's number in his address book—so after finding Jack's number, he placed the call.

They talked for a bit about Jack's two kids, Jack had asked how Debbie was doing—she was married and living in Merrimack—then Bill asked if Jack had any new info on "Johnny's killing." Jack said he didn't, though that was a lie; he hadn't had the courage to tell Bill about Mike Ferreira's statement at the pig roast five years earlier. He'd considered doing so when it had happened, but he'd made the excuse to himself that he'd needed to talk to the police first (which he'd never done). And as time went by, the shock of Mike's confession had faded…and Jack's lack of courage became a lack of memory about the incident with Mike. In other words, he'd forgotten about it.

But Bill's phone call rekindled Jack's awareness about what Mike had told him—and with it, a new spark of anger over the murder of his childhood friend. Though it was several months after Bill's call that Jack finally contacted the police, Bill's query was the seed. And one day in early August of '02, a phrase—one that little Jackie Ward had vowed to Bill over thirty years before to uphold—reasserted itself in his memory: "As long as it takes…" He called Detective Wayne the next day.

And after learning from Ward what Mike Ferreira had allegedly said at the pig roast, Wayne and Sullivan decided to redouble their efforts on the case. Though they had some doubts about how much of Jack Ward's story was true—and how much of it was Jack's own exaggeration—they agreed that it was as good a focal point as any from which to move forward with the investigation. They'd familiarized themselves with it back in '99, when Wayne first received the assignment; he'd spent several weeks reading through hundreds of police reports, reviewing forensic evidence, and looking at crime scene photos. But he quickly realized this was not a job for just one man, so he first enlisted the help of Lieutenant Dennis Peterson from the Tewksbury PD—it would be good to have a Tewksbury man working the case, he figured—then he'd brought Sullivan in the next year.

And as they dug into the files together, it became clear to Wayne that, despite his pride in his own investigative skills, he'd been smart to bring Sullivan in—because Sullivan was no ordinary detective. He possessed a lightning-quick mind, and he was a fountain of creativity in connecting seemingly unrelated facts about the case. Sullivan had a natural knack for understanding almost anyone's motives too; Wayne decided that with Sullivan's understanding of personality types, it might be better if Sullivan did most of the interviewing, as Wayne admitted that his own persona could at times be…less than pleasant. Still, armed with such cerebral gifts, the McCabe murder was as much a puzzle for Sullivan as for anyone else. His way of putting the pieces together—in this case, or any other—was to methodically collect information, let the clues be uncovered, then make a determination after as much info as possible was revealed.

So when Sullivan began reviewing the McCabe case files, it was this method he utilized—a sort of "don't make it happen, *let* it happen" approach. This unnerved Wayne at first; he was more of an old-school, "if it don't fit, force it" type of investigator. They finally agreed to compromise and use both approaches, as two different ways of looking at the case might prove more beneficial than just one.

First they made a list of suspects: Walter Shelley, Mike Ferreira, and Kevin Bevilacqua (though Bevvie had died in '72, there was still a strong possibility he'd committed the crime, or, at least, had a part in it) topped the list. And, Sullivan posited, a combination of any two—maybe even all three—could have conspired to do it.

Against Wayne's protests, Sullivan also listed more peripheral suspects like Robert Morley, who'd moved to Florida around the time of the murder, and Frank Espinola, the alleged member of the Hell's Angels who'd been accused by an anonymous caller of killing McCabe over drugs. Sullivan thought it interesting that those suspects hadn't been investigated further; Wayne found that logical, since he believed that St. Peter and the other original detectives were on the right track by focusing on the Shelley/Ferreira/Bevvie contingent. They finally decided to keep the focus on Shelley's group, since they had more evidence on them and could therefore get closer to finding out who the true killer was—regardless of who it might be.

Sullivan's reason for including even minor suspects on the list was this: it all tied in with the caller to the two priests, particularly the one to Father Walsh. The caller had told Walsh "he" (or whoever the killer was, if not the caller himself) had worn gloves.

"And in the initial forensics test, they found black cotton fibers, the kind used in gloves, in the adhesive tape over the vic's mouth," Sullivan told Wayne one day in November 2002. They'd just finished going through the case files with a fine-toothed comb—again—and were brainstorming ideas and theories about the crime. "To my knowledge," he went on, "the fact about the gloves wasn't made public. So following the logic, odds are the caller to the priests was the doer. If it wasn't, he made a lucky guess about the gloves…but my guess is it was him."

"Well…maybe," Wayne muttered. He didn't sound very convinced.

"The caller said something else to Cahill, the other priest: 'I have John's belt.' And remember, McCabe wasn't wearing a belt when he was found. Same logic applies."

"Maybe," Wayne repeated. Sullivan figured that in Wayne's mind, they needed to be focusing on the Shelley posse and no one else and that exploring any other possibilities was a waste of time.

Sullivan offered up a compromise. "The next question is: did Shelley—or Ferreira, Bevvie, or any of those guys—make the calls to the priests? If not, then who? That's why I included the others on the list. Because *any* of them could've made those calls."

"True," Wayne admitted. "Wonder if we can find out somewhere in all this"—he patted the case files stacked haphazardly on the table—"what our suspects' whereabouts were when the calls were made? Remember what date that was?"

"Hmmm…it was…" Sullivan looked through the folders until he found the one containing the relevant report. He opened the folder and glanced at the date on the top. "October 1. Five days after McCabe was found." He scanned the rest of the report. "Doesn't say here anything about allegations of who made the calls." They spent the next few minutes searching through various reports trying to find any relevant info but located none. They devoted the rest of the day to more brainstorming but came up with nothing new.

In the months following the Jack Ward interview, the two detectives also dug into the forensic evidence—of which there was comparatively little. There were, of course, a number of disadvantages to investigating a thirty-year-old case—but in one aspect, time was on their side: in three decades, there had been exponential advancements in forensic technology. So they sent all the physical evidence to the state police lab down in Sudbury for extensive testing. This included the rope and adhesive tape found with John's body, swatches of each piece of clothing he'd worn, and trace samples of dirt and other substances found on the bottom his shoes. The testing packet also contained various pieces of evidence from the vacant lot in Lowell where the body had been discovered (photos of the tire tracks found there, soil samples, and miscellaneous debris collected the morning after the murder), along with samples of material and paint chips from Walter Shelley's car. (That evidence had been taken—literally *taken*, Sullivan figured, as cops hadn't bothered with petty nuisances like warrants back in the 1960s—when St. Peter and Jop had staked out Shelley's residence a few nights after the murder.) Another interesting item in the packet was an Allstate Insurance card belonging to Robert Morley, the twenty-five-year-old Lowellian whose brother had reported him as a suspect in November 1969; it was a curious item because whoever included it with the other physical evidence (in the original investigation, presumably) hadn't specified when or where it had been found, or even how it was relevant to the case.

Once the evidence reached the lab, analysts tested it in two ways: first, they gathered all the evidence with non-porous surfaces (meaning it would be more likely to have fingerprints), and subjected it to cyanoacrylate (or "fume") tests. This method, not available in the 1960s, consisted of placing a piece of evidence in an airtight chamber and exposing it to cyanoacrylate (super glue) vapors. The vapor would adhere to any prints present on the object, allowing them to be viewed under a "white light" source, then photographed with a special camera designed for fume tests. If any prints were found, they would be compared to the prints of the suspects; barring a suspect match, they would be run through the Integrated Automated Fingerprint Identification System, or IAFIS, the FBI's database containing fingerprints and criminal histories of seventy million subjects from around the world.

After days of fume-testing every possible piece of evidence, the only relevant prints found were those belonging to John McCabe.

The analysts also performed thorough examinations of all the evidence looking for hair fibers, skin cells, or any other material not consistent with the object. Hopefully, they would identify any foreign material (or in the case of hair or skin, find a specimen containing human DNA) and use it to reveal information about that piece of evidence. If any DNA was discovered, that would possibly compel a judge to issue a warrant for one or more of the suspects' DNA information, depending on the nature of the DNA evidence found. On the second day of testing, an analyst actually found some DNA material…but it was only cross-contamination from a crime lab employee named Carlos Seino.

The analysts used a microscope to examine the black cotton fibers found in the adhesive tape over John's mouth, and determined the type of cotton in the glove was of a higher grade than most, meaning if the fibers were from gloves, they probably came from a pair designed to be worn by a lady, since ladies' gloves usually had a higher thread count (and were therefore softer) than men's.

Once again, the forensic analysis was a total failure. Aside from the detail about the gloves, the analysts found no relevant information the detectives didn't already have.

Sullivan and Wayne were obviously disappointed, but they weren't ready to give up. Their next step, Sullivan thought, should be to try and find out more about the "peripheral" suspects like Morley and Espinola, but Wayne insisted they stay on the same track they'd been pursuing— Shelley and company, in other words. And after several days of debate, the detectives decided to continue following Shelley's trail.

EX PARTE[1]: An Introduction to Eric Wilson

My name is Eric Wilson. I'm the attorney who represented Mike Ferreira, and I will tell you right now: *Michael Ferreira did not murder John McCabe.*

There are a multitude of reasons why I believe this is so, but I'll get to those eventually. First I'd like to tell you how I came to represent Mike, and how (and why) I became an attorney in the first place. I'll get the bio part out of the way so we can move on to more important matters:

I was born in 1963 in Nashua, N.H., not long before Kennedy was assassinated. After graduating high school in '82, I served in the Marine Corps for four years, then enrolled at Keene State College a few miles from my hometown. I thought about becoming a history teacher, so I studied history and political science, but…that's not quite the direction my academic career ended up taking.

During my four years of undergraduate work, I befriended one of the college deans, and he convinced me to get involved in student government. (I was a "non-traditional" college student, since I started school at twenty-one instead of the usual eighteen, so possibly my bit of extra maturity played a part in that.) In any case, I somehow ended up as student body president. And oddly enough, the student government policies stipulated that the only person allowed to advocate for a student facing a

---

[1] *(Latin for "on one side only." A judicial term referring to motions, hearings, or orders granted on the request of and for the benefit of one party only. This is an exception to the basic rule of court procedure that both parties must be present at any argument before a judge, and is many times off the record.)*

disciplinary issue was—you guessed it—the student body president. So I assisted students in disciplinary matters on numerous occasions, which laid the groundwork for my current career as a defense attorney.

At my college dean friend's urging, after graduating from Keene I entered law school at the University of New Hampshire, and received my law degree in '92. I passed the New Hampshire bar exam shortly thereafter, and the next year I became certified to practice law in Massachusetts. And I've been a criminal defense attorney ever since.

In case you're wondering why I do criminal work, I can give you a simple answer: everything changes. Criminal cases—especially jury trials—are like snowflakes, in that no two are the same. Every client has a different story, which means a different set of facts, different evidence, and therefore a different strategy. A tax attorney, for example, basically works with the same set of circumstances on each case—which I would find very tiring. Criminal law is *never* boring. My work is an important part of the legal system; whether a client is guilty or not, it's my duty to make sure his or her rights are preserved, and to make sure he or she receives a fair, just trial.

And as I would eventually learn, representing Mike Ferreira would certainly put my duties to the test.

2. Thursday, June 5, 2003

"Mom! Phone!"

Forty-seven-year-old Marla Shiner put down the knife she'd been using to spread mayo on the ham sandwich she was making her son for lunch. Unfortunately, ham sandwiches were a staple of his diet—of hers, her daughter's, and her Aunt Charmaine's too, really—because they couldn't really afford much else. A teacher's salary wouldn't stretch very far when you were a single mother with two teenage kids and an aging aunt to support.

Marla walked over to the phone on the wall by the fridge and picked it up. "Hello?"

"Is this Marla Shiner?"

"It is."

"Miss Shiner, I'm Lieutenant Tom Sullivan with the Massachusetts State Police. How are you today?"

"Fine." Marla immediately wondered why a Massachusetts cop would be calling her. She and her kids had loaded a Ryder truck and made the four-day drive to Southern California back in '96 to live with her aunt, and nobody she knew—or, at least, cared about, anyway—lived in Tewksbury anymore. So he couldn't be calling about some kind of emergency. "What's this about?"

"Miss Shiner, I'm Detective Gerry Wayne. The lieutenant and I are talking to you on speakerphone—is that all right?"

Her answer was even frostier this time. "It's fine. Why are you calling?"

"Well," Sullivan said, "Detective Wayne and I are investigating an old case. The murder of a boy named John

McCabe, back in 1969. You were living in Tewksbury then, correct?"

"Yes." Fear and anger—disguised as adrenaline—shot through her system, and a single thought entered her mind: *Walter. That bastard.* "Why are you calling *me* about it?" Back in Massachusetts, the two detectives glanced at each other, eyebrows raised.

Sullivan: "Well, we've learned some new information about the case, and we'd like to ask you some questions. Is this a good time? We don't want to interru—"

"It's fine." She sighed. "What do you want to know?"

"Thank you." He and Wayne had agreed that he'd take the lead on the questioning. "If you can start by telling us what you remember about John."

She paused. "Um—you mean about the murder, or about John when he was alive?"

"Sorry—about John, as a boy in general. Before he was killed."

"Oh. Well…I didn't know him very well. We lived in the same neighborhood, we saw each other once in a while…that was about it. He was a couple years older than me, so we didn't hang out together or anything." There was a pause that stretched for a few seconds. "That's about it."

"Okay. Now, what do you recall about John's death?"

She uttered a brief, humorless laugh. "Wow—a lot. Where do you want me to start?"

"Anywhere you like, Miss Shiner." Though he knew she couldn't see him, Sullivan smiled broadly when he said it. It was a trick he'd learned growing up with his salesman father, a trick that served him well in telephone interviews: if he wanted his voice to emote a certain feeling, he consciously applied a corresponding expression, even if—

especially if—the listener couldn't see him. If he wanted to sound happy, he grinned; to sound angry, he scowled, and so on.

"Um…okay," Marla began. "Well…the rumor was that he was killed because of drugs. Maybe he saw somebody doing a drug deal, or something like that. I don't…that was a long time ago. I don't remember what the rumor was, exactly, but I think it was that it happened because of something bad like that."

"Okay. What else do you remember?"

"Hm…I heard he was hogtied."

"Okay." The detectives looked at each other again, and Wayne moved the tape recorder he was using to document the interview closer to the phone's speaker. "And…do you remember where you heard that?"

"No. But a lot of people were talking about it—that he was tied up so that if he moved, it choked him. I don't remember who told me that."

"Okay." Marla heard what sounded like papers being shuffled. Then Sullivan asked: "Do you remember hearing about John's death?"

"Oh yeah. I heard the next day. It was awful."

"And do you remember exactly how you found out, or who told you about it?"

"No. But it was everywhere—in the paper, on TV, and everybody was talking about it." *Why don't you just go ahead and ask me if Walter told me about it,* she thought but did not say. "I don't remember how I heard. It…just awful," she repeated.

Marla heard more papers shuffling, then, as if Sullivan could read her thoughts: "Now, let me ask: do you remember a boy named Walter Shelley?"

"You already know the answer to that—of course, I do," she said. "I ended up marrying him. I'm sure you know that too."

"We do," Sullivan said. "And thank you. Miss Shiner, by no means are we trying to patronize you, or run some kind of mind trick, or routine or anything. We're just doing our very best to get our facts in this case correct. If you perceived something else, that's my fault, and I apologize."

The heartfelt plea seemed to do the trick because Marla softened a bit. "Okay. It's just…this was awful," she said again. "It's not my favorite childhood memory, ya know? So I'm sorry if I seem touchy…it's just not the greatest thing to talk about."

"I understand," Sullivan said. "And thank you again. Now…you do remember Walter, we've established that. What was your relationship? Were you two close?"

"Yes. We started dating around then."

"You were dating when John died?"

"I…that's a good question. I don't remember exactly when we started going out. I *do* remember that he'd just started a new job."

"Do you remember where his new job was?"

"Uh…it was…" She thought for a moment. "No. I don't—oh! Astro Circuits? Was that…yeah. Astro Circuits."

"Okay." There was a pause while Marla imagined—correctly—that the detectives wrote this info down. Then: "How old were you when you started dating him?"

"Twelve or thirteen. I forget exactly. But he was six years older than me."

"Right. And did you know that he was questioned by the police several times back then?"

"About the murder? Yeah, I knew."

"Did Walter ever talk to you about it? The police questioning him, I mean."

There was a pause. Then she said, "No. And you know what? I thought that was bizarre. I found out from other people that the police were asking him about it—he never told me about it himself. But that was the kind of relationship we had." The brusqueness had crept back into her voice. "For me, it was a 'speak only when spoken to' sort of thing."

"Okay." There was a pause, and Marla thought she perceived the detectives whispering. Then Sullivan said aloud, "Did you know a boy named Mike Ferreira then?"

"Yes. He and Walter were good friends."

"All right." More whispering. Then Sullivan blindsided her. "Were you ever aware of John McCabe having a crush on you?"

Marla was speechless for a moment as she tried to process the question. "Wha…no. Why would—no! Who told you that!?"

"He never exhibited any type of romantic behavior toward you, like flirti—"

"No! Why would you ask me that? Where's this coming from?"

"That's not important. But it *is* important that you're honest with us, Marla. He never made a pass at you? You really weren't aware that he was interested?"

"*No.* I don't know where you heard that, but it's not true. I never thought of him that way. At *all*." She was mentally piecing it together: their theory was that Walter killed John out of jealousy. Over *her*. She knew Walter was a bastard, but…*killing* somebody? She refused to believe it.

When her thoughts returned to the present, Sullivan was asking another question. "…Friends, or people you knew, who did drugs?"

"Say again?"

"Do you remember if any of your friends, or just people you knew around town, did drugs at all?"

"Oh." Her brain was still reeling from his question about John's alleged crush. "Um…yeah. My brothers. And Bevvie—that's Kevin Bevilacqua, everybody called him 'Bevvie'—was a druggie. Big-time. He died of a drug overdose, actually."

"Yes. In '72."

"That's too bad," she said with no remorse at all. "Let's see…Joey Richard. He was a good friend of mine. He died in 2008."

"Sorry to hear that, Marla," Sullivan said. "What about Walter?"

"Never. At least that I knew of. He just liked his booze." The acidity was returning again. "That was his problem—he liked it *too* much."

"You said he and Mike Ferreira were friends, right? Did they hang out a lot?"

"Almost every day. There was a guy named…Allen. He was around a lot too."

More papers shuffling, then: "Allen? Remember his last name?"

"Um…no. Red-headed kid. *He* was nice, actually. Don't remember much about him, just that he was…what's the word? Gullible. Yeah. He'd do pretty much anything Walter and Mike asked him."

"Okay." More whispers. "Do you remember if you went to the K of C dance the night John died?"

"Hm…I'm sure I didn't. I would've been too young to go then."

"Okay. Now…you said you ended up marrying Walter?"

"I did. When I was eighteen." Full-blown bitterness now. "Biggest mistake I ever made."

"And you joined the military not long after that, right?"

"Yes I did."

"Can I ask why, so soon after you were marr—"

Marla barked a short, sharp laugh. "To get away from *him*! Walter…he was abusive. Very physical. Sober or drunk—it didn't matter. Thinking back, I now question his mental capabilities. He just…he was just not right. He would blindly fly off the handle—didn't matter who was around." She sounded near tears. "I got out of there first chance I had."

"Okay. Was he violent with other people?"

"Just *me*! I never understood that. He could be so nice to other people, and here I was getting black eyes left and right. I just…ahh, it was awful."

"Okay. Thank you, Marla. Sorry to make you revisit what must've been a difficult time…but these were questions we needed to ask."

"I understand." Deep-seated anger in her response.

"Well…I don't have any other questions. Anything you'd like to say? Anything we didn't talk about?"

"Hm…you may want to talk to my sister Daryl Ann. She was closer to John's age; she probably knew him better."

"We will. Anything else?"

"Nope."

"All right. Thank you for your time."

After the call ended, Sullivan and Wayne faced each other. Neither spoke for a moment. Wayne finally broke the silence. "Well? Whaddya think?"

Sullivan pursed his lips as he thought. "I think she was telling the truth about everything. And she sure doesn't have any love for Walter Shelley. In her eyes, he's a monster."

"She wouldn't be wrong about that." Wayne paused, then: "What about McCabe? Think she thought he liked her…and maybe she just wasn't telling us?"

"Oh no. She was genuinely shocked when I asked her about it. Didn't have to see her face to know that. And she seemed to feel some honest remorse about the murder. She wasn't remorseful about much else, but about that, she was."

They both sat lost in thought for a moment. Then Wayne asked: "What about Mike Ferreira?"

Sullivan raised his eyebrows. "What about him? Listen: the only thing we can take from this is that one, she didn't know about any crush John had on her, and two, Walter Shelley is a piece of shit. And that—about Walter—we already knew. As far as Ferreira goes…I say we talk to him again. He married Nancy Williams, right? Are they still together?"

"They are."

"Then let's find them."

Wayne grunted. "Okay. Bet that bastard'll give us something. He better."

EX PARTE: Eric Wilson Takes the Case

Currently, I'm the founding member of Wilson, Bush, Durkin & Keefe, a firm in downtown Nashua. We handle an assortment of criminal cases, ranging from DWIs to homicides. And in 2008, I believe, I represented Mike Ferreira on a motor vehicle violation. A family member of his, Mike said, was a police officer, and the officer gave Mike my name because he remembered me from previous cases. Mike drove a commercial vehicle at the time, and wanted to avoid having a traffic offense on his record, so I helped him get the violation dismissed.

In early 2011—I think it was March or April—Mike called me again to ask for representation...for something more serious. The police, he said, wanted him to come in for an interview concerning a murder that had been committed in Tewksbury in 1969, when Mike was sixteen years old. Mike knew nothing about it, he told me, and had no idea why they were still wanting to question him so many years later, but he wanted to have an attorney lined up just in case.

As soon as we ended that phone call, my mind started racing. I briefly researched the 1969 murder case, and slowly realized that it had the potential to become an enormous one. I knew from the other homicide cases I'd tried that the commitment involved in a murder trial would require hundreds (if not thousands) of hours of preparation. At that point, I had no idea if I would be involved, but if an indictment came down for Mike Ferreira, I was going to be a very busy man.

3. Tuesday, July 15, 2003

Brian Gath had just exited the main office of the Tewksbury Water Department—his employer for nearly two decades—and was headed to his work truck when he heard his name called. He turned and saw two men dressed in suits walking toward him; as they got closer, he could see a badge pinned to the taller man's suit coat. The other carried a legal pad. *Great,* he thought, mentally replaying the last few days, trying to remember whether he'd broken any laws. But as they drew near, he observed friendly smiles on both their faces and he relaxed a bit.

When they reached him, the taller one asked if he was Brian Gath.

"I am." He smiled, trying to look as innocent as possible.

"I'm Lieutenant Sullivan with the State Police, and this is Detective Wayne with Lowell PD." Gath shook hands with both men. "May we speak with you?"

"Um…" Gath looked at his watch. "Sure. Got a water main to take a look at on Whipple Road, but…it can wait. What's up?"

"We're investigating an old murder case, actually," Sullivan said. Wayne pulled a pen out of his coat pocket. "Do you recall a boy named John McCabe? He was killed back in '69?"

Gath suddenly looked serious. "Of course. How can I help?"

"Well…start by telling us anything you remember about John."

"Okay…well, I went to school with him as a kid. I remember he went to a high school dance and nobody ever saw him again. They found his body in a field the next morning over in Lowell." He shrugged. "That's about it." Wayne was documenting this on his pad.

"Do you remember if the police asked you about it back then?"

"This is the first time anybody's asked me about it."

"Okay. Do you ever remember any rumors going around about what happened?"

"Oh yeah. People say Walter Shelley had something to do with it. Jealousy, over his girlfriend, Marla."

Gath noticed the men glance at each other. "Okay. Do you remember who you heard that from?"

"I'm sure it was Jack. Jack Ward? He works with me here. We've talked about it some over the years." He smiled. "Jack thinks of himself as some kind of amateur detective."

"He does, huh? Well…" Sullivan looked away, considering that for a moment, then looked back at Gath. "You're talking about Marla Shiner, right? Did you know her?"

"A little bit. Just to say hi here and there, you know. Not much. I do remember hearing that Walter gave her a beating from time to time."

Wayne was writing away on the pad. Sullivan said, "Yeah. So…do you remember any other rumors about the murder?"

"The other theory was that it was the Hell's Angels. Something having to do with drugs." He paused to think. Then, shrugging one shoulder: "That's all I remember."

"Okay." Now Sullivan withdrew a small notepad from his own coat pocket and briefly consulted it. "Do you remember having a pig roast at your house a few years ago?"

Gath chuckled. "I've had many."

"Well—do you remember one, specifically, when Jack Ward and Mike Ferreira were both there?"

"Oh…yeah. In about '97."

"Do you remember them talking?"

"Not specifically, no. I have these kinds of parties a lot…I'm always running around, getting drinks and food and stuff. So I'm never in one place for very long. But do I remember Jack and Mike talking? No."

"You didn't hear them talking about John McCabe?"

"I didn't hear anything."

"Okay." Sullivan consulted his pad again. "That's all we have, Mr. Gath. Anything else you'd like to add?"

"Hm." Gath looked away, thinking, then: "You know what? Yeah. I remember hanging out with Mike and his brother Brian one time. We were having drinks at a bar…we got to talking about John McCabe. Mike said he was called in for questioning back then, and he couldn't understand why." Gath paused. "Just thought you might want to know about that."

"Okay. Thank you. You said you were talking about John McCabe? Remember anything else that was said?"

"Just that Mike and Brian thought the same thing Jack does—that it was Walter doing it over a girl. I remember them saying, 'We're leaning that way.' And Jack? Jack's said that more than once." He smiled. "I don't know if he gets much right, but…Jack's theory about McCabe *is* right, I think."

"Okay. Anything else?"

"Think that's it."

"Have a good one." They shook hands, and Gath walked over to his truck.

In the car on the way back to the station, Wayne said, "Boy…this Walter Shelley's turning out to be a piece of work."

"I don't know if 'work' is the word I'd use, but yeah," Sullivan said, "he's something."

"So…do we pull the trigger? Shelley lives right here—think we should go see him?"

Sullivan thought for a moment. "Not yet. All the info we have doesn't directly tie him to it. It's starting to seem like he's capable…he definitely has the temperament. But let's dig a little more. Maybe we can find something more useful, so if—when—we go talk to him, we have something to wave in his face, and he cracks." Sullivan paused, then looked over at Wayne. "*If* he's the one."

"Again with that?" Wayne nudged Sullivan's arm. "Why do you keep thinking he isn't? Marla Shiner, Gath just now—they both say he's a crazy man. He's the one, Tom. Think about it."

But Sullivan wasn't convinced. "Maybe." He stopped and thought. "I just…I don't see it. Not yet."

"Then you're blind, my friend." They drove in silence for a bit. Then Wayne said, "How 'bout we go see Mike Ferreira then? I bet my first wife he knows more than what he told us way back when."

EX PARTE: The Arrest of Mike Ferreira

In early April 2011—two weeks or so after my initial conversation with Mike about the McCabe homicide—I received a call from Tom O'Reilly, Assistant D.A. of

Middlesex County, inquiring whether Mike would be coming in to discuss the case. Apparently, someone behind the scenes—maybe Detective Linda Coughlin, or Tom Sullivan from the state police—had talked to Mike, who told them that I would be representing him. A.D.A. O'Reilly wanted to know whether Mike would "be on the prosecution train" or not (in other words, whether he would cooperate with the Commonwealth in the pursuit of Walter Shelley in exchange for his own lighter sentence—something to which Ed Brown had already agreed). Mike told me he had "no interest in that at all," since he had absolutely no involvement.

On April 14, Mike Ferreira was arrested at his home in Salem, N.H., on a Fugitive from Justice warrant out of the Commonwealth of Massachusetts. The charge was murder. So I appeared in Salem District Court the next morning for his arraignment; we waived extradition, which brings up yet another interesting aspect of this case.

At the time of McCabe's murder in '69, Mike was sixteen years old. So under the law—both then and in 2011—he would've been a juvenile, for which a different set of laws would apply. I had conversations with both Mike and with A.D.A. O'Reilly about it, and in the end I didn't think we could challenge the issue of extradition—long story short, I didn't see a legal basis for contesting Mike's extradition from New Hampshire, and a Juvenile Certification hearing would eventually take place in Massachusetts anyway. So we waived extradition, and Mike agreed to be transferred from New Hampshire to Lowell. He was held in the Middlesex County House of Corrections without bail.

As I just mentioned, my first order of business was a hearing in Lowell Juvenile Court in July of '11—what's commonly called a "transfer hearing," or a "72a"—to determine whether Mike would be tried as an adult. O'Reilly was pressing us to just go ahead and transfer the case to the adult court without the juvenile hearing, but in retrospect I'm glad we didn't do that. Because in the transfer hearing I had several hours of cross-examination of witnesses—particularly Ed Brown—that basically planted the seed for my defense. In the end, the juvenile court determined that Mike would be tried as an adult, but from that hearing I learned that the basis for our case would be the total disqualification of Ed Brown as a reliable witness.

In the meantime, I'd started receiving "open file discovery" materials—basically, by law the Commonwealth had to share with me all the evidence they planned to use at trial. By the time the trial started eighteen months later, the discovery was over a thousand pages of materials. Needless to say, it was time to get to work.

4. Thursday, October 30, 2003

Mike Ferreira was drying himself off after a steaming hot shower—part of his daily ritual upon returning home from his job driving a truck for the local Pepsi distributor—when, through the closed bathroom door, he heard the doorbell ring.

He heard his wife Nancy walking down the hall to answer, and he dried himself, then put on a T-shirt, gym shorts, and flip-flops. He heard three sets of footsteps make their way into the kitchen as he dressed, his wife making small talk as they passed.

Nancy: his wife of twenty years. They'd known each other since they were kids. They'd partied together in high school; she'd still been in Tewksbury when he'd returned from Vietnam in '73, and they'd had an on-again, off-again relationship for several years before they'd married in '83. Even so, it was as if they'd known even as children that they would spend the rest of their lives together. They'd been soulmates, and had been in love with each other—though it hadn't started as romantic love, they'd shared a kinship since they first met one fall afternoon on the school playground—even before they were old enough to understand the concepts. His sweet Nancy. Sure they had their differences…but even when they were fighting like cats and dogs, Mike knew he loved her dearly.

He entered the kitchen and saw two men—cops, he concluded immediately—sitting at the table in the dining area adjacent to it, while Nancy was at the stove making spaghetti with meat sauce for their dinner. The doorway between the two areas was big enough that the detectives were able to see and converse with Nancy too.

"Mike, this is Lieutenant Sullivan and Detective Wayne. They're up from Lowell PD." Mike shook hands with both men.

"I didn't do it," he said with a laugh, holding both hands up with palms next to either shoulder. Sullivan joined in with a chuckle of his own, but Wayne's face remained cold. *Hm,* Mike thought. *What's up with this guy?* Aloud he said, "How can we help ya?"

"Well," Sullivan began, "we're h—"

"They wanna talk to you about John McCabe," Nancy cut in. "They've been—"

"*Nance.*" Mike held up a hand to her. "Let the men talk?" From the table, Sullivan guessed this particular occurrence—Nancy interrupting, Mike shushing her—was an all-too-common one. And sure enough, she quieted and returned her attention to the spaghetti.

"McCabe, huh?" Mike joined them at the table. "That was, what…back in 1970?"

"'69, actually," Wayne said. "We're re-investigating the case. Came to ask you about it." His short, clipped statements told Mike that if they were pulling the old good cop/bad cop routine, Wayne was definitely playing the mean one. And Mike was both surprised and not surprised to see them sitting in his kitchen; while not aware that the McCabe case had been re-opened, the fact that it had been explained their desire to speak to him again. Back in '69, the cops had been all *over* him for months after the murder.

Sullivan: "Will you answer some questions, Mike?" He looked over at Nancy as he pulled out his notepad. "You too, Mrs. Ferreira. I'm glad you're here too…we might need help from both of you to clear some things up."

"Sure," Mike said, and Nancy, apparently trying to exhibit some good—and quiet—behavior, simply nodded.

"Okay," Sullivan said. He picked up the pen on the legal pad on the table to his right, and Wayne readied his own pen and pad. "Start by telling us what you remember about the murder."

Mike laughed a bit. "What I *remember* is being hassled by you guys. For something I had nothing to do with."

"Well…let's start with the night it happened. Can you tell us about it?"

"Oh yeah. I remember 'cause I told this story several times back then." He drew in a deep breath, then: "It was a Friday night. Me and Walter went over to Waltham to clean a restaurant. It was pretty late, going over."

"It was just you and Walter? Was there anybody else with you?"

Mike stared into space to think for a moment. "Maybe? There might've been someone else…jeez, it's been a long time." Wayne and Sullivan both wrote on their pads, Wayne alternately looking up at Mike with a slight scowl.

Sullivan stopped writing to continue the questions. He looked over at Nancy: "How about you, Mrs. Ferreira? Remember what you did that night?"

"Home for the night," she answered without turning from the stove.

Sullivan to Mike: "Anything else you remember about that night?"

"Um…we went to Cunningham's store to get cigarettes." Pause. "That's about it."

"Okay." Both detectives wrote. "You said the cops 'hassled' you. You remember how many times you talked to them?"

"Oh, multiple times."

"Were your parents with you, do you remember?"

Mike mulled the question. "Don't think so. My mom, maybe…I know my dad didn't go. He just didn't care."

"And how 'bout you, Mrs. Ferreira, you were interviewed too, right?"

She was busy dumping noodles into a colander. "Went to the station twice with my mother."

Sullivan put his pen down and leaned forward, honoring Mike with the most honest, open expression he could muster. "So Mike: how do you think this happened?"

Mike's answer was immediate: "No idea."

"No idea, huh?"

"No idea," Mike repeated, a little more forcefully. "If I'd've known, I woulda told you back then."

"Do you know how John died?"

"Yes I do. Strangled. I know because a cop threw a picture right in *front* of me. And I'll tell you what I told him then," he said, his eyes locked on Sullivan's. "I had *nothing to do with this*." They stared at each other for a few moments, the space between their faces practically crackling with tension.

"All right, Michael," Sullivan said abruptly, breaking the standoff by looking down at his notepad. "Let me ask you this: do you remember a girl named Marla?"

"Sure. Marla Shiner. Walter's girlfriend."

"Do you know if Walter ever hit her?"

"Yeah. A few times…why?"

Sullivan ignored the query. "Was Walter a…was he a tough guy?"

Mike grunted. "Tough? Not really…but he could snap like *that*." He snapped his fingers.

156

"Know if they ever got married?"

"No idea."

Sullivan wrote on his legal pad for a moment, then looked up. "Do you remember being at a pig roast at Brian Gath's house?"

"Hmmm…I've been to a few of them."

"Well, do you remember being at one a few years ago and telling somebody that Walter probably killed John McCabe?"

At that, Nancy slammed a knife—she'd been using it to cut up veggies for a salad—onto her cutting board. She spun to face them. "*What*!? Why would you say that?"

"I don't know," Mike said. He stared at the table.

Nancy was yelling now. "You knew that and you *never told me*!??"

"I don't fuckin' know, I just said it!" Now Mike and Nancy had a staring contest of their own.

"Okay," Sullivan said in an attempt to cut the tension. "Mike, let's go over that night again." Mike turned to face him, still seething. "You said you were with Walter?"

"Yeah," Mike answered in a slow exhale. "Him and Marla."

"Hey," Wayne interjected. "You never said—"

"Gerry," Sullivan said, holding up a hand to interrupt him. To Mike: "Go on."

"We went over to Cunningham's to get cigarettes. We got out to go in…Walter and Marla said they had to go take a leak. They weren't gone long. Then Walter dropped me off at the restaurant, then he went to go clean a bank."

"Where was Marla during this time?"

"Don't remember." Sullivan could tell Mike was shutting down.

"And how long was Walter gone?"

"Maybe an hour, at least. Maybe more."

"Okay." Sullivan and Wayne both documented this on their pads. Then Sullivan to Nancy, who was finishing up with dinner: "You picked up John earlier that night, correct?"

"Yeah. He was on his way to the dance."

"How do you know that? Did he say?"

"No...but he was dressed for it. Said he was going that direction on Main. So I just figured that's where he was headed."

"Got it." The detectives wrote for a bit, then looked up. Wayne leaned over and whispered in Sullivan's ear, but Sullivan shook his head. He looked at his notepad briefly, then: "Well...I think that's all. For now, anyway. Anything else either of you want to say?"

"No," they answered simultaneously. Mike got up and walked over to Nancy, and they hugged. Mike put his arm around his wife, then said, "Well...we're about to have some spaghetti. You're welcome to stay—ow!"

Nancy had elbowed him in the ribs. "Sorry," she said. "I only cooked for two." She plastered on a fake smile. "Have a good trip back."

Wayne was unusually silent in the car during the twenty-minute trip across the Massachusetts line and into Lowell. Just after they'd left New Hampshire, Sullivan inquired about his state of mind.

"So?"

Wayne was looking out the passenger's side window, and kept his gaze there. "So...what?"

"So whaddya think? Think he's telling the truth?"

Wayne slowly turned his head to Sullivan. "I think…he's full of shit. Nancy too."

"Really? Why do you say tha—"

"C'mon, Tom. When she acted 'surprised'"—he made quote marks with his fingers—"about what he told Jack Ward at the pig roast? Bullshit. They've both known that all along."

Sullivan pondered this. "Hm…I don't know. I think she really didn't know about that."

"What about his discrepancies when he was telling us about the night of the murder? I'm sure you caught that too. First he doesn't remember who else was there, then later he says Marla was there. Then—*then*—he says 'we' got outta the car at Cunningham's, but that Walter and Marla left to take a piss. Who's '*we*'? There was somebody else there. He was lying." Wayne turned to look out the window, then immediately turned back. "Thanks for shutting me down from questioning him about that, by the way."

"Gerry…" Sullivan thought about how to diffuse Wayne's anger. "Look: I just don't see it, okay? Sure, his story didn't always match up with what we know, but I'm not surprised. It's been *thirty-four years.* Hell, I can't remember what I had for breakfast, much less something from that far back. So to me his discrepancies make sense." He breathed for a moment. "They're on the up-and-up, I think. They have their differences, yes—but what married couple doesn't? They…" He looked over at Wayne. "They're telling us what they know. And I believe them."

Wayne kept looking out the window. Finally, without turning: "If you say so."

They drove on a bit more, then Sullivan asked: "So…what do you think we focus on next?"

"I don't know," Wayne said, still staring at the passing countryside. "Do you?"

EX PARTE: A Thousand Pages of Discovery

After the transfer hearing in July of '11, Mike went back to the House of Corrections, where he was incarcerated for a lengthy period of time until I was able to get him out on house arrest late that year. His family posted a substantial cash bond to make that happen, and Mike had to wear an ankle bracelet and live in Lowell with his brother, since he was not allowed to leave that jurisdiction.

Meanwhile, I was receiving the discovery material by the boxload from the Commonwealth, so I began the monumental task of organizing the sheer mountain of information, then deciding what was most important. But the first thing I had to do before anything else: read it, then try my best to commit it all to memory.

In a major case like this one, I generally wait until I've read and digested every bit of relevant information before I even start to think of a strategy. As I'm going through it all, I jot down ideas about my defense; sometimes I keep the ideas, sometimes I get rid of them when another, better idea jumps out—and sometimes I try to combine two (or more) ideas when planning a defense. It all depends upon the specifics of each case. To come up with a strategy before you've familiarized yourself with everything— *everything*—you're handcuffing yourself, so to speak.

So for Ferreira, as I do in any big trial, I made what I refer to as a Discovery Index. It's a shortcut I learned from an excellent defense attorney under whom I worked when I was fresh out of law school in the early '90s. Simply put, the Discovery Index is a detailed outline listing each individual item of discovery, and highlights of each: the type of the item—police report, official letter, handwritten note, etcetera—along with names, dates, and the central ideas the item contains. It's an excellent way to quickly reference any particular item, and I put the index to great use during trial, when I may have only seconds to find a specific bit of info that would otherwise be buried beneath the mountain of discovery files.

And I read most of the Ferreira discovery on a stationary bike at 5:00 a.m.

I work out at the YMCA near my house three or four times a week, and I like to go first thing in the morning, so for much of the fall of 2011 I read through the discovery while either riding a stationary bike or walking on a treadmill. I made both mental notes and physical ones—the latter on a legal pad I kept on the handlebars next to the files. And from my notes I wrote the Discovery Index—an outline that, in the end, was itself fifty pages long.

So by December, around the time I was able to get Mike released on house arrest, I was ready to begin building my defense. I finally decided that there were two key points to gaining an acquittal for Mike Ferreira: Edward Allen Brown, and hogtying.

5. Tuesday, July 12, 2007

In the four years since their last interview with Mike Ferreira, Sullivan and Wayne had made absolutely zero progress on the case, and were beginning to think that, with the evidence they had, they wouldn't be able to solve it at all. Wayne had wanted to go after Walter Shelley (and by proxy, Mike Ferreira) with what they had, but Sullivan had said it would be a fruitless effort; they needed *solid* evidence—like a confession or an eyewitness to the actual crime—before they'd be able to get anywhere with Shelley or anyone else.

After their 2003 meeting with Mike and Nancy had revealed nothing very useful, they'd stepped away from the McCabe cold case, and both detectives had started focusing on other more current crimes in their respective police units. But each spring, emboldened by Bill McCabe's annual March 13 phone call requesting an update on the investigation, the detectives had put in a few weeks' work trying to solve it—and each year their efforts, and with them their hopes of catching the killer (or killers, plural), diminished. And each spring they shifted their focus: in 2005, they'd tried to learn still more about what they called "the Shelley-Ferreira Gang," to no avail; the next year they'd looked into Sullivan's "peripheral suspects" (Robert Morley, Richard Santos, and others), and again came up empty.

In 2007, they'd decided to combine the parameters of their previous searches and investigate the peripheral members of the Shelley-Ferreira Gang. On May 29, they drove to the Pepsi bottling plant in Ayer, Mass., about ten miles west of Lowell, to speak with a man named Robert

Brown. Brown had been mentioned—albeit briefly—in several reports from the original investigation, including a 1969 interview with Mike Ferreira.

And once again, from Bob Brown they learned very little. "Mr. Brown related that he was 19 at the time of the murder," Wayne wrote in the report he typed up two days later. "He never met John McCabe or heard of him before the murder occurred. At the time of the murder, Mr. Brown had already been drafted and believes he was in Florida for training, or may have already gone to Vietnam." Toward the end of the interview, Wayne reported, they asked Brown for the whereabouts of his brother Ed. "Mr. Brown stated that he and his brother were not close. He thought his brother lived in Londonderry, N.H. He said he didn't have Ed's address or phone number."

Upon the detectives' return to Lowell, Sullivan performed a quick search of the New Hampshire DMV database and learned that Edward Allen Brown, fifty-five, resided at 7 Brookview Drive in Londonderry, another ten-mile drive from Lowell PD. So one afternoon a few weeks later, Sullivan and Wayne made the short trip across the state line to Londonderry. During the drive Sullivan noticed some ugly, purple storm clouds drifting into the area.

He pointed at the oncoming gloom. "Got an umbrella?" he asked Wayne.

"Uh…" Wayne looked on the floorboard, then in the back seat. "No. Do you?"

"Nope."

"Ah, we'll be fine."

They were anything but. As they made their way up the walk to Brown's front door, they were pelted by a smattering of fat raindrops. Sullivan rang the bell, and a few seconds later a short, scrunchy-faced woman opened the door. The rain was intensifying by the second.

She looked at them through thick eyeglasses. "Yeah?"

Sullivan flashed his badge. "Mrs. Brown?"

"Yeah…I'm Carolyn Brown."

"I'm Lieutenant Sullivan with Mass State Police, and this is Detective Wayne with Lowell PD. Is your husband Edward Allen Brown?"

"Ed Brown, yeah," she said, her face expressionless.

"Is he home right now? We'd like to speak to him, please." By now the drizzle had become a full-on shower; the detectives knew that by law, unless they had a warrant they were not allowed to enter a private residence without being invited in, so they leaned as far into the doorway as they dared. Sullivan hastened a glance up to see if any overhang extended from the roof over the doorway—of course, there was none—and with the slight wind at their backs, they were getting soaked. And their only option was to stand there and take it.

Meanwhile, Ed Brown's wife was looking at them, her face even more scrunched. "Yeah, he's here. What's this about?"

Sullivan ignored the question. "Could you get him, please?" He had to raise his voice a bit to be heard over the downpour.

"One second," Mrs. Brown said, and closed the door with a decisive snap.

The detectives stood in the driving rain for nearly a full minute. At one point they looked at each other with identically glum expressions. "*Really?*" Sullivan said, perfectly summarizing the situation.

At last the door opened, and Edward Allen Brown stood in the doorway surveying them. His once-burly, soft physique revealed a man who probably hadn't exercised in years; he had a ruddy, acne-scarred complexion, and the gray was starting to overtake what little bit of auburn hair remained on his head. His eyes darted between the detectives as he scrutinized them both. He didn't invite them inside. Instead, he said, "What can I do for ya?"

Sullivan introduced himself and Wayne again, then: "We're investigating an old case—the murder of a boy named John McCabe, in 1969—and we'd like to ask you some questions."

"Who?" Brown had trouble hearing them over the spatter of rain on the concrete landing.

Sullivan repeated himself, nearly yelling: "John McCABE? He was murdered in 1969!?"

"Oh." Brown looked down and to the left while he thought. Then, meeting Sullivan's eyes with his own: "I don't remember anything about that."

The detectives glanced at each other, then Sullivan said, "You grew up in Tewksbury, right?"

"Yeah, I lived there for a few years."

"Were you living there in 1969?"

"Let's see…" His gaze, this time, was to the right. "I woulda been sixteen, seventeen…yeah, I was there in '69."

Sullivan wiped the rain from his face. "And you don't remember anything about a boy being murdered?"

"No, I don't."

Wayne cut in: "Mr. Brown—Tewksbury was a small town. Still is, actually. Word gets around quick. *Everybody* knew about that murder. I'm finding it really hard to believe that you're the only person who didn't."

"I'm telling you the truth," Brown said, looking directly at them now. "I left for the service in '70. Master Sergeant. So maybe that's wh—"

"Mr. Brown," Wayne interrupted, "the murder was in '69. You said you left in '70. So: you following me here? You were still living in Tewks when it happened. And you say you don't remember *anything* about it!?"

"I don't," he said again. "Sorry."

The detectives looked at each other. Thankfully, the rain had started to ease a bit. Sullivan said, "Have a nice day." They turned and jogged through the drizzle to their car, and Edward Allen Brown closed the door.

* * * *

Three hours later, Detective Wayne was sitting at his desk at the Lowell Detective Bureau, catching up on paperwork (though writing the report on the Edward Allen Brown interview wasn't part of it; Sullivan had said he'd do it), when his desk phone rang.

"Gerry Wayne."

"Um…hi, this is Carolyn Brown," the caller said softly. Wayne could hear a TV blaring in the background. "You came to my house earlier today?"

"Oh—yes. What can I do for you?"

"Well…" She paused as if to gather her courage. "Eddie doesn't know I'm calling. He's watching the Red Sox game in the living room. I…" She hesitated, then plunged forth. "I was in the living room when you talked to Eddie today, I overheard what was said, and…I think he was lying about that murder."

She had Wayne's full attention now. "Okay. What makes you say that?"

"Well…I dunno if this has anything to do with the Tewksbury thing, but…he told me once that he was involved in a murder when he was young."

Wayne was documenting this on a notepad, and a shot of adrenaline ran through his body. "Okay. Do you remember if he told you anything about it?"

"Um…not much. He just said he may have been involved. I do remember him saying something about a body in the river in Manchester."

"Manchester, New Hampshire?"

"Yeah." There was a pause, then: "I just thought you'd wanna know."

"Okay. Anything else?"

"No sir."

"Thanks for the call."

Wayne didn't even hang up the phone. He clicked the disconnect button with his finger, then dialed Sullivan's extension from memory.

"Sullivan."

"Hey, Tom. Gerry."

"Heya, pal."

"Write that report yet?"

"Ah, I'll get to it. Unless you want t—"

But Wayne was too excited for small talk. "Listen to this: I just got an interesting phone call." He detailed his conversation with Carolyn Brown.

"Wow," Sullivan said when he'd finished. "Think she was telling the truth?"

"I don't know why she'd lie about it."

"Wow. So what would you like to do?"

"Not sure yet. But what I *am* sure about: Ed Brown was full of shit."

167

"I'm with ya there, pal."

EX PARTE: Trial Preparation

After I familiarized myself with all the discovery info, it was time to start preparing for the trial itself. We decided that I would be lead counsel and one of my partners here at the firm, Timothy Bush, would assist me as second chair, so in early 2012 Tim and I went to work. And once Mike Ferreira was out of jail on house arrest, he started helping us by doing research at the Lowell library and compiling information about the crime scene.

Probably the most important part of trial prep in a case of this magnitude is preparation of witnesses. I'll tell you that preparing defense witnesses is easy. They're almost always testifying of their own volition, and your main objective in prepping them is to go over the questions you'll ask them at trial so they can practice their answers (and not be surprised by the questions). Preparing to cross-examine witnesses for the prosecution, meanwhile, is altogether different—mainly because you *won't* know what their answers will be, and the answers will almost always be antagonistic and argumentative. So the trick is to devise a line of questioning that hopefully emphasizes the theories of your defense. For example: in the Ferreira trial I knew one of the prosecution witnesses would be Detective Gerry St. Peter, who was several years retired but was one of the main detectives who worked on the original McCabe investigation in '69. And because of the time and energy he'd invested in it back then, I knew he'd prove difficult on cross, so I spent many hours working on his questioning.

But then you have a sensational subject like Dr. Tom Andrew, whom I consider the star witness for the defense. He's the chief medical examiner of the state of New Hampshire, and worked for years as a medical examiner in the Bronx, so he's seen more murder cases than ten lawyers put together. I mean, the guy just oozes credibility. He's also an adjunct professor at the Dartmouth College med school, and often consults as an expert witness on cases in other states. I knew of Dr. Andrew from other trials I'd been involved with, and I knew he'd provide some brilliant, truthful testimony.

I met with him mainly to find out what he thought about the medical evidence (the characteristics of livor and rigor mortis in John McCabe's body, and his opinion of the possibility that John had been hogtied). And I liked what he told me. One of the greatest things about Dr. Andrew is that he's a straight shooter—in other words, he'll give you his unbiased opinion about the facts and characteristics of a particular case. If those facts won't be helpful to your case, he'll tell you so. So I knew Dr. Andrew would be a vital witness for our defense.

Over the next few months, I prepared other witnesses as well…and those would be much more interesting.

6. Thursday, November 15, 2007

"How do you wanna play this?"

Sullivan and Wayne were making the short drive to Tewksbury to talk to Walter Shelley at his Nelson Avenue home. The detectives had hoped that when they finally did speak to Shelley, they would have some solid evidence to throw at him, and maybe he would confess. ("*If* he even did it," Sullivan had said once more when they were planning the interview, which had garnered a nasty look from Wayne.) Unfortunately, in the years they'd been working on the case, Sullivan and Wayne had found almost nothing new.

And now, as they were entering Tewksbury proper, Wayne asked Sullivan how he wanted to conduct the interview; Wayne was hoping his partner had an idea for some magical interrogation technique—which Sullivan didn't.

"I say we play it by the book. Get a feel for him, just see where it goes. I'll lead off the questions…then we'll see what happens from there. Sound good?"

"Got it. Just make it good."

"Don't I always?" And they both laughed.

Walter Shelley himself answered the door. The fifty-five-year-old had a slight build, close-set eyes behind thick glasses, a thick mustache, and an unfortunate mouth that always made it seem as if he were frowning. He blinked behind his glasses as he inspected the detectives. "Yes?"

They flashed their shields. "Walter Shelley? I'm Lieutenant Sullivan, Mass State Police, and this is Detective Wayne with the Lowell Criminal Bureau. May we speak with you?"

Shelley blinked again, then surprised both detectives: "Um…sure. Come on in." He stood aside while the other two entered. "Let's talk in the kitchen. This way." The detectives followed him through a doorway connecting the den and the kitchen.

As they all sat down, Shelley asked, "What can I do for you?"

The detectives were both a bit shocked by Shelley's utter calm. "Well," Sullivan said as he brought out his pad and pen, "we're here to talk to you about the murder of John McCabe, back in 1969."

A lightning-quick glimmer of fear crossed Shelley's face, then it was gone; he instantly reverted to the picture of serenity. "Oh." His next statement came out of nowhere: "Mike Ferreira had my car that night."

No one spoke for a moment; the detectives were simply lost for words. Sullivan finally recovered, then said, "Okay. But Mr. Shelley: in the reports from when the police interviewed you back in '69, you never said anything about anyone—not Mike or anyone else—borrowing your car. So what you're telling us now is different from what you said back then. Care to explain that?"

Shelley remained calm as glass. He even managed to turn his perma-frown into a slight smile as he gazed at the detectives. "Like I said: Mike Ferreira had my car that night."

Sullivan documented this on his pad. As he was writing, he glanced up to see who he presumed to be Shelley's wife standing in the doorway. He looked over at Walter, and he noticed that Walter's sense of calm had disappeared; he was suddenly fidgety and nervous, his eyes darting back and forth between the detectives and his wife.

"Everything okay?" Mrs. Shelley asked.

"Uh, yeah," Walter said, visibly uncomfortable. "They...they just wanna ask me about something that happened a long time ago. We'll be done in a minute."

"Okay...if you say so." Mrs. Shelley went and sat on the couch in the den and picked up a magazine, then pretended to thumb through it as she obviously eavesdropped.

Sullivan continued the interview. "Anything else you remember about that night, Mr. Shelley?"

"Nope," Walter said immediately. "Don't remember anything."

"Do you remember anything at all about the murder?" When Sullivan said the word *murder*, he noticed Walter wince. "Any rumors? Anything about your interviews with the police? Anything at all?"

"Nope." It was obvious to both detectives that Walter Shelley had shut himself down.

Sullivan wrote briefly on his pad. "Well...okay." He nodded to Wayne, then both men stood. "Would you mind coming by Lowell PD to look at the police reports from back then? Maybe they'll refresh your memory?"

"Okay."

"We'll be in touch." And the detectives left without another word.

In the car on the way back to Lowell, Wayne said: "Boy. Whaddya make of *that*?"

"Hm, I don't know," Sullivan said. "But it's obvious he's keeping something from his wife. I'd bet money on that."

"What do you think that would be?"

"Don't know that either."

The last paragraph of Sullivan's report detailing the interview—a report which, as it turns out, he didn't write for another three and a half years—read: "Mr. Shelley later telephoned Detective Waync and informed him that he (Shelley) was respectfully declining his invitation to come to the police station."

EX PARTE: More Witness Prep

I said before that prepping defense witnesses was easy. But I'm going to rescind that statement somewhat. Because for various reasons, some witnesses either change their story at some point, or they have a story they don't want to tell in the first place.

I'll give you a perfect example: In the Ferreira trial, I had a perfect "alibi witness," Michael Richard, who told police back in '69 that he saw Ferreira and Shelley outside his house—*in another part of Tewksbury*—between 11:30 and 12:00 the night of the murder. That means they couldn't have abducted John McCabe after the K of C dance let out, as others would testify because they were not in the area. So I added Mike Richard to the defense witness list.

Mike Richard lives in Lowell, but he works in Manchester, N.H., and passes through my town of Nashua on Route 3 on his way to and from work. So three or four times during 2012 I met Mike at a Park n' Ride next to Exit 8 in Nashua to discuss his testimony. (I like to make it as easy as possible for witnesses, since they're helping us by testifying.) I showed him the police report with his interview from '69. "Yep, yep, I remember that. They interviewed me sitting at the kitchen table." In the fall I met with him again to review the info, give him his subpoena, and so on. Again: "Yep, that's what I said, I remember that."

I called him once more, just a few weeks before trial, to prepare him one last time. And this time it was, "You know what? I don't remember any of this." He changed his tune completely. My guess? The Commonwealth got to him. I won't directly accuse anyone, but he basically shut himself down on the stand—and at the end of his testimony, we were able to give the jury a clue as to why he did so.

Marla Shiner was another defense witness—and she was reluctant from the beginning, mainly because in the indictments of Ferreira and Shelley, her name was mentioned as the subject of motive for the murder (i.e., Walter's jealousy over John's "crush" on her). Marla has always maintained that, though she knew who John was, she had no romantic interest in him, and he definitely had none for her; that was simply a theory posited by several people—Jack Ward, among others—and the detectives just ran with it. Another interesting fact, one that would come up during the trial, was a glaring inconsistency between the detectives' allegation of Walter's jealousy and Marla's memory of when they actually started dating. (As you'll read, there was a dispute at trial over whether Marla and Walter had even begun seeing one another at the time of the murder.)

Regardless of her reluctance, Marla agreed to testify. Since she lived in California, she and I had several lengthy phone conversations, then we met in person the night before she testified so we could go over it all one more time. And as I predicted, her trial testimony was crucial to our defense.

And then you have a wild card like Detective Gerry St. Peter. As one of the few police officers from the original investigation that was even still alive, I knew he'd be testifying for the Commonwealth, especially since he was the main detective on the case back then. So I wanted to at least have a conversation with him prior to the trial.

So I contacted Tom O'Reilly and asked him to pass along my number to St. Peter. And a couple of days later, he actually called me and agreed to meet with me. But the day before we were scheduled to meet—November 12 of 2012, I think it was—he called again to tell me he'd changed his mind, that he "didn't think it was appropriate to talk to me." And that was the only reason he gave.

I won't try to say I know what was in his mind, but I believe he was doing what he thought was best for "his side," which was the Commonwealth. To me, a trial—*especially* this one—is about finding the truth of the matter at hand. It has nothing to do with which "side" you're pulling for. And I got frustrated when St. Peter refused to talk to me because I felt that if anybody would know about the value of truth, it would be a career detective like him.

And as it turned out, when St. Peter took the stand, I was able to use his refusal to talk to me against him.

7. Wednesday, April 16, 2008-Wednesday, April 8, 2009

Under Massachusetts law—as is the case with many states—citizens can be charged with a felony only after a grand jury has reviewed the merits of the case. So as a matter of course, courts in Massachusetts convene a grand jury each month in order to decide if assorted criminal charges deserve the issuance of a formal indictment. A representative from the district attorney's office will present evidence pertaining to the case, then members of the grand jury determine whether the case will move forward with an indictment, then a subsequent trial. No judge presides over the proceedings, so the hearings are usually a lot more loose and informal.

For the April 2008 session of the Grand Jury of Middlesex County, Assistant D.A. Tom O'Reilly presented several witnesses in the investigation of the John McCabe murder. Because grand jury proceedings are kept secret, very little is known about the details of this hearing; names of witnesses, types of evidence presented, and possible suspects of the crime are all sealed, and, therefore, unavailable to the public.

The one notable exception to this is the testimony of Mike Ferreira on April 16. His statements were made public when part of his 2008 testimony was read—word-for-word—at his trial in 2013. Apparently, Mike's memory was completely exhausted thirty-nine years after the alleged crime, because his statements in the grand jury hearing about the events of September 26, 1969 differed greatly from those in his 1969 interviews. It was also revealed at Ferreira's trial that Ed Brown was summoned to the hearing, but after being informally questioned outside the courtroom by A.D.A. O'Reilly, he was excused.

It is assumed that at least one detective working the McCabe cold case testified in the 2008 proceeding; odds are it was Lieutenant Sullivan, because Detective Wayne had been diagnosed with cancer the preceding December, and had taken leave to fight the illness.

When the grand jury formally issued its indictments at the end of that session, no charges were brought forth in the murder of John McCabe.

* * * *

On a bright, cool morning in April 2009, Gerry Wayne, even after numerous chemotherapy treatments, died of cancer. He'd told Lieutenant Sullivan upon his initial diagnosis that he had to "take some time off for some tests, maybe some treatments, and then be right back on the case." Sadly, Wayne never returned to work.

After his death, Sullivan stopped investigating the John McCabe murder, and shifted his focus to more active cases. So once again, the investigation went cold. It remained frozen until January of 2011, when Lowell Detective Linda Coughlin brought it back to life.

And for better or worse, Detective Coughlin wasted no time in bringing the McCabe murder case to a close. Whether or not she apprehended the correct suspects, though, remained to be seen.

EX PARTE: Pre-Trial Motions

In the months leading up to the Ferreira trial, A.D.A. O'Reilly and I had numerous hearings before Judge David Ricciardone, the Superior Court judge who would adjudicate the case. The subjects of these hearings were numerous—and, I'll admit, often boring—but a couple were extremely important: the motions on "third-party culprit" evidence, and those on what's called a "Bowden defense." Those two judicial rulings are closely related, and I'll explain each.

First, third-party culprit. By law in Massachusetts, a defendant has the constitutional right to offer evidence that another person committed the crime for which he or she is accused. That right is not absolute, though, because the trial judge determines whether the evidence is relevant, and decides how much (if any) of the evidence the jury will hear. In the Ferreira case, I presented motions that evidence should be heard about suspects like Frank Espinola, the biker who'd been accused by an anonymous caller; Robert Morley, suspected by his brother Raymond; Richard Santos, who'd abducted a woman in '74 (and admitted to the woman that he'd done it before!); and the unknown male who'd called the two priests.

The Bowden defense is named after Horace Bowden, a Massachusetts man who, back in 1980, was wrongly convicted of murder. (On appeal, it was revealed that police did not investigate other suspects, including the one who actually committed the crime.) Another name for Bowden evidence is "Inadequate Police Investigation" evidence. Prior to the Ferreira trial I sought to prove that, in the McCabe investigation, the police were so focused on Shelley and Ferreira—and now, Ed Brown—that they failed to properly investigate the above-named suspects.

In the end, some of my motions were granted, some not, but overall I was pleased with Judge Ricciardone's rulings.

8. Tuesday, January 11, 2011

"Mr. and Mrs. McCabe: I'm gonna find the people who killed your boy."

Bill and Evelyn sat on their living room couch, listening to Detective Linda Coughlin make her promise. She said it simply, as if it were a matter of fact—but it was a promise they'd heard several times before. Still, Coughlin had actually called *them* to arrange this meeting; she wanted to speak with them, she'd told Evelyn on the phone, because her boss had asked her a few days before to take a fresh look at the forty-two-year-old case. ("New year, new eyes on it," she'd said.) After the 2008 grand jury hearing had failed to return any indictments, Bill had increased the frequency of his calls to the Lowell criminal bureau, making sure the investigation stayed active. His last call had been just after Christmas, when he'd felt particularly reminiscent about his long-dead son, and Coughlin's commander, Captain Jonathan Webb, had promised to follow up.

And apparently, Captain Webb had kept his word, because here Detective Coughlin sat.

Bill spoke first. "Detective, I kn—"

"Call me Linda. Okay?" She smiled. Bill mentally appraised this woman sitting before him: pretty (but tough-looking, which probably served her well as a detective), dirty blonde hair, just a touch of makeup, and a total no-bullshit attitude. Bill liked her instantly and returned the smile.

"Okay. Linda: a few guys have already told us that. Never found anybody. Whaddya think you're gonna do different?"

Her eyes locked on Bill's. "I'm not sure yet. I just got finished reading the case history…it's a big one. But I'm meeting with Tom Sullivan this week, and he and I will go over everything he knows. I know he and Gerry Wayne—may he rest in peace—they've done a lot on it already, but maybe I can see something they missed."

"All right." Bill said it doubtfully, but a glimmer of hope planted itself in his mind. "I've always thought it had to be Shelley…maybe Ferreira too. Shelley and some others. The thing is, why? Was it over drugs? A girl? I think if we find out the *why*, we'll figure out the who."

"That's my first order of business—digging into those individuals," Coughlin said. "I know that nobody's looked much at their associates at that time—guys and gals they ran with back then. It's been investigated a little, but not enough, I think. I'll take a harder look at their friends—hopefully that'll tell me where to go next."

Evelyn finally spoke. "Thank you, Det—Linda. We've…" She leaned forward, her eyes pooling. "We've been waiting forty years to find out who did this." A tear escaped her eye, and Bill reached over and put his hand over hers. "Even so many years later, I think about our Johnny every day. He didn't deserve this."

Coughlin leaned forward and put one hand over Evelyn's, and the other on top of Bill's. She looked first at Evelyn, then at Bill. "I know you've been waiting a long time. But you won't have to wait much longer. That I promise you."

Over the next few weeks, Detective Coughlin worked nearly nonstop to fulfill that promise. She enlisted the help of fellow Lowell Criminal Bureau members Sergeant Joe

Murray and Detective Todd Fenlon, and the three got down to business.

Just as Coughlin had told Bill and Evelyn McCabe, the detectives decided to focus on people close to Walter Shelley and Mike Ferreira. They started with Nancy (Williams) Ferreira, and on the evening of January 21 the three drove up to the Ferreira residence in Salem, N.H., just as Sullivan and Wayne had done eight years before. According to Coughlin's report on the interview, when they began speaking to Nancy, the detectives realized Mike was also home, so they persuaded Nancy to get in her car and follow them back to Lowell PD—their own turf—so they could speak to her alone.

Once they were all seated in an interview room at LPD, the questioning resumed, and just as she'd done years before, Nancy maintained her (and Mike's) innocence. When asked what she remembered about the night of the murder, she responded by saying she "couldn't remember yesterday, never mind forty years ago." When told that her husband had always been considered a suspect, Nancy replied that Mike "wouldn't hurt a fly." Then Coughlin said that Walter Shelley had also been under suspicion, she told the detectives that "Walter was jealous of Marla," and that he got angry when anyone paid attention to Marla—or even when he suspected that to be the case.

At the end of the interview, Coughlin asked Nancy about Ed Brown, and Nancy responded by saying that her sister, Debbie, was married to Ed's brother, Bob. Coughlin ended Nancy's interview by asking if Nancy would agree to a polygraph test. Nancy said she would; when she took the polygraph on February 9, she denied having any knowledge of the murder, and passed the test with flying colors.

Meanwhile, Coughlin spoke with other friends and associates of Shelley and Ferreira. On February 3, she and Fenlon interviewed Deb Brown, who provided very little useful information; on February 9, they spoke to Jack Ward. Interestingly, during that interview Ward suddenly recalled having a second conversation with Mike Ferreira either at the same 2002 pig roast or shortly after it. "Ward told us that Ferreira told him during this conversation that on the night McCabe was killed, Mike drove to Lowell with Walter Shelley," Coughlin's report read, "and a third boy whose name he could not recall." And later: "I asked Ward why he hadn't previously disclosed this information about a second conversation with Mike, and he told me he thought he had but couldn't say for certain." Aside from Ward's conveniently refreshed memory about his additional talk with Mike, the detectives learned nothing new.

Then, on February 17, Coughlin and Fenlon traveled to Salem, N.H., to talk to Ed Brown. And it was there, at a Park n' Ride where they spoke with Brown for nearly an hour, that Detective Coughlin began to put her plan into action.

EX PARTE: Last-Minute Discovery

The Ferreira trial was originally scheduled for either late September or early October of 2012—I forget which—and then, for various reasons, it got pushed back to December. So I had a two-week opening in my schedule that I'd originally set aside for the trial. I told my wife and kids that we could go to Florida for a few days, as I suddenly had a gap in my trial calendar, so we went to Siesta Key and had a marvelous time.

Just prior to that trip, I had a weird feeling in the back of my mind that I didn't have everything from the Commonwealth in the Ferreira case—that maybe there were some discovery materials I still needed. So I went to the Lowell Detective Bureau to meet with A.D.A. O'Reilly, Detective Coughlin, and Lieutenant Sullivan so we could go through all their stuff and make sure I had it.

Well, it started raining during my drive down there, and by the time I got to the Lowell station it was absolutely pouring. I couldn't find a parking place, and had to park maybe a quarter-mile away, and I didn't have an umbrella. So I got drenched—I mean, soaked to the bone. I walked about halfway there, and I thought, *Know what? This is stupid. I should go back to my car, call and cancel the meeting, and just review the discovery over the phone when I get back to my office.* But I decided to go on anyway, and I was dripping wet when I got to LPD. And I'm glad I went ahead and went.

We start going through all the boxes, and it was all stuff I already had. But then I saw a box in the corner, and I said, "What's that box over there?" Sullivan started pulling stuff out of it, and there were photos and reports I'd never seen. O'Reilly said, "Oh, I gave you copies of all that stuff." And to his credit, Lieutenant Sullivan replied: "Tom, *I've* never seen this stuff. So I'm sure Wilson hasn't." I made copies of all of it and went on my merry way. (Luckily it had stopped raining by the time I left.)

Our Florida trip was sort of a working vacation for me. So here I was, my wife and kids are having fun, and I'm sitting in a beach chair on Siesta Key reading Ferreira discovery. That last-minute material included info about a guy named Richard Santos, who was arrested in '74 for abducting a woman, taping her eyes and mouth shut, tying her up with rope, and leaving her for dead near some railroad tracks—a crime with numerous similarities to the McCabe murder. When I read the part about Santos telling the victim that he'd *done that before*, I literally cursed out loud, prompting my wife, who was sitting in a chair next to me, to ask if everything was okay.

Obviously, the info on Santos was a huge piece of evidence. And the scary thing is that if we'd gone to trial in September like we'd originally planned, I would've never known about Richard Santos.

On a side note: the week after I got back from Florida, I went to review the Santos material, and when I dumped the manila envelope onto the table, guess what trickled out with it?

A good amount of beach sand. True story.

9. Thursday, February 17-Wednesday, March 2

After two days of snowfall had pounded New England, a warm front was passing through, so Coughlin and Fenlon drove through a dozen miles of dirty slush on their way to meet Ed Brown at the Park n' Ride in Salem. As they pulled into the parking lot, they saw Ed leaning against his car, which was parked near the front of the lot. They pulled in next to him and got out.

In preparation for the interview, the detectives had reviewed what little info they had on Ed: first, Mike Ferreira had stated in his 2008 grand jury testimony that he was with Ed the night of the murder. To Coughlin's knowledge, Mike had not previously revealed that information; though she knew Mike had probably just confused his memories in his testimony, she decided to gamble on the possibility that Mike, while under oath, had finally decided to tell the truth about something about which he'd previously lied.

Coughlin also knew that detectives Sullivan and Wayne had spoken to Ed Brown several years before, but after digging through multiple boxes of McCabe case files, she couldn't find the report detailing that interview. (Coughlin made a mental note to ask Sullivan about it at some point, if it turned out she still needed the report.)

And now, as Coughlin and Fenlon approached Ed, Coughlin sized him up: arms crossed, trying to appear relaxed (but failing), amicable enough expression on his face—but was there a hint of nervousness beneath his easy smile?

Coughlin applied a disapproving smirk—one of her go-to expressions—as they drew near. "Thanks for meeting us, Mr. Brown."

"No problem." He extended his hand. Coughlin looked down at it for a moment, as if deciding whether it was safe to touch, then shook it with her own. Ed said, "What do you wanna know?"

"Like I said on the phone, Detective Fenlon and I"—she gestured toward her partner—"are looking into the John McCabe murder. We'd like to see what you know about it."

Ed gave a nervous chuckle. "Nothing. Not really."

"What do you remember about the murder?"

"Well…I really have no memory at all. But some detectives came to talk to me about it back several years ago, so after that I started asking around. I asked my mother…she said she definitely remembered it. She says, 'It's a good thing you weren't with them that night.' She—"

Fenlon cut in: "'Them'? Who would that be, Mr. Brown?"

"Oh. Mike and Wally. That's who you think it was that did it, right?"

Coughlin ignored his question. "You mean Ferreira and Shelley? Were they friends of yours?"

"Ah…yeah. I'd say so, yeah."

"Did you guys hang out a lot together?"

Another chuckle. "With Wally and Mike? Yeah, I guess so…" He paused. "I mean, separately, yeah. But I don't…I can't ever remember the three of us running together."

Coughlin acted as if this were an absolute lie. "Never, Mr. Brown? You're telling me the three of you *never* spent any time together? I find that hard to believe."

"Well, we didn't. Not that I remember."

"If you say so." Coughlin gave Ed a moment. Then: "Is it possible that you were with Walter and Mike on the night John McCabe was killed?"

"Is it possible? Yeah—anything's possible." He gave them an odd smile. "But like I said, I don't ever remember being with them both. Hell, Wally and Mike didn't like each other anyway."

Coughlin frowned and glanced at Fenlon, who was returning the quizzical look. Shelley and Ferreira didn't like each other? That contradicted everything they'd already learned—that the two were close friends. Still, Coughlin let it go—for the time being.

The interview—now closer to an interrogation—continued. Coughlin repeated her disbelief that, with the McCabe murder being such big news, Ed had no memory of it, and he, in turn, repeated his lack of recall. They discussed the fact that Ed was helping Walter clean businesses at that time, and Ed said that Walter would often leave him to clean one place while Walter went to clean another. He talked about how he and Walter had gone together to the recruiting office when they'd joined the Air Force in 1970, the different kinds of cars he and his friends had driven then, and that he'd known Kevin Bevilacqua but hadn't liked "that punk." He also said that he hadn't seen Walter and Mike in many years.

Coughlin decided to wrap it up. "One more question: would you be willing to submit to a polygraph test concerning this case?"

"Um…sure. I don't have an objection to that."

"Okay. We'll be in touch to set it up." Then the detectives got in their car and left. As they were merging onto I-93, Fenlon asked: "How 'bout it? Think he knows more than he's saying?"

"Hm," was all Coughlin said in response.

* * * *

Even though his appointment for the polygraph wasn't until 10:30 a.m. on February 2, Ed Brown arrived at Lowell PD thirty minutes early. So he and Coughlin sat down to review what he'd told the detectives at their previous meeting, and again Ed maintained his complete lack of memory concerning the McCabe murder. Coughlin then brought in Special Agent Brenda Malloy of the U.S. Department of Justice, who would be administering the polygraph. (Coughlin had worked with her on other cases, knew she was an outstanding polygraph expert, and had called to request that she come up from Boston for the day.) Malloy advised Ed of his Miranda rights—it was standard procedure to do so if there was a possibility that the examinee would fail the polygraph, meaning an interrogation would likely follow—then Coughlin left the room. She stepped into the viewing area behind the two-way glass to watch the test.

In the interview room, Agent Malloy went to work preparing Ed for the polygraph. The situation was eerily reminiscent of one four decades earlier, when Ed's friend Mike Ferreira had undergone the same process—but in forty-one years, polygraphs had changed, both in mechanics and in questioning methods. The manner in which a person's heart rate, perspiration, blood pressure, and perspiration were measured was essentially the same, but they were now analyzed by a computer program designed to give much more precise measurements than its analog predecessor. And the questions themselves were formulated to provide extremely accurate results: the "relevant" questions—the ones about the crime—were asked more than once, often in a varying order, to gauge the participant's answers to each one. The manner in which the interviewer asked the "irrelevant" (or control) questions had advanced, too; the interviewer asked a wider variety of "truthful" and "deceptive" questions in order to measure the interviewee's different reactions, thereby ensuring a more accurate readout.

Agent Malloy, who'd administered scores of polygraphs in her twenty-year career, was excellent at her job. Coughlin had briefed her on the circumstances of the McCabe murder and its suspects, and they'd come up with three relevant questions that Malloy would ask Ed at random intervals. So with her equipment in place, Malloy began.

"Is your name Edward Allen Brown?"

"Yes."

"Do you live in Salem, New Hampshire?"

"Yes."

In the viewing area, Coughlin looked on. As she watched, she thought about the utter gravity this case carried—not just for her, but for the McCabe family, and the entire community. *Forty-two years*, she thought. *Two suspects—and now, maybe three—who a lot of folks think are guilty. But only circumstantial evidence. Nothing solid.*

Malloy now asked Ed a "possible lie" question, meaning she couldn't be sure of a truthful answer. "Have you ever cheated a friend out of something?"

Ed, beads of sweat on his brow, was staring at his lap. He looked up briefly. "N…no."

"Have you ever been caught masturbating?"

"No." He sat very still.

In the viewing area, Coughlin thought: *We need…an eyewitness. But seems like they would've found one by now. Murder weapon? We already have it—the rope, and it's useless. One other thing would solve this case: a confession.*

Malloy asked the first relevant question. "Did you participate with anyone in causing John McCabe's death?"

"No."

Coughlin: *Ed Brown says he doesn't remember anything about that night.*

"Did you yourself do anything to cause John McCabe's death?"

"No."

Then maybe…maybe I can "help" him remember.

"Do you know who left John McCabe's body tied up in that field?"

"No."

I'll just keep the pressure on till he remembers how it really *happened.*

In the interrogation room, Malloy kept the barrage coming. She repeated the relevant questions multiple times, randomizing their order and interspersing them between meaningless questions like "Is Carolyn your wife's name?" and "Did you drive a motor vehicle to get to the police station today?" As the onslaught continued, Ed became more and more withdrawn, prompting Malloy to request near the end of the test that he repeat his answers.

I can make this work, Coughlin thought from her place in the viewing area. *He's going to fail this test.*

And Coughlin was right. When the test was finished, Malloy asked Ed to leave the interview room while she examined the results. She read the findings on her laptop for a couple of minutes, comparing the graphs displayed there to the questions she'd written on a legal pad. Then she called Ed back in and asked him to have a seat.

"Mr. Brown: according to my findings, in all aspects of questioning related to the murder of John McCabe, you failed. You were asked three questions about your knowledge of, and participation in, that murder. Those three questions were asked four different times, and for each question you generated four separate responses. That constitutes a failing score."

Ed said nothing. He dropped his head and, after a moment, only nodded.

Malloy looked at the two-way glass, behind which she knew Coughlin was standing, and nodded. Coughlin entered the room two seconds later. Malloy asked: "We'd like to give you an opportunity to explain why you failed, Mr. Brown."

He looked back and forth between the two women. Any semblance of stillness and calm he'd previously shown was now completely gone, replaced by sheer desperation. "I'm telling you—I *don't remember.* Sure, it's possible I was with Mike and Wally. But I have no memory of it!" He looked as if he would start crying any moment.

Coughlin acted like she wasn't buying it. "Let me get this straight: you've told me details about your job with Walter Shelley back then. *Details* about you and Ferreira joining the service. *Details* about what car you drove.

Details about a lot of things from that time. But you're saying you don't remember *anything* about the night a boy was murdered?"

Ed wiped the sweat from his brow. And then he scratched the side of his face with his fingers, as if his upper jaw itched. "That's what I'm saying."

Coughlin abruptly stood. She looked at Malloy and gestured to the door. "A word?" As the two women were exiting: "Sit tight, Mr. Brown." Once they were in the hall, Coughlin told Malloy she'd be right back, and hurried up the corridor toward the administrative offices at the front of the station.

Agent Malloy stood and watched her go. Malloy and Coughlin had immense respect for each other as colleagues, but were not close personally. Geographical distance aside, Malloy considered Coughlin to be standoffish, even aloof…but if that was part of the package, that was okay with Malloy. Because she knew that Linda Coughlin was an extraordinary detective.

After a couple of minutes Coughlin came hurrying back. "Sorry about that," she said. "Now Agent, let me ask you: do you think he's telling the truth about not remembering that night?"

"I…Detective, I'm not sure."

"Do you think it's possible for someone who claims to have a repressed memory about something—a specific time or event—to fail a polygraph if they were asked about that event?"

Malloy pursed her lips while she thought. Then: "It is not. These results were clear and conclusive. When I asked him about the death of John McCabe, he failed—on knowledge and participation. All four graphs indicated deception. His failure points were significant. There's no doubt in my mind he was lying."

Coughlin's reaction was unreadable. "That's all I needed to know," she said, and breezed past Malloy to the door of the interrogation room. Malloy just shrugged and followed her.

Ed was sitting with his face in his hands, and he didn't remove them as the women sat at the table.

Coughlin asked: "Mr. Brown, are you on any medication?"

"Prilosec," he responded in a small voice. His hands were still over his face, so Coughlin had difficulty understanding him.

"What's that?"

He pulled his hands away. "Prilosec, I said."

"That's for heartburn, right?"

"Yeah."

"Do you see a doctor for any type of physical or mental condition?"

"No."

"What I'm getting at, Mr. Brown, is that there's no medical reason for you to have failed this test. Therefore, the only conclusion is that you're lying. You remember what happened that night. Don't you?"

"I'm telling you, I don't!"

"I don't believe you. I think you killed that boy. Or you were with whoever did." Coughlin continued with a merciless stream of questions, Ed repeatedly denying each one.

"Did you take part in that murder?"

"Don't remember…"

"Did you help tie that boy up?"

"…Don't remember…"

"Why did you leave him in that f—"

"I DON'T REMEMBER!"

The room was still as Ed's shout reverberated off the walls. After a moment Coughlin spoke, and now her tone was soft and sympathetic. "Edward. What happened to John?"

"I don't *know*," he said, nearly groaning. "I'd only be telling you my fantasy."

Coughlin thought that was an odd response. "What do you mean? What's your fantasy?"

"I don't know…maybe Wally killed John 'cause he was jealous over Marla."

"Is that your 'fantasy,' or is that what really happened?"

Deep sigh. "I just…don't…remember!"

Coughlin switched gears in an instant. "Edward!" She slammed her fist on the table, making Ed jump. "You need to start working with us here. Mike Ferreira and Walter Shelley already are." That was a lie, but Coughlin thought that if it could get her what she needed, so be it. "Is there anything at *all* you remember about this crime? *Anything*?"

"Well…" He thought for a moment. "Now that I'm thinking about it…I do remember driving Wally to the police station." He looked at Coughlin. "They questioned him about it back then, you know."

Coughlin grunted. "Of course I know. And now we're getting somewhere! Do you r—"

"Detective Coughlin?" They turned and saw a young lady poking her head through the door. "Sorry to disturb you, but…" She held up a manila folder.

194

"Oh," Coughlin said, and reached for the folder. "Thanks."

"Sorry," the girl said and disappeared. Coughlin just put the folder on the table. Ed eyed it like it was a bomb, but Coughlin picked right up where she'd left off.

"So: you were talking about taking Walter Shelley to be interviewed. Tell me everything you remember about that."

"Well…not much to tell. I took him to the station in Tewks, waited in the car while he went in. He was in there for…jeez, forty-five minutes? He came out, I took him home. That's it."

Coughlin continued the line of questioning for another thirty minutes; Ed's responses became repetitive variations of either "I don't remember" or "I'd only be telling you my fantasy." Finally, when Coughlin realized they were getting nowhere, she decided to at last level with him.

"Ed, listen to me: Bill McCabe has been waiting forty-two years to find out who killed his son." She leaned in close, and nearly whispered: "Don't you think he deserves an answer?"

"He does," Ed said, equally soft. "He…he deserves an answer."

"Then Ed: why won't you give us one?"

"I…I'm scared."

"What are you scared of?"

"Go…going to jail."

"And why would you go to jail?"

"I…I…" He looked at Coughlin, his eyes shining. Then in an instant, his face hardened. He collapsed back in his chair, almost as if he were physically powering down. "I don't know."

Coughlin held his gaze. After a few moments, it was clear he wasn't going to give it up—at least not yet. "Okay," she said, and reached over and grabbed the manila folder. She withdrew a sheet of white paper and slammed it on the table in front of him.

"What's this?" He picked it up and started scanning its contents.

"A subpoena, Mr. Brown," Coughlin spat. "You're to appear at a grand jury hearing one week from today, March 9, 9:00 a.m. at the Middlesex County D.A.'s office. Don't be late. Your failure to appear at that location at that date and time will result in a warrant being issued for your arrest."

EX PARTE: Final Preparations

The weeks leading up to the trial were chaotic and nerve-racking. I remember coming down with bronchitis at some point, probably because I was only sleeping three or four hours a night.

One big issue we had to deal with: in November 2012, I think—this was not long after the trial got continued to December—Tim Bush, my firm partner who was to be my second chair for Ferreira, needed some time off to deal with his mother's failing health. So I recruited Stanley Norkunas, a defense attorney in Lowell whom I liked and respected, to replace him. Stan and I had a good professional relationship—we'd thrown cases each other's way from time to time—and I knew he'd be a great addition to the team. (Rather, he'd actually *make* it a team, since I was the only other defense attorney involved.)

Once Stan was on board, one of our biggest tasks was the preparation of what I'll call "witness folders," for lack of a better term. In a big trial like this one, I like to have a separate folder for each witness —whether it's my own or one for the prosecution—containing an informal outline of my trial examination of him or her, along with every single piece of evidence, discovery material, and even newspaper articles, remotely related to that witness. That way, during trial, I have all the relevant evidence pertaining to each witness at my fingertips; in an instant, if I need to, I can look at something in that witness's folder and say, "On this date, at this-or-that proceeding, you said such-and-such." It's a really valuable tool.

For Ferreira, we spent several weeks prepping those folders. Some, like Detective St. Peter's, were very thick, with many, many entries; folders for collateral witnesses like David Beek (who would simply testify that he saw McCabe immediately after the K of C dance, and whose testimony I imagined would be comparatively brief) contained only one or two pages. For Ferreira, I think we prepped about forty folders altogether. (The number of witnesses who actually testified was fewer than that, but we had to prepare for everybody on the witness list—thirty-nine of them, if memory serves—and we couldn't be sure who the Commonwealth would and wouldn't call to the stand.)

Once the witness folders were finished, it was time to start planning my defense strategy. And my intention was to start planting the seed for my defense even before the trial began—I'd do it while selecting the jury.

10. Wednesday, March 9-Thursday, April 14

As Ed Brown mounted the steps of the Middlesex County District Attorney's office just before 9:00 a.m., his mind was a veritable storm of worries. His wife Carolyn was going to the doctor every other week, it seemed like, after discovering yet another ailment. His kids were giving him nonstop fits. (Yeah, they were teenagers, and that's what teenagers did, but that didn't make it any easier.)

And now…this. After all these years. He'd been telling the truth when he'd talked to the cops on those previous occasions—he just didn't remember what happened. And if he didn't remember, why the hell would he have failed the polygraph? But Ed took a bit of solace in the fact that, for better or worse, he'd probably learn what his future held once he testified to a grand jury. Whether that included time in jail, he had no idea…but at least after today, he'd *know.*

He inquired at the front desk, and a receptionist directed him to Interview Room Two on the third floor. *An interview room?* Ed thought as he got on the elevator. *Aren't grand jury hearings held in a courtroom?*

When he reached the third floor, he exited the elevator and walked down the hall—which looked like doors to offices, not courtrooms, he thought—searching for the correct room. He found it at the end of the hall. Sweat glistening on his brow, he reached with a shaky hand and turned the knob.

When the door swung open Ed saw not a courtroom, but a nondescript meeting room with a large table at its center. Sitting around the table were four people: Detective

198

Coughlin, Lieutenant Sullivan, A.D.A. O'Reilly, and a man Ed didn't recognize.

"Uh...hi," Ed said. "Am I...I thought—"

"Come in, Mr. Brown," Coughlin said. She gestured to the others as she introduced them. "You remember the lieutenant...the district attorney...and this is Sergeant Murray—he works at LPD with us." Murray nodded, stone-faced.

"But...I thought I was—"

"Have a seat, sir," O'Reilly said, gesturing to a chair at the head of the table. O'Reilly was old-school, had been practicing law for decades, and he knew no explanation was required for misleading Ed Brown about his visit to the D.A.'s office. "The grand jury testimony isn't necessary." He raised his bushy eyebrows. "Not yet."

Ed slowly sank into the chair, nerves electrified. "But..." He looked at Coughlin. "You gave me a subpoena. I th—"

"Mr. Brown, we asked you here because we need to get to the bottom of this matter," Coughlin said. (She neglected to tell him that the grand jury subpoena was fake, and its only purpose was to assure that Ed would appear that day. And it worked.) "These men are all familiar with the case—and familiar with *you*—and they're here to help me. And we're going to help *you* remember what really happened to John McCabe that night."

Ed sighed heavily. Sweat now dripped down the sides of his head. "I've told you a million times, I don't remember anyth—"

"That's not going to work anymore. You remember, Mr. Brown. Don't you? Why else would you have failed that polygraph? You remember. Maybe your memory is...I don't know, repressed or something. But we're going to help you get your facts straight. Okay?"

Ed was obviously terrified. He began scratching the side of his face—a gesture Coughlin had noticed him make a week earlier—and when he raised his hand to do so Coughlin could see his fingers quaking. His eyes darted from face to face. Amidst his jumble of thoughts, though, was one of clarity: *They're not recording this. Why? Far as I know, they didn't record it last week either. Shouldn't th*—

"Edward!" Coughlin slapped the table. "You need to get with it. You told me last week you don't want to go to jail, right?"

Ed's bottom lip was quivering. "No. I don't."

"Then think about that. With you in prison, who'll take care of your family?"

"I dunno. Nobody."

"Mr. Brown." It was A.D.A. O'Reilly. "Detective Coughlin's right. You're looking at a homicide charge. That carries with it a possible life sentence. You'll spend many years—maybe the rest of your life—in prison. I know I wouldn't want that. So if you know something, you need to tell us what it is. And you need to do so now."

As O'Reilly talked, Ed's eyes overflowed with tears. As they continued to roll down his face, he stopped glancing nervously around; instead he clasped his hands together on the table and bowed his head, almost as if he were praying. (Coughlin thought she wouldn't be surprised if that's what he actually *was* doing.) He stayed in that position for a few seconds, then raised his head. His cheeks were wet with tears, but no more rolled down his face.

"If I tell you what I remember…then what happens?" he asked. Coughlin, along with everyone else in the room, looked at O'Reilly.

"That depends," he said.

"On?"

"On the information you give us. Then we can discuss the possibility of a lighter sentence, if you work with us. If what you remember matches what we already believe happened. Do you understand?"

Ed paused to think. His eyes were still on the move, but Coughlin thought he was beginning to show a semblance of calm. Finally he took a deep breath. "Okay."

"Okay," Coughlin said, scooting her chair closer to him. "Can you tell us what happened that night?"

"Well…like I say, I don't remember much. And a lot of this will be a guess. 'Cause I really don't…maybe my mind's blocked it out, or whatever. But…maybe Walter did it because he was jealous of Marla."

"Right," Coughlin said. "But Ed, you've told us that before. Can you remember any details? Who were you with?"

"Um…Walter. Mike. And Marla?" He looked at Coughlin, almost as if he needed confirmation. "It's hard to remember."

"Okay. What happened?"

And for at least the next two hours, according to Coughlin's report on the interrogation, Ed told them. But instead of details of what he and the others did to John McCabe that night, Ed changed his story every few minutes, telling a total of five more versions of it in all. And therein lay the crux of the entire case: did Ed keep changing his story because of a repressed, faulty memory, or did he do it in an attempt to match what the detectives and the A.D.A. believe happened? The five people in that room that day are the only ones who know.

In the second version of Ed's memory of the night's events—the first being his previously repeated claims that he had no involvement at all—he said he was cleaning a restaurant in Waltham, and upon being picked up by Walter, Mike, and Marla, they told him that they'd killed John and had his body in the trunk; the four then drove to the vacant lot in Lowell, and Walter and Mike dumped the body there while Ed remained in the car.

Version three went back to Ed's proclamation that he was not involved, but that Walter and Mike told him the next day that they'd killed John accidentally. In version four, Ed said that he was present for the murder, then modified the story again by saying that Walter and Mike dropped him off at home prior to the killing. At some point during this two-hour period, A.D.A. O'Reilly suggested to Ed that they'd tied up John "just like in *The French Connection,*" a suggestion to which Ed shakily agreed. Also during that time, Coughlin showed Ed the crime scene photo that showed John's body as it was originally found by the two young boys: lying on his stomach, bound with rope, tape covering his eyes and mouth.

It was revealed later that the interrogation, as Ed Brown suspected, was not recorded. Coughlin wrote her report from memory (and from notes she or one of the other detectives presumably took) about seven weeks later, on April 27, and it filled multiple pages. After Ed Brown told the multiple versions of the events, Coughlin wrote that "it was obvious to all officers present that Ed Brown was lying.

"He was confronted with our beliefs," she continued. After that confrontation, Coughlin wrote, Brown told them one last version of events—a version almost identical to the one he told at Mike Ferreira's trial nearly two years later. According to the report:

On the night John was murdered, Ed was with Walter and Mike. They rode around for a while drinking, then picked up Marla from the K of C dance. Shortly after that, they dropped Marla off, presumably at home. "Because Walter believed John McCabe had been paying attention to her," Coughlin wrote, "they decided to find him and 'teach him a lesson.' Brown went on to say that the three of them set out to find John and that they'd 'fix his ass.' Brown told us that they decided they would tie him up 'like in the movie.' Brown explained that he was referring to a movie they'd seen prior to the murder in which someone was bound and tied." (It is assumed that the movie to which Ed referred—at least, according to Coughlin's report—was *The French Connection.* This, Eric Wilson would later prove at trial, was an impossibility.)

They found John hitchhiking on Route 38, Coughlin wrote, headed in the direction of Lowell. When they saw him they pulled over, and Mike grabbed him and put him in the back seat. "Shelley was the driver and Ferreira the front seat passenger. Brown told us that when they got McCabe into the vehicle, Michael Ferreira was hitting him. Shelley continued to drive and they headed to the vacant lot on Maple Street." When they got there, they forced John out of the car, threw him to the ground and held him down. "Ed Brown held his legs as he was being tied at the hands and feet by Ferreira and Shelley," the report read. "Brown claimed that Ferreira had the rope and a knife, and that he cut sections of the rope with the knife."

During all of this, Brown recalled, John was "yelling, crying, and screaming," so one of them—the report didn't name which boy—covered John's mouth with tape. And then the report read: "Brown told us that the three of them left John tied and struggling. He was bound at the neck, wrists, and legs, with a rope connected from his ankles to his neck." (In other words—at least, according to Coughlin's report of Brown's recollection—John was hogtied.) "Brown stated that as they left, John continued to struggle. At one point he was on his stomach trying to get on his side. He appeared to have his legs in the air. Brown stated that this was how they left John McCabe."

The three drove around for an hour or so, the report explained, then returned to the lot. "They approached John. Brown told us that John was not moving. Brown stated that one of them removed the tape from his mouth and found that he was not breathing. After they realized John was dead, they put the tape back over his mouth.

"We asked Brown what they thought at that point. Brown told us, 'We were screwed.' Brown then said they panicked and left the field."

After they left, Coughlin wrote, the three tried to figure out what to do. "Brown stated that they swore they wouldn't tell anyone what had happened, and maybe they wouldn't get caught. Brown said, 'We thought if we didn't tell anyone, we'd be okay.'" Mike Ferreira threatened him at one point, Brown said, saying that "if he (Brown) told anyone what had happened to John McCabe, Michael would kill him."

At the end of the report: "Brown stated, 'How long am I going to jail for?' I asked him if that were the reason he'd lied to us, and he said yes, he didn't want to spend the rest of his life in jail. We asked Brown if what he now told us was the truth about what had happened to John McCabe. Brown told us that it was. At the conclusion of our interview, Brown was served with a subpoena. Allen 'Ed' Brown is scheduled to appear before the Grand Jury of the Commonwealth on March 15, 2011, to provide testimony regarding the death of John McCabe.

"Investigation to continue."

* * * *

Over the next two days, Lieutenant Sullivan went on a report-writing rampage. After Ed Brown's March 9 interrogation, Coughlin mentioned to him that she'd been unable to locate the report on Brown's 2007 interview with Sullivan and Wayne; after further discussion, Sullivan and Coughlin realized that that report, along with several others from the previous decade, simply didn't exist.

So on March 9 and 10, Sullivan wrote numerous reports, including those on the 2003 interviews with Mike Ferreira and Brian Gath, and the 2007 interviews with Walter Shelley and Ed Brown. Like Coughlin's lengthy report on Brown's 2011 interrogation, Sullivan relied on his notes and his memory to write them. It is possible there had been confusion between Sullivan and Wayne over which detective would write the reports; another scenario is that until Brown's "confession," Sullivan simply didn't consider those interviews important enough to warrant a written record of them.

On March 23, Ed Brown testified before a grand jury, during which he recounted details of the alleged murder of

John McCabe on the night of September 26, 1969. Indictments were issued for Brown, Ferreira, and Shelley, and on April 14, Walter Shelley was arrested at his place of employment. The charge was first-degree murder.

That same day, Ed Brown was arrested and released on his own recognizance. The charge was manslaughter. Since he'd agreed to testify in the trials of Ferreira and Shelley, Ed served no jail time.

Also on April 14, Mike Ferreira was arrested in Salem, N.H., on a Fugitive of Justice warrant out of Massachusetts. The charge was first-degree murder. Five days later, Mike and his attorney, Eric Wilson, waived extradition, and Lieutenant Sullivan and Detective Coughlin brought Mike back to Lowell, where he was held in the Middlesex County House of Corrections.

Once news broke of the arrests, word spread quickly across the country. CNN dedicated an entire news segment to the forty-three-year-old murder. The *Boston Globe* and *New York Times*—along with dozens of smaller newspapers—published feature stories on it. And in Lowell, Middlesex District Attorney Gerry Leone held a press conference, during which he said that the arrests were "the result of an incredible turn of events." The men were charged, he told the swarm of media, because of "excellent work by detectives of the Lowell Criminal Bureau."

Detective Coughlin, from her place behind D.A. Leone on the dais, gave a wry smile while Leone heaped praise upon her and her cohorts. After four decades, she thought to herself, she'd finally gotten results. The manner in which she'd gotten them wasn't important.

EX PARTE: Jury Selection

For a time, we thought the trial would take place in December—but for a number of reasons that I won't even get into, it was continued again, now to January. We began selecting the jury in early December, and after the continuance, finally empaneled it on January 14, the day before the trial began. And by now, the Ferreira trial was getting national attention: *Good Morning America* was already reporting on it, and it was being covered extensively by CBS's *48 Hours,* the *Boston Globe,* and by numerous TV news stations. For that reason, both parties wanted to find potential jurors who didn't already know a lot about the case (and therefore already be biased about whether or not Mike Ferreira was guilty).

In a first-degree murder case, the attorneys get to question potential jurors with what's called "individually sequestered voir dire." Here's how that works: all the potential jurors will fill out a jury questionnaire consisting of about twenty stock yes-or-no questions ("Do you have any relatives in law enforcement?" and "Have you formed any judgments or opinions with respect to this case?" are a couple of examples); the attorneys also have the opportunity to add specific questions related to their particular case.

Once the questionnaires are completed, the potential jurors are brought into the courtroom individually and questioned by the judge and the attorneys for both parties. And potential jurors can be "challenged"—in other words, dismissed—in one of two ways: first, they can be "challenged for cause," meaning they give a valid reason, on which the attorneys and the judge agree, that they cannot be fair and impartial. ("My brother was murdered, so I hate all murderers" would be an example.) Both parties are also given a number of "peremptory challenges," meaning they can dismiss a juror for any reason whatsoever. In Ferreira each side was given fifteen peremptory challenges, and I was very careful about using mine.

As I said before, I wanted to plant the seed for my defense right from the start. So one of the questions I added to the juror questionnaire was: "Would you find it more difficult to assess the credibility of a person who made several statements about an event as opposed to someone who made only one?" And the potential jurors who answered "Yes" were obviously the ones I favored. Because one idea I wanted to express to the jury: *Edward Allen Brown is not to be believed.* During my questioning of each juror I would get more specific, with questions like "Can you envision a person lying to the police about their involvement in a crime?" and "If someone admitted their commission of a crime, how would you determine whether their statements were credible?" And depending on what a juror's answers were, I would start a dialogue with them to find out how they felt.

I used this whole process to pare down the jury to my liking (as much as was possible, at least). When the jury was empaneled, I was…moderately happy, I'll say. Regardless of that, though, it was time to try the case. And I was ready.

11. Tuesday, December 11, 2012

In the twenty-month period between the arrests and Mike Ferreira's trial, investigators interviewed (and in some cases, *re*-interviewed) numerous people in an attempt to fortify the Commonwealth's case. Among them was Marla Shiner, who was interviewed in June 2011, in person at her home, by two detectives from the Escondido (Calif.) Police Department. During that interview, Marla reiterated her previous assertion that there had never been any romantic involvement between her and John McCabe. She recalled attending only one or two K of C dances back then, and said she would've gone to them with Walter. And Walter, she said again, had never shown any feelings of jealousy about John; "Believe me, I would've known," she told the detectives.

Investigators also spoke with Bob Ryan, Carol Ann (McFrederies) Roberts, and Bob Brown, none of whom gave them any useful information they didn't already have. In late April 2011, not long after the arrests, Ed Brown was arrested for threatening to shoot his wife, then himself, with the .38-caliber handgun he owned. "Edward has been under a great deal of stress due to the pending trial," the arresting officer wrote in his report, "and he has had violent outbursts in the past." Ed was later released on $25,000 bail.

In early December 2012, Coughlin spoke with Frs. Walsh and Cahill, both of whom had received anonymous calls in 1969 from a man claiming to be the killer. Walsh remembered taking the call, but provided no further info; Cahill, who was several years retired, could not remember receiving such a call at all.

Then, on December 11, Coughlin interviewed Mary Ann (Richard) LaCourciere, the babysitter whom Mike Ferreira had said he was with around the time of the murder, who'd traveled to Lowell PD from her Hooksett, N.H. home at Coughlin's request. And during their talk, LaCourciere provided quite an interesting piece of information.

"What do you remember about that night?" Coughlin asked to begin the interview. Lieutenant Sullivan and two representatives from the district attorney's office, A.D.A. Gina Kwon and victims' advocate Dora Quiror, were also present, and now they leaned forward to hear Mary Ann's answer.

"I remember I was babysitting for the McCarthys...some boys came by at one point. Mike, Walter...and I think there was another boy with them. I can't remember."

Coughlin and Sullivan shared a quick glance. "Could it have been Ed Brown? Think he went by Allen back then?"

"Allen Brown? Maybe...I just don't remember. That was...what, forty years ago?"

"Forty-three years, but yeah," Coughlin said. "Do you remember if Nancy came by too?"

"Nancy Williams? Well, Ferreira now...but no. She wasn't there."

"Okay. Tell me what you remember about when the boys came over."

"Let's see...I'm sure I talked to them at the door. The McCarthys didn't allow me to have people over when they weren't there. And..." She frowned for a moment trying to retrieve the memory. "I think we talked about Carol Ann."

"Carol Ann McFrederies, that would be?"

"Yeah. She was a good friend of mine."

"Do you remember if she went to the dance?"

"She did. I remember because when Mike mentioned her, I said she was still at the dance."

"Hm. So when they were there, it was before the dance let out?"

"Pretty sure it was, yeah."

"Okay." Coughlin looked at Sullivan, who just shrugged. "Well, Miss LaCourciere…anything else you'd like to tell us?"

"Actually, there is." She paused for a moment. "I…I've been thinking about this ever since I heard about them being arrested. I…this was a few weeks after John was murdered. It was me, Mike Ferreira, and another friend of ours, Jackie Spencer. We were in the kitchen at my house, we were talking about John's murder, about how he was strangled and all that…all of a sudden, Mike comes and puts a scarf around my neck…and he pulls it tight, like he was choking me." She'd gotten very quiet.

The others were a bit stunned. After a moment, Coughlin said, "What did you do?"

"I told him to stop. He just laughed, didn't really say anything. He…he acted like it was just a joke, but…it scared me to death."

"What happened next?"

"Nothing, I guess. He just kind of laughed it off…but I stayed away from him after that. He scared me."

The interview continued, with Mary Ann explaining that her brother, Joey, who'd died in 2008, took a trip to California shortly before his death to visit Marla Shiner; upon his return, Mary Ann said, he warned her to "stay away from those people" (the "people" in question being

Walter, Mike, Nancy, and Ed), and that they were all involved with the McCabe incident.

Coughlin wrote her report on the interview later the same day. And again, her report contained information not attributed to anyone, information that read as facts, but may very well have merely been Coughlin's own speculation about the given info.

For example: near the end of her report, when she was detailing Mary Ann's statements about her conversation with her brother, Coughlin wrote this standalone sentence: "Joey, Marla, and John McCabe were all childhood friends." Nowhere in the one thousand-plus pages of McCabe evidence is that confirmed; Marla Shiner herself, in fact, repeatedly refuted that claim.

EX PARTE: Last Minute Thoughts

Interestingly enough, the night before a big trial like Ferreira begins, I always sleep like a baby. Because in cases of this magnitude, I like to over-prepare, rather than under-prepare; the odds are more likely to be in my favor if I've done everything humanly possible to be ready. Usually, by the time the trial begins I've covered all the bases, so I like to get some good rest the night before the big show starts.

And as usual, the night before we had opening statements in the Ferreira trial, I slept like a rock. As I lay in bed I considered my strategy, and found it to be a pretty damn good one: in summary, the prosecution would be relying almost solely on Ed Brown's testimony to make their case. So my main objective was to ruin his credibility—and to hopefully start doing that even before the jury saw his face, so that by the time he took the stand to testify, they would already be convinced he was a liar. The other minor points O'Reilly would bring up—Mike's "I did it" joke during the beer run in '69, the incident with Mary Ann Richard and the scarf, etcetera—I would address during my opening and at relevant points during witness testimony. And I knew that I probably wouldn't be able to deal a "death blow" to the Commonwealth's case with one witness or piece of evidence; I would have to employ a "death by a thousand cuts" strategy, whereby I damaged the state's case with many minor blows, which when put together would mean an acquittal.

For my opening statement itself, I wanted to cover several major points: for one, I would acknowledge that John McCabe died a horrific death. But instead of hiding behind that fact, I wanted to amplify it. I wanted John McCabe to speak. Not through his words, obviously, since he was dead…but through his body. The placement of it, the physical evidence related to the ligature marks on his neck, and the overall condition of the body itself would tell a much more credible story than the one they would hear from Ed Brown.

I also wanted to introduce the issues of Richard Santos, the caller to the priests, and other suspects that all related to the third-party culprit evidence. But above all else, I knew that the Commonwealth's ability to convict Michael Ferreira was going to be predicated on the believability of Brown, so I want to plant in the mind of the jurors the fact that they just weren't going to be able to believe him.

In this case, more than any other I've tried—and I've done other murder trials, but certainly none with the complexity and notoriety of this one—I knew that it could be won or lost in my opening. And one way I planned to get the jury on my side was to set the focus on *me*. Hopefully I could have the jurors pay more attention to the defense, and whether or not we were proving our case, than whether the Commonwealth was proving theirs. In other words, I wanted the case to be mine to win or lose.

Part Three:
The Mike Ferreira Trial

1. Tuesday, January 15, 2013: Ferreira Trial, Day One

"All rise."

As a door on the side of the courtroom opened and Judge David Ricciardone strode through it, the hundred or so people in the courtroom stood. The gallery, consisting of spectators and members of the media in about equal numbers, was packed with people, all of whom had stood in line before the courtroom had even opened that morning in order to gain the seats they now held. *In Session TV*, which planned to broadcast daily highlights of the trial in the following weeks, was filming the proceedings with cameras at the front and rear of the room. CBS's *48 Hours* was also on hand to tape footage for an upcoming episode of the show.

Interestingly, after the trial had been continued the previous December, the litigants had discovered that no courtrooms were available in the Lowell Superior Court building until April. In the interest of time, both parties had agreed to move the trial to the closest available Superior Court in Woburn, a few miles southeast. And the Woburn courtroom itself, unlike the polished brass and hardwood rooms usually depicted in the movies, was businesslike and drab, with plain gray carpet and unflattering fluorescent lights.

Standing regally behind the prosecution table was the lead prosecutor, A.D.A. Tom O'Reilly, along with A.D.A. Elisha Willis (who would act as the Commonwealth's unofficial "bulldog," objecting to the defense's tactics whenever possible and examining some essential witnesses) and A.D.A. John Mulcahy, essentially the prosecution's "technical" attorney; Mulcahy would note all the details of the litigation in case the Commonwealth needed to appeal the verdict to a higher court. Seated mere feet behind the prosecution table, in the first row of the gallery, were Evelyn McCabe and her daughters Debbie and Roberta, who all planned to attend every second of the trial. (Since Bill McCabe was the first witness scheduled to testify for the prosecution, he was not allowed in the courtroom prior to his testimony.)

At the defense table, Mike Ferreira stared down at his feet, his face expressionless, while the judge walked to the bench. To Mike's right was lead defense counsel Eric Wilson, his bright eyes inspecting Judge Ricciardone as the judge took his seat. Stan Norkunas, the tall, salt-and-pepper-haired attorney who would serve as the defense's second chair, stood next to Eric. Behind them, taking up nearly the entire first row of gallery seats on that side, were members of the Ferreira clan. Mike's niece Danielle sat amongst them with a notebook on her lap, ready to take notes. (Eric had asked her to pay extra-close attention to the jury, and their reactions to the various testimony, during the trial.) Mike's wife Nancy, like Bill McCabe, was absent because she was scheduled to testify for the defense.

"Good morning," Ricciardone said to the group, eliciting murmured responses. (Eric himself was truly pleased to have David Ricciardone presiding over this trial; the judge brought with him a reputation of fairness and attention to detail, and Eric knew Ricciardone wouldn't allow the notoriety the case was already garnering to affect his judicial readiness.) After covering a few logistics issues, including a stern warning to the *In Session* cameramen that they were "under no circumstances" to film any member of the jury, Ricciardone asked the bailiff to bring the jurors in.

And one by one, they entered through the same doorway through which the judge had passed. Sixteen men and women—twelve true jurors and four alternates—filed into the jury box and took their seats. Once they were in place, Ricciardone, who was known for being a stickler for making sure his trials remained on schedule, wasted no time.

"Mr. O'Reilly, your opening statement, please?"

"Thank you, Your Honor." O'Reilly stood and ambled to the podium to the right of the juror box. With thousands of hours of litigation under his belt and a three-decade career as an attorney to his credit, Tom O'Reilly didn't hurry for anybody. Silver-haired and -bearded, he exuded quiet, effortless power…but a casual courtroom observer might wonder if, after over twenty years of putting criminals in jail as an A.D.A, he'd grown a wee bit too comfortable.

He cleared his throat and surveyed the room. "Your Honor, Madam Clerk, counsel…if I cough, I apologize." He smiled and leaned in to the jurors seated about ten feet in front of him. "Unfortunately, when I've been speaking lately, I cough, which is bad for a district attorney," he said, then chuckled. (As Eric Wilson watched from the defense table, he noticed that not one of the jurors shared in O'Reilly's mirth; they simply stared at him.)

O'Reilly suddenly turned serious. He eyed the jury for a moment, then: "On the morning of September 27, 1969—a Saturday morning—two young boys were cutting through a field by the railyards in Lowell, on their way to catch some frogs. While walking across the field they spotted a young boy. He was bound hand and foot, rope around the neck, face down. The boys ran and got the police. When the police showed up, they discovered the body of John McCabe, fifteen years old, last seen in Tewksbury. His father had been out looking for him the night before, so they had John as a missing person. His father went and identified him at the funeral home where they did the autopsy."

O'Reilly left the podium and stood directly in front of the jury box. "This trial is about how John McCabe reached that point. And the evidence will show that it was based upon jealousy—jealousy by Walter Shelley, because, supposedly, John was flirting with his thirteen-year-old girlfriend, Marla Shiner." O'Reilly scowled. "So a plan was hatched. Shelley and his best friend Michael Ferreira, the defendant in this case"—he turned and gestured toward the defense table—"decided to go looking for John to teach him a lesson. Only no one knew what the lesson was until the final resting of John McCabe."

O'Reilly explained that on the night in question, Mike and Nancy Williams had picked John up at the novitiate and given him a ride to Main Street, then John had gone on down Main to the K of C Dance. After the dance let out, O'Reilly said, "a boy named David Beek, who you'll hear from in the coming days, looked out the window and saw John thumbing in the direction of Chandler Street, just by the pay phone in front of The Oaks."

O'Reilly paused for a moment. "Now, why is that important? It's important because Edward Allen Brown was the third person in the car with Shelley and Ferreira. Ed Brown did not know of the lesson they planned to teach

John McCabe until he got in the car. Did not know what the lesson was to be.

"They picked up Ed Brown at his home and came up Shawsheen Street, which is right across from The Oaks. They turned onto Main Street…and they saw John McCabe thumbing just past The Oaks. Shelley pulled his car up—his '65 Chevy Impala, maroon in color—and Michael Ferreira hopped out, grabbed John in a bear hug, and pushed him into the back seat of the car. John was now sitting behind Michael Ferreira, wanting to get out. 'Let me out…let me out…where are we going? What are we doing?' Edward Allen Brown described it as fear in his voice."

O'Reilly was in a groove, the jurors hanging on his words. The A.D.A. slowed his pace a bit while he told the jury how the boys had driven to the lot off Maple, pulled in, and thrown John onto the ground outside the car. They'd taken him further into the field, put adhesive tape over his eyes and mouth, then Shelley and Brown had sat on him while Ferreira tied his ankles and wrists together.

"Then they got off, and Ferreira put a rope around the neck down to the waist, bending his knees up so that they were almost straight up in the air, the rope running from his feet to his neck," O'Reilly said. "And they were taunting him: 'That's what you get for messing with Marla. Stay away from Marla.' And as they walk away Brown sees John struggling and moaning.

"Then they got in the car and they drove away."

Several of the jurors were crying softly. Others looked angry. O'Reilly paused a moment for dramatic effect, then continued his narration of the events—or at least, Ed Brown's version of them, which had in turn been described by Detective Coughlin in a police report. The three had driven around for at least an hour, O'Reilly said, then Brown had said they needed to return to the field. "When they drove in, John's feet were still up in the air. Brown said he didn't get out of the car this time, but Ferreira and Shelley did. They went over to the body…and they were there for thirty to forty seconds, then came running back to the car. 'What's going on?' Brown says. 'He's not breathing.' Then they backed out and took off again."

O'Reilly repeated the info about the two young boys discovering the body, how they'd found the police, and that the medical examiner had determined at the autopsy that John had died from asphyxiation due to ligature strangulation. As O'Reilly went on describing details of the early investigation, John's funeral, and Mike's "joke" confession during the beer run, Eric noticed that some jurors started shifting in their seats and letting their eyes wander around the courtroom.

But O'Reilly seemed to take no notice. For the next twenty minutes, he got lost in his own story, telling the jury—many of whom seemed to grow increasingly bored, Eric saw—about how the investigation continued through the decades. He talked about the cold case's resurgence with Jack Ward's story about Mike's statement at the pig roast, the continuing investigation by Lieutenant Sullivan and Detective Wayne (which, by and large, had ended with Wayne's 2009 death), and Detective Coughlin's resumption of the case in 2011. By the time O'Reilly neared his conclusion, even Judge Ricciardone was glancing impatiently at the clock.

O'Reilly finished his saga of the investigation with an account of Ed Brown's last interrogation. And at its end:

"Ed Brown told what happened that night as I've related it to you. He fully expected to walk out of there in handcuffs. In exchange for his testimony to a grand jury several weeks later, an agreement was reached with him. He was indicted and charged with manslaughter. In exchange for his testimony, he will not do jail time. But Michael Ferreira gave us his name…and Ed Brown gave us the information.

"Ladies and gentlemen, John McCabe was kidnapped off the street by Shelley, Ferreira, and Brown. Mr. Brown was a full participant. When he gave his statement to the police, he had no deal, no promise—he fully expected to go down for life. So you'll have to judge his credibility. After he was arrested for John McCabe, he was picked up again for domestic violence up in New Hampshire, for which he pled guilty and was put on probation. That's his only record other than manslaughter. Mike Ferreira was arrested and brought back to Massachusetts; Walter Shelley, arrested, brought back too. So it's an issue of credibility, simple as that. *You* judge. *You* make the decision. I suggest that at the end of this trial, you will find Mike Ferreira guilty of first-degree murder.

"They left John McCabe writhing on the ground, a rope around his neck. You'll see the furrows in his neck in the autopsy photos. You'll see the marks on his hands and his feet. One can only infer that he was struggling for air, struggling to breathe. And the three of them just walked away. Taunting him. I suggest to you: Why would a rope go around his neck other than with an intent to kill?

"Thank you." The courtroom was silent as O'Reilly walked back to the prosecution table.

Judge Ricciardone, true to form, kept things moving. "Thank you, Mr. O'Reilly." He looked down at the defense table. "Mr. Wilson, on behalf of the defendant…?"

"Thank you, Your Honor," Eric said as he rose. He skipped the podium altogether and walked directly to a few feet from the jury box, where he planted himself and looked the jury members over for a moment; his good looks and intelligent, piercing eyes caught the glance of every juror in the box. And it was an instant Eric loved. In his twenty years as a litigator—half of that as the founding partner of a law firm in his hometown—there was nothing quite like the flash of adrenaline he got when he began a murder trial, especially one as notorious as this one. This was the moment he'd dreamed about during law school. And it was a moment he was built for.

"Forty-three years ago, John McCabe died. He left his family, he left his friends, he left this very *world* in a field that we're going to go to in an hour or so, off Maple Street in Lowell." Eric shifted his focus to a juror in the middle of the back row. "Throughout this trial, John McCabe—not through his words, because he cannot talk—but through his injuries, and through the placement and condition of his body, is going to tell you what happened. In the course of this trial, you're going to learn what happened to him through science. Through physical evidence. Through photographs. And the evidence just doesn't match what Edward Allen Brown is going to tell you." Now he looked at a female juror in the front row, then repeated: "It will not match anything he'll tell you.

"Photographs. Medical evidence. Science. These are the things that will bring you to the end of this case…not the words of Ed Brown. It will be tangible things, measureable things that you'll be able to rely on. It won't be through faded memories, fed and fabricated stories. That's what I anticipate the evidence will show you with respect to Ed Brown: fed and fabricated testimony."

Eric took a few steps over to meet the eyes of yet another juror, this one at the end of the back row. "Cold cases don't get better with memories. Cold cases get better with science and facts—things that don't change over forty-three years. Although there is no DNA, there is documented evidence with respect to the crime scene. You will see that. I'll point out to you today, when we view the crime scene, things like buildings. The location of buildings hasn't changed. Billboards haven't changed. The location and manner in which John's body was left in that field won't change—and that's what will convince you. The facts you learn through this trial will render your verdict of not guilty for Michael."

Similar to how O'Reilly had just laid it all out, Eric continued his opening by outlining the four-decade investigation—but unlike O'Reilly, Eric subconsciously invited the jurors in. As he spoke, he shifted his focus from one juror to another every few seconds, as if he were holding a one-on-one conversation with each of them. And, as Eric noticed while he was addressing the sixteen jurors, they seemed to welcome the change; they looked captivated.

Also unlike O'Reilly, Eric's description of the forty-three-year investigation included its numerous holes—holes that were often overlooked, or simply ignored altogether: the detectives' confusion when questioning Mike in 1969; Jack Ward's speculation about the motive—jealousy over Marla—which detectives seemed to treat as fact; and Ed Brown's memory of the events, which morphed from no recall at all in 2007 to five different versions of how the murder happened during his 2011 interrogations—which hadn't been recorded.

"You'll hear during the course of this trial that it's okay for the police to fabricate things," Eric said. "For example: Ed Brown was told, 'Ferreira says you were with him that night and you guys are involved.' Mike Ferreira never said to the police or anyone else he was involved, other than a joke he told Elaine Callahan. But Ed Brown was told, 'Mike is saying you did this with him.' So Allen Brown—unrecorded—is hearing all of this evidence. Then on March 2 he tells the police, 'Listen, you guys are telling me I'm involved, you're telling me I'm lying. You guys are accusing me of murder. I'm afraid to go to jail.' Later he tells the police, 'Maybe I was involved and I have repressed memory. Maybe I was involved and I just don't remember this.' And then the police say, 'No, you're lying, you were involved.' And he said these words: 'If I told you I was involved, it would just be fantasy, Detective. I wasn't involved.'"

Eric paused to survey the entire jury. "It would just be fantasy. I wasn't involved." He let those words sink in before continuing his narration of the March 9 interrogation. He continued to hammer home the fact that the longer Ed Brown continued his denial, the more the detectives maintained his involvement. And slowly but surely, Eric explained, the pendulum began to swing. Eric ticked off the five versions of events Ed had confessed, then brought his point home.

"Then the interview stops. He is told by Detective Coughlin what she thinks happened to John McCabe. And

Detective Coughlin tells him that Shelley and Ferreira are the prime suspects, and she says they've told her that Ed is involved too. And then Coughlin shows him a troubling photograph—which you'll see during this trial—of fifteen-year-old John McCabe tied up in a field, his hands bound, his feet and neck bound, his mouth and his eyes taped. Tells him, 'This is what you did.' And just by looking at those photos, anyone could tell what happened to John McCabe. Anyone could give their own version. So what happens next? Ed Brown tells version six—not recorded—that, coincidentally, exactly matches what the detectives thought."

Eric paused to breathe. As he did he noticed that all sixteen people in the jury box were transfixed on him and every move he made. At that point, he knew, he had everyone's attention. He picked up his pace while informing the jurors of O'Reilly's *French Connection* theory he'd suggested to Ed on March 9, noting that *The French Connection* hadn't been released until three years after the murder. Then Eric switched gears and talked about the third-party culprit evidence: he recounted the details of the caller to the two priests, during which he highlighted the fact that the caller claimed to have John's belt (and that police never revealed to the public that John wasn't wearing a belt when his body was found), and explained that Richard Santos, upon his 1974 arrest, had disclosed that he'd abducted and assaulted other people. "Linda Coughlin never even looked at the possibility of the caller to the priests, or Richard Santos, or numerous other suspects that have come and gone over the last forty-three years. She focused her attention on Ed Brown, and she got him to say what he'll tell you during this trial."

Eric ended the opening with the introduction of a single theme—one he'd return to repeatedly over the next seven days. "Ed Brown is going to testify before you. And the biggest question that will remain in your minds after this trial—one you probably don't have to answer—is: Why is he telling you what he's telling you? Like I said, you don't have to answer that. But one thing in this trial is clear:

"Ed Brown didn't have his facts straight." Eric paused to look the jurors over once more, then headed back to the defense table.

Judge Ricciardone was silent for a moment while he let the jurors collect their thoughts. Then: "Thank you, Mr. Wilson." He glanced at the clock on the wall opposite the jury box. "Well, ladies and gentlemen, looks like it's a little past 1:00, so I'm going to take the lunch recess now. We'll meet back here at, say, 2:15? We'll be boarding a bus to go on the view, wherein we'll visit the crime scene and other locations mentioned during this trial." He leaned in toward the jury box. "In the meantime, of course, the ongoing instruction not to discuss the case with anyone—including amongst yourselves—will apply. All right? We'll see you at 2:15." And with that, the bailiff led the jurors out.

As Judge Ricciardone left the bench, Eric turned to Mike and whispered: "How you holding up?"

"I'm okay," Mike answered, but his face was drawn with worry. Eric looked over his shoulder to Danielle in the first row, then raised his eyebrows and shrugged in a gesture that asked, *Well...?* Danielle gave him a big smile and a thumbs-up. *You're doing great.*

* * * *

When the jurors were back in their seats after lunch, Judge Ricciardone gave them a brief instruction on what would happen on the view—"We're about to go on a field trip, so to speak," the judge joked—while the bailiff distributed notebooks and pencils with which the jurors could take notes during the trial, if they so desired. "If you wish to take notes, you may do so," Judge Ricciardone instructed them. "I'm not suggesting that you have to. You should do whatever makes you feel comfortable. It may be that your memories will suffice…but I did want to give you the choice." When he finished, the jurors departed to board the bus—a school bus on loan from the Woburn Public Schools District—that would take them to and from the crime scene in Lowell. The attorneys remained in the courtroom for a brief meeting to discuss some logistical matters, then boarded the bus behind them; after the judge was settled in the front seat, the bus departed. State police cruisers, their emergency lights flashing, drove directly in front of and behind it.

Fifteen minutes later, the procession was on Main Street in Tewksbury. Not much there had changed since 1969, including the location of the Knights of Columbus Hall; O'Reilly pointed it out on the jurors' right as the bus rolled slowly past. At the next intersection, O'Reilly indicated the spot where The Oaks restaurant once stood (a locally owned gas station was there now). Store patrons stared as the caravan breezed through the stoplight. The vehicles turned left onto Chandler Street, A.D.A. Willis pointing out the corner—another gas station, a Texaco, had been there for years, but it was now a Shell—at which Nancy Williams and Mike Ferreira had supposedly dropped John off after they'd picked him up hitchhiking on his way to the dance; as they passed the novitiate, Willis indicated the area where Nancy and Mike had stopped to give him a ride. After a right on Whipple Road, the caravan entered Lowell, and after winding its way through several side streets, turned off Maple Street into the vacant lot that was the site of the 1969 crime scene. The entire trip had taken about thirty minutes.

Though the lot itself had changed somewhat, the skyline behind it—and for the most part, the city of Lowell itself—hadn't. The concrete foundation near where John's body had been found had been removed in the 1980s; gone, too, was the shallow mound of dirt upon which the body had lain. And New England had been blessed by an unusually warm spell just prior to the trial, so there was no snow on the ground as the jurors stepped off the school bus.

Once the group was together again, O'Reilly indicated the remnants of the trail that had once led to the dirt mound. Then, pointing at a sign in the distance, he told the jurors: "Notice the billboard on that building just toward the bridge there. And right over there"—he moved his hand a few inches—"is the train tower." He brought the group up the trail a short distance, then stopped. He pointed at the ground. "This is where the body was found. Notice the marshland is a ways further over there, and back the other direction is the dirt road coming in from Maple Street." He looked at Ricciardone, who was standing a bit behind the cluster of jurors. "That's all, Judge. Thank you."

"Thank you, Mr. O'Reilly." He looked at Eric. "Mr. Wilson?"

Eric sprang into action. "Ladies and gentlemen, follow me," he said as he continued up the trail. The group followed, many of them puzzled as to where they were going. After they'd walked about sixty yards, Eric stopped. "Look at the billboard Mr. O'Reilly pointed out. See it? Now look to your left—there's the railroad tower. And over there—that smokestack." He pointed to each item as he mentioned it. "Now what I'd like you to do is, one at a time, come stand next to me." Visibly curious now, the sixteen jurors formed a haphazard line to do so. And as each one stood with Eric, he again referenced the landmarks in question, and asked them to create a mental snapshot of what they were seeing. One by one they stood with the defense attorney. And Eric offered no explanation of what he was doing; he only asked the jurors to remember what they saw.

O'Reilly frowned while Eric commenced with his unconventional (yet perfectly legal) presentation. But the demonstration was part of Eric's strategy: in the months before the trial, he'd visited the crime scene more than once, sometimes alone, other times with Mike Ferreira and/or his second chair Tim Bush (the latter before he'd taken leave to care for his mother). Then Eric had literally used a microscope to go over the crime scene photos, including one that showed John's body from a distance; the billboard, train tower, and smokestack were all visible in the photo's background. Finally, using a "triangulation" method he happened to remember from high school geometry, Eric was able to calculate the precise location of John's body when it had been found. And this location— the exact spot where he'd had each juror stand—was different from where the prosecution claimed the body had been. During his cross-examination of Ed Brown (and possibly Detective Coughlin), he planned to have them point out on a diagram where the body had been, then show that photo in hopes that the jurors would notice the difference in location, thereby damaging the witnesses' credibility. Certainly, Eric was going to great lengths in order to prove a relatively minor point—but it was all part of his "death by a thousand cuts" game plan.

Once Eric had stood with each of the sixteen jurors, he let Judge Ricciardone know he was done. The group walked back down the trail and boarded the bus, and forty-five minutes later were again gathered in the courtroom in Woburn. The judge gave them his instructions—which he would repeat daily—before discharging the jurors for the evening. It was a boring but necessary speech, one that he'd memorized.

"Ladies and gentlemen, I'm going to release you for the day—with a caution. And I'll give you some version of this caution when we quit every day. The caution is this: keep an open mind. Do not form any judgment, conclusion, opinion, or belief as to any aspect of this case until it is given to you for deliberations." He paused to look the jurors over. "Do not talk to anyone about any aspect of this case. This includes spouses, family members, friends, fellow employees, acquaintances, strangers, or even to your fellow jurors. No one. Understand? If anyone asks, you may advise them that you've been selected to sit as a juror in a criminal case here in the Middlesex County Superior Court, and that it may take about a week to try."

Riccardone flashed a smile, then: "And finally, don't conduct any independent investigation as to anything you've heard about the case. When it comes to the Internet, do not divulge any information about this case through use of computers and websites and things. Do not seek any information from the Internet—or from any other source—

regarding this case, whether it's good old-fashioned books or anything like that.

"We need jurors who will keep an open mind and decide this case fairly, based on the evidence presented to you here in the courtroom. Any independent or outside information or influence would be unfair to both parties. So if you as jurors avoid any outside contact, we can ensure a fair, just, and equitable trial. Any questions?" The jurors shook their heads. "Okay. With that, have a great night and we'll see you bright and early tomorrow morning. It's my intention to begin right at nine o'clock. Thank you." The sixteen jurors rose and filed out behind the bailiff.

EX PARTE: Trial Day 1 → Day 2

Stan Norkunas and I rode together to and from Woburn every day, and our drives were a good opportunity to discuss the trial, plot our strategy, and talk about what was coming up the next day. Luckily I had a good relationship with A.D.A. O'Reilly, so throughout the trial he and I would give each other a heads-up each night about who we would call to testify the following day. (Which isn't always the case; oftentimes at trial, the only way I know who is testifying next is when the prosecutor calls the witness to the stand. That's when those witness folders I use come in extra-handy.)

On the drive home that first night, I remember feeling pretty good. My own opening statement went well; now I had to be sure and follow through on the promises I'd made the jury—namely, that they'd be able to examine the other evidence I presented, *then* decide whether or not Mike Ferreira was involved. Ed Brown's testimony, I hoped, would end up being irrelevant in making that determination.

I felt like O'Reilly's opening was pretty typical. I believe that for this trial, O'Reilly was sort of forced to play his hand, and the only card he was holding—albeit a potentially very strong one—was, again, Ed Brown's testimony. So I knew I had to take the wind out of O'Reilly's sails, especially when it came to Brown, and I think I did that pretty well on the first day.

O'Reilly told me the witnesses scheduled to testify the next day were Bill McCabe, Lieutenant Tom Conlon (a detective, now retired, who'd worked on the original investigation), Judy Schaffer (the supervisor of the Lowell PD lockup; a minor witness whose sole purpose for testifying was to positively ID Mike Ferreira), Linda (King) Locklear (the stenographer in the original investigation), and Detective Gerry St. Peter (one of the main investigators back in '69).

Two of those witnesses I want to mention: First, Bill McCabe would be tricky. I knew he was in his eighties at that point, and frail, and would automatically gain a lot of sympathy from the jury. (And deservedly so. Here was a guy who'd waited forty-three years to get justice for his son—a position I would never want to be in.) Two issues I wanted to touch on with Mr. McCabe were John's belt, and whether or not he knew it was missing when the body was found, and whether or not it was raining when he'd gone to look for John the night of the murder. (Depending on how that line of questioning went, I planned to tie that in with other evidence later in the trial.)

And second: Detective St. Peter. He was going to be a complex one. In a nutshell, I wanted St. Peter to confirm certain pieces of information that I knew would conflict with what I anticipated witnesses like Brown and Coughlin would later say, in essence undermining the later witnesses' believability.

I knew the first day of testimony would be an interesting one. As I discovered, "interesting" was putting it mildly.

2. Wednesday, January 16: Ferreira Trial, Day Two

In forty-three years, Bill McCabe had, of course, aged significantly—but the weight of four decades of uncertainty over who'd taken his son's life seemed to have added even more years to his eighty-five. He shuffled—painfully, it seemed—to the witness stand and sat down with a sigh. His head shook slightly from palsy, and his voice had a similar quiver when he spoke. When Bill looked up at the court clerk, though, those in the courtroom saw eyes that were still burning bright with intelligence.

"Sir," the clerk asked him, "would you please state your name, and spell your last name?"

"William J. McCabe. McCabe: capital M, small C, capital C-A-B-E."

O'Reilly, who'd been standing back while Bill was sworn in, now walked to the center of the room. "Good morning, Mr. McCabe."

Bill cupped a hand to his ear. "Could you speak a little louder?"

"I said, good morning, sir," O'Reilly repeated with more volume.

Bill relaxed and smiled. "Good morning."

"Mr. McCabe, what town do you live in?"

"I live in Tewksbury, Massachusetts."

"And how old are you, sir?"

"Excuse me?"

"HOW O—" O'Reilly paused, exasperated. "Your Honor, with the Court's permission, may I get closer to him? I'll keep my voice elevated."

"Yes," Judge Ricciardone said. "And I'm having trouble hearing the witness. Could you pull the microphone closer to him?"

O'Reilly walked to the witness stand and adjusted the mike, then remained next to Bill. "Now, how old are you, sir?"

"Eighty-five years old."

"And, sir, how long have you lived at your home in Tewksbury?"

"Since 1962."

"Now, did you have children back in 1969?"

"Yes. Two girls, one boy."

"And what was the boy's name?"

"His…his name was John J. McCabe," Bill said, his throat tightening.

O'Reilly walked to the prosecution table and picked up a photo. He held it up as he approached Bill again. "Do you recognize the boy in this photo?"

"Yeah."

"Who is this, sir?"

"That's our son."

"John McCabe?"

"John McCabe, yes."

"I'll put this up on the Elmo," O'Reilly said, and stepped over to a table near the witness stand. On the table was a piece of equipment known as a visual presenter (or an "Elmo," as it was called in courtrooms, since that was the brand name of visual presenters most courtrooms employed). The Elmo was essentially the next-generation overhead projector: a small video camera pointed down to a lighted surface, upon which photos, documents, and other evidence would be placed; the camera was connected to a large video monitor hanging from the ceiling so the jurors and witnesses could view evidence on a larger scale. (A smaller monitor sat next to the witness stand so that the person on the stand could get a closer view.)

O'Reilly turned the Elmo on, and an image of John McCabe—the yearbook photo taken a few months prior to his death—filled the screen. A few jurors and spectators issued quiet, involuntary gasps. From his seat at the defense table, Eric noticed many jurors looking at the monitor—and at Bill McCabe—with expressions of near-heartbreak. O'Reilly looked at the judge. "May this be marked as an exhibit, Your Honor?"

The judge looked at Eric. "Any objection?"

"None, Your Honor."

"It may be marked," the judge said, then added: "Sorry to interrupt, Mr. O'Reilly, but I need to talk to the jury about exhibits." Ricciardone then explained—as he did in every trial—the difference between testimony ("questions and answers between attorneys and witnesses," he told them) and exhibits ("tangible things: photographs, drawings, or what have you. You'll be able to have these things with you during your deliberations"). When he finished he asked O'Reilly to continue.

"Thank you, sir," the A.D.A. said. "Now, Mr. McCabe: do you remember September 26, 1969?"

"Yes sir."

"How old was John that day?"

"September 26 of '69 he was fifteen years, six months, and two weeks old," Bill said it with practiced ease.

"And how tall was John?"

"He was five-four, five-five, around there, sir."

"Thank you." O'Reilly paused to look at the jury, then at Judge Ricciardone. "I have nothing further for this witness, Your Honor."

Smart, Eric thought as O'Reilly crossed to the prosecution table. *He called Bill McCabe for one reason only: sympathy from the jury.*

"Thank you, Mr. O'Reilly," the judge was saying. "Mr. Wilson? Would you like to inquire?"

"Thank you, Your Honor." Eric rose and crossed to the witness stand. "Good morning, Mr. McCabe."

"Good morning, sir."

"Sir, my name is Eric Wilson."

Bill cupped a hand to his ear again. "Eric what, sir?"

"Wilson," Eric answered more firmly.

"Wilson, you said?"

"Yes sir. Eric Wilson. We've seen each other in court before and I wanted to introduce myself."

"Thank you." Bill smiled at him. "I don't think we've officially met."

"Well, it's a pleasure to meet you. I've got a couple of questions for you, sir. And I know this is probably difficult for you…it's difficult for me, but these questions need to be asked. All right, sir?" Bill nodded once in acknowledgment. "Okay. The early morning hours, Mr. McCabe, of the 27th of September of 1969. Do you remember that time?"

"Yes, I do."

"I understand from police reports that your wife had woken you up to tell you John hadn't come home."

"That's right."

"Okay. And y—"

"Wait a minute. No, she woke me up at about 11:30 p.m. on the 26th. I was already asleep."

"Okay. And after driving around in efforts to find John, you contacted the Tewksbury police, right?"

"Well, I didn't drive around. My wife and daughter did. I rode around in a police car."

"Right. An Officer Walter Jamieson drove you around, in the early morning hours of the 27th, looking for John, right?"

"Yes."

"You were in a police cruiser driving around Tewksbury, and it was raining. Do you recall that, sir?"

Bill frowned. "Well, it was kind of misty. Not a heavy rain…misty."

"Okay. And later that morning—early that Saturday morning—the rain was heavier. Do you recall that, sir?"

"I don't remember that. I was in the house, and we—I fell asleep around 2:00 or 3:00, and I didn't wake up till maybe 6:00 or 7:00." Bill was starting to look agitated, so Eric knew he had to tread lightly.

"All right. Thank you, sir. Now: I know you kept journals over the years about this crime, and about John's life, right?"

"Yes."

"And in your journals, you recall that on that Saturday morning the field where they found John was rain-soaked. Correct, sir?"

Bill's face clouded. "They wouldn't let me go to the crime scene, sir."

"Thank you." Eric decided not to press the issue. He quickly stepped over to his table and referenced Bill McCabe's witness folder. He walked back over to the stand, then: "Mr. McCabe, you were aware that John's belt was never recovered, right?"

"I heard that. It was never told to me officially, but I heard it from rumors, yeah."

"It was never returned to you or your wife, never located at the funeral home, right, sir?"

"No."

"Thank you." To Judge Ricciardone: "Nothing further."

O'Reilly popped up. "A question on redirect, Your Honor?" The game of judiciary cat-and-mouse had already begun.

"Yes, Mr. O'Reilly," Ricciardone said.

"Thank you." O'Reilly strode over to Bill. "Mr. McCabe, were you at home when John left to go to the dance?"

"No."

"Do you know if John was wearing a belt when he went to the dance?"

"I don't know that. I wasn't there."

"Thank you. Nothing further."

Now it was Eric's turn. "Just briefly, Your Honor?" He walked to the stand. "Mr. McCabe, a follow-up question regarding the belt. Over the years you've been quoted in newspaper articles, have you not, sir?"

"Objection," O'Reilly quickly responded. "Beyond the scope."

"Do you want to be heard further?" the judge asked.

"Yes sir." As O'Reilly and Eric walked to the judge's bench, Ricciardone explained to the jury what was happening, and the purpose of sidebar conferences— another example of his thorough courtroom control. When he was finished, the judge and attorneys had a brief discussion over whether or not Eric's question about newspaper articles (the testimony about which the judge had, during pretrial motions, strictly forbidden) was hearsay. In other words, O'Reilly argued, since testimony about newspaper stories was not allowed, Bill would only be testifying to information he'd heard from someone else, which was therefore factually irrelevant. In the end, Ricciardone ruled in O'Reilly's favor, and asked Eric to rephrase the question.

"Sorry for the interruption, Mr. McCabe. One last question or two. After the morning of September 27, the Saturday when John was found. a search of your home was done—a search for the belt. And none was found, was it?"

"I don't know the answer to that."

"Okay. Thank you. Nothing further, Your Honor." The judge asked O'Reilly if he wanted to redirect—O'Reilly didn't—so the judge told Bill his testimony was finished, and that he could join his wife in the gallery. As the jurors looked on with commiseration, Bill took nearly a full minute to shuffle back and sit next to Evelyn in the first row of the gallery.

* * * *

If one were to describe his or her idea of the typical retired cop—paunchy, sallow-skinned, mostly bald, probably reeking of onions—he or she would unknowingly give a perfect description of Lieutenant Thomas Conlon, former detective with the Lowell Criminal Bureau. As Conlon took the stand as the prosecution's next witness, Eric dug through the witness folders and found Conlon's; it was thin, as Conlon was mentioned only a handful of times in reports from the original '69 investigation. Eric assumed that O'Reilly wanted his testimony simply for descriptions of the crime scene the morning the body was found.

And Eric was right. O'Reilly spent nearly an hour presenting to his witness various photographs of the crime scene from assorted angles and distances, photos of the ropes used to tie John up, and a roughly drawn diagram of the overall area, sketched by Detective St. Peter during the original investigation. As O'Reilly displayed the items on the Elmo, Conlon, in a gruff voice also typical of a retired detective, explained their relevance. O'Reilly ended his questioning without a flourish, then Eric began his cross-examination—one he knew wouldn't be pretty.

Again, Eric was correct in his assumption; the lieutenant treated Eric with not-so-subtle disdain from the very start.

"Lieutenant, my name is Eric Wilson," he began. "We've not met, true?"

"True." Conlon stared at him, his expression flat and dismissive.

"You're aware that we reached out to talk to you prior to your testimony today?"

"Yes."

"You refused to talk to us, right?"

"That's right."

And so the cross-examination went. But even as Conlon was answering questions with as few words as possible, usually in a brief, "you're-a-piece-of-crap" tone, through his testimony Eric was able to start painting a picture for the jury—one that would differ from the description of the crime Eric anticipated Ed Brown and Detective Coughlin would give. Conlon admitted that when John's body was first seen by police, it had no rope connecting the ankles to the neck (and therefore no evidence of hogtying); when Conlon had arrived at the scene, he said, the field was wet from rain, but John's body had appeared dry ("I didn't touch the body, so I dunno if he was wet, but he looked dry," Conlon testified).

Eric's last line of questioning concerned John's belt, and whether Conlon and other detectives in '69 had discussed the issue that one was never found. Simply put, Eric attempted to use a combination of third-party culprit and Bowden evidence to reveal the fact that police had failed to properly investigate the caller to the priests (who claimed he had John's belt with him). The line of questioning, though, was essentially futile, as Conlon answered Eric's questions with varying versions of "Don't remember" and "Can't recall." Though it was too soft for the assorted microphones to pick up, Conlon was grumbling to himself as he left the witness stand.

The next prosecution witness took the stand simply to present collateral evidence. Judy Schaffer, who was the Lowell PD lockup supervisor, positively identified Michael Ferreira and testified to his correct birthdate, and Eric had no questions for her. Next was Linda (King) Locklear, who'd been the stenographer for numerous interviews and meetings during the '69 investigation; a majority of her direct testimony with O'Reilly was a reading of the transcript of one of Mike Ferreira's first interviews with detectives in the days following the murder.

Then, after a break for lunch, Eric performed a brief (though effective) cross-examination of her, during which he emphasized several main points: for one thing, the police had never, to Locklear's knowledge, questioned Ed Brown (meaning he wasn't considered a suspect until

Detective Coughlin took over the investigation). Eric also had Locklear reread Mike's '69 interview statement that "the windshield wipers were working most of the night (of the murder)." In other words, according to Mike it had definitely rained. Lastly, Eric had her confirm that the statements she transcribed from Mike's interview were accurate. (This was pure strategy on Eric's part; he knew that Mike's statements from that interview would be called into question at some point, so he wanted the jury to hear, from the person who actually transcribed them, that the statements were correct.)

In the midst of Eric's cross-examination of Locklear, he asked her if she'd taken a statement from a teenager named Robert Ryan. When she said she had, Eric took the opportunity to ask the judge about a stipulation—in legal terms, a formal agreement between the prosecution and defense that certain evidence or testimony can be submitted to the jury, and, therefore, require no court argument— concerning Ryan's 1969 statement to police. (Ryan had since moved to Florida, and for various reasons was not able to testify in the Ferreira trial; Eric and O'Reilly had formally agreed that Ryan's '69 statement—or a summary of it, at least—could be read in court, then presented to the jury as an exhibit.) O'Reilly read the stipulation aloud, which essentially stated that Robert Ryan said he'd been Nancy Williams's boyfriend at the time of the murder, and that on the night in question he'd ridden to Lowell with Walter Shelley and Mike Ferreira in an attempt to get beer. They'd left Nancy's house at about 9:30 p.m., Ryan had told police, then returned shortly after; Ryan said Walter and Mike had left again at approximately 10:30, "stating they were going for a ride." According to Ryan's statement, the stipulation read, "he did not see Walter or Michael again that night."

After Locklear was finished, O'Reilly introduced his next witness: Detective Gerald St. Peter, retired officer of the Lowell Criminal Bureau. And as Eric had anticipated, his testimony would get ugly—in more ways than one.

* * * *

"I call Detective Gerry St. Peter."

As the retired detective walked to the stand, Eric began looking through his witness folder, which was quite thick compared to the others; as the lead detective in the original investigation, St. Peter had obviously invested enormous amounts of time and energy on the case, so the reports and other documents in Eric's "St. Peter folder" numbered in the dozens.

And the detective himself, though aged, was as sharp as ever. The amount of hair still left on his head was inversely proportional to the supply of still-active brain cells firing in his skull. Now a grandfather, his personality had softened somewhat, but his desire to see this forty-three-year-old case closed had adrenaline racing through his body as he sat down at the stand.

"Good afternoon, sir," O'Reilly said from the podium.

"Good afternoon."

"Detective, are you employed at this time?"

"No sir, I'm retired, for going on fourteen years."

"And what was your employment?"

"I worked for the Lowell Police Department. For most of my career, I was a detective for the Lowell Criminal Bureau."

"And how long did you work at LPD?"

"Let's see…I retired in my fortieth year."

244

"Okay." O'Reilly referenced his notes for a moment, then: "Now, sir, were you a detective in 1969?"

"Yes sir, I was."

"And on September 27—a Saturday morning—were you working at home?"

"I believe I was at home, and I got a call to go to an area off Maple Street."

"What were you called there for?"

"I was told that a body had been found. I was also told that I would be the officer in charge."

"I'm going to show you Exhibit 5." O'Reilly put a photo of McCabe's body—one he'd previously shown Lieutenant Conlon—up on the Elmo. "Do you recognize that photo?"

"Yes I do."

"And what do you recognize it to be?"

"It's the body of a young boy, lying on the gravel."

"Is this the body you were sent to the scene for?"

"Yes it is."

"And what did you do at the scene? After you saw the body, I mean?"

"Well…first I wanted to see if there were any witnesses, obviously. So I ordered a canvass of the houses in the area, then—I knew there were people at the railroad relay station at all hours of the day, so I went up there to talk to personnel who may have been on duty."

O'Reilly came around from behind the podium. "And did you talk to anyone?"

"I talked to the switch operator. He said he'd been on duty since 7:00 that morning, and he hadn't seen anything."

"Okay. And where did you go from there?"

"I went back to the scene where the other officers were. By that time the dogs from the state police had arrived."

"And did they track the area?"

"They d—"

"Objection," Eric interrupted. "Foundation. I can't cross-examine the dogs." A brief titter rose from the gallery.

"I'll hear you on this," Judge Ricciardone said as he motioned for the attorneys to approach. Once O'Reilly and Eric were before him, the judge said quietly: "I didn't know anything about dog evidence. That's why I wanted to talk to you over here."

"Your Honor," O'Reilly whispered, "we're not going to say the dog found anything. But I understand...I'll withdraw the question."

"Thank you," Eric and the judge whispered simultaneously. The attorneys stepped back, and O'Reilly continued.

"Sorry about that. Moving on: where did you go once you left the scene?"

"I went out to the McCabe home in Tewksbury." St. Peter glanced over O'Reilly's shoulder at the McCabe family sitting in the first row. Evelyn McCabe gave him a smile.

"Were you at the O'Donnell Funeral Home in Lowell at any time that day?"

"I was. I went there for the autopsy of John McCabe's body."

Back in '69, some autopsies were conducted in funeral homes, correct?"

"Yes, they were."

O'Reilly walked over to the clerk's table and picked up a manila folder. "Detective, I'm going to show you a series of photos. Mr. Wilson, I'm—" He looked over at the judge. "Your Honor, may we go to sidebar so I can explain?"

"Yes." Ricciardone motioned them forth.

"Your Honor," O'Reilly whispered once the attorneys were before him, "I'd like to enter as exhibits almost every photo I have of the autopsy, except the ones where the body is cut open. My medical expert relied on these photos for her opinion on cause of death."

"As did mine," Eric interjected.

"His too," O'Reilly said. "So I can introduce them now, then the medical experts can pick which ones they want to use."

"Okay," the judge said. "Mr. Wilson? Any objection?"

"No objection, Your Honor. Although"—he glanced over his shoulder at the gallery, then leaned in closer and whispered softly—"this is probably something we should be cautious about the family seeing."

"Yes," O'Reilly said. "I'll show them just to him—I won't put them up on the Elmo. But I want them introduced so the jury can see them when they deliberate." He was looking at Eric while he said the last part.

Eric smiled widely. His eyes never leaving O'Reilly's, he whispered: "No objection."

"Okay, gentlemen," Ricciardone whispered, adding: "Notice my wording." As the attorney stepped back, the judge snickered to himself.

O'Reilly spent a couple of minutes with the clerk, entering the photographs of McCabe's body at the autopsy as official exhibits, then carried the stack of photos over to St. Peter at the witness stand. During the brief break in the action, Eric took the opportunity to glance over his shoulder at the McCabe family. Oddly enough, Bill McCabe was nowhere to be seen.

"Exhibit 26," O'Reilly said as he showed St. Peter the first photo. "Do you recognize that photo?"

"Yes sir."

"And what do you recognize it as?"

"The body of John McCabe, on the table at the funeral home."

"Are there markings on the neck area?"

St. Peter made a guttural sound. "Ligature marks around the throat."

"Exhibit 27. What does this photo show?"

"Rear view of the body, rope marks on both wrists." From the gallery arose a muffled cry of misery. Eric— along with most others in the courtroom—turned and saw Evelyn McCabe with her face buried in her daughter Debbie's shoulder, her body shaking as she sobbed silently. The spot next to her, where Bill had been sitting, was still empty.

O'Reilly soldiered on. "Twenty-eight. This one?"

"Ligature marks above the ankles."

O'Reilly repeated the process for the next ten minutes, showing St. Peter twelve photos in all. He also had the detective positively ID the red shirt and green trousers John had worn, and these were entered into evidence as well. Then, returning to the more typical question/answer format, O'Reilly queried the detective about his interviews with Mike immediately following the murder.

"Sir, you've reviewed a number of reports you authored back then, correct?"

"Yes sir, I have."

"Do you remember an interview you conducted with Mr. Ferreira on September 28 at 3:25 in the afternoon?"

"I do."

"And what, sir, sticks out in your mind about that report?"

"Well, when interviewing Mr. Ferreira, part of the way through it we stopped…and then when we started again, there were inconsistencies that developed when he gave his version of events that night."

"Okay. Do you have a memory of what those inconsistencies were?"

St. Peter took a couple of minutes to explain that, when Mike had recounted details of his night the second time, he'd included the fact that he and Nancy Williams had picked up John McCabe hitchhiking—something he hadn't told them before the break. This, St. Peter said, constituted an important difference between the two versions of events Mike recalled, which caused St. Peter to wonder why Mike had left it out the first time.

After a few more routine questions about the interviews, O'Reilly walked over to his table and retrieved a poster-sized drawing, a detailed topographical map of the crime scene and surrounding area, depicted from overhead. (Eric and Mike exchanged an amused glance; it had been Mike, at Eric's request, who'd done some research on the vacant lot at the Pollard Memorial Library in Lowell, and he'd found the map purely by chance. And now the prosecution was using it to try and convict the very man who'd found it.) Noticeably absent from the map was any indication or marking of the exact location in which the body had been found. As he crossed to St. Peter, O'Reilly asked: "May I offer this as an exhibit, Your Honor?"

The judge looked at Eric. "Mr. Wilson?"

"No objection."

O'Reilly's only intention for displaying the drawing, it seemed, was to have it entered into evidence so the jurors would consider it credible, maybe even "official." O'Reilly set the drawing on an easel next to the witness stand, then asked St. Peter to point out on the drawing several important details of the area: Maple Street and the dirt road that ran off it into the lot, the stone foundation, and finally, the location of the body itself. And then, surprisingly, O'Reilly was finished.

"No further questions for this witness, Your Honor."

"Okay, thank you," Ricciardone said. "Mr. Wilson?"

"Thank you, sir," Eric said as he stood. Though he was normally a cool customer during litigation, Eric could feel his heart racing. Which was good, actually; his plan was to attack St. Peter at the beginning about his (and in retrospect, Lieutenant Conlon's) refusal to talk to the defense attorney prior to trial. His objective for doing this was quite simple: to hopefully have the jury recognize that St. Peter's (and Conlon's) unwillingness to cooperate with Eric meant they were unfairly biased toward the prosecution, and, therefore, unreliable. And Eric knew that showing aggression with a witness was risky, but it was a risk he was willing to take.

He was quick and snappy when he introduced himself. "Mr. St. Peter, my name is Eric Wilson."

"Yes sir." St. Peter was equally short with his answer.

"We spoke back in November, right?"

"I believe it was then, yes."

"Mr. O'Reilly was kind enough to give you my phone number, correct?"

"Yep."

"And you called me thereafter?"

"Yep."

"I wanted to have an opportunity, before we got in front of this jury, to sit down and talk about the very things you're testifying to today, did I not?" The acidity in his voice was obvious now.

"Correct."

"You initially agreed to sit down with me, right?"

"I did."

"And then you called me back and told me, 'I'm not going to meet with you,' right?"

St. Peter must have realized where Eric was going with his questions, because he immediately softened. "I…I told you that I'd thought about it, and I did not feel it would be appropriate to talk to you."

"You met with the prosecutor though, didn't you?"

"Yes, I d—"

"You met with him, he gave you all the reports from forty years ago so you could refresh your memory for this jury, right?"

St. Peter was getting flustered. "Ye—yes sir."

"Yet you didn't think it was appropriate to meet with *me*?"

"It just depended what team you were on."

Eric was stunned by the answer. Not angry, just stunned. Because St. Peter couldn't have given a more perfect acknowledgment of Eric's point. He uttered an involuntary laugh, then said, "Oh. It depended on what team I was on, huh?"

St. Peter realized his mistake. "I…I just felt it wasn't appropriate. I did return your call. I did agree to meet with you. I sat home and thought about it, and I decided it wasn't appropriate. So I called you and relayed that."

But Eric wanted to drive his point home. "Because I'm on the wrong team, right?"

"Not in that perspective. It was prosecution and defense. My personal feeling was—"

"I'm on the wrong team," Eric repeated. "Right? Those are your words."

"Objection," O'Reilly said, trying to rescue his witness.

"I didn't say that," St. Peter shot back. "You're putting words in my m—"

"Objection, argumentative!"

Ricciardone banged his gavel once—*crack!*—but it was enough; the room was instantly silent. "Mr. Wilson, that's enough."

"I apologize, Your Honor."

"Why don't we move along, okay?" It was a gentle warning, but an unnecessary one; Eric knew his point was made. *Actually,* Eric thought as he approached St. Peter again, *you made the point for me.*

Eric's strategy with St. Peter's cross-examination was to start "taking bites from the apple." Like his "death by a thousand cuts" analogy, the apple idea—one he'd learned early in his career, as a trial associate for a former judge who was an extraordinary defense attorney—was that in the absence of what was known as a "magic bullet" (a single, crucial witness or piece evidence that firmly implanted reasonable doubt in the jurors' minds), some trials required the acknowledgment of numerous smaller holes in the prosecution's theories. These individual "apple bites" were meaningless by themselves, but when put together during jury deliberations, they hopefully added up to the consumption of the entire apple—which would mean an acquittal.

Eric's questions to St. Peter put the apple theory into play. First he had St. Peter admit that it would be difficult to remember the events of a particular evening, even a significant one like the night of John's murder, after three decades. (Mike had been questioned by Sullivan and Wayne in 2003, and again by a grand jury in 2008, during which his memory of the night's events changed yet again. Eric anticipated that O'Reilly would use these varying versions to show that Mike was being dishonest, so Eric was trying prior to that to show exactly why Mike's story had changed.)

Next, Eric had St. Peter expand on the so-called "inconsistencies" in Mike's story during his '69 interview. Eric, reading from that interview transcript, pointed out that during the version of events Mike told before the break, St. Peter asked him specific questions about that night— questions that did *not* include an inquiry of whether they'd picked John up by the novitiate. Then in Mike's version he told after the break, St. Peter simply asked him to give a "narration" of his events, so Mike added the detail about picking John up. Logically, Eric revealed through his questioning, this wasn't an "inconsistency," it was the statement of a fact about which Mike hadn't been previously asked. St. Peter had no choice but to acknowledge this as true.

"In fact, the only thing that changed between those two versions," Eric said to end the line of questioning, "was that Mike Ferreira was afraid to tell you till the end of the interview that he was wanting to find some beer. Right, sir?"

"I…" St. Peter seemed utterly flummoxed—which was quite unfamiliar territory for a decorated detective. "I just don't recall."

"That's okay. We can move on."

Eric shot a quick glance at the clock—it was 3:15—and he knew he wouldn't be able to finish his cross-examination before they adjourned at 4:00, so he relaxed, knowing he'd continue with St. Peter the next morning. He took a few more bites of the apple: first, Eric asked a few questions about St. Peter's memory of the morning he'd first arrived at the crime scene, and St. Peter acknowledged that there had been no rope connecting John's neck and his ankles—again, no hogtying. Eric then had the detective admit that he'd not seen John wearing a belt at the scene (St. Peter smiled to himself when he recalled the "mental wardrobe inventory" he'd done way back then); nor, St. Peter said, had he seen any belt during John's autopsy. And when Eric asked about the part of St. Peter's police report from that day which stated that "the weather at 4:00 a.m. that morning was cold and damp," the retired detective conceded to learning that detail from Bill McCabe instead of actually knowing it himself.

Just as Eric was beginning his final line of questioning, Judge Ricciardone asked to speak to both attorneys at sidebar.

"Mr. Wilson, how much more time do you think you'll need?"

"About twenty minutes?"

"Hm. Why don't we just quit early and resume tomorrow?"

Eric and O'Reilly agreed. As the attorneys were packing up their materials, Ricciardone gave the jury a condensed rendition of the instructions he'd laid out the day before: no discussion of or seeking out any information regarding the trial. No Internet communication about it, and no viewing or listening to news reports. Then he sent the jurors on their way.

Five minutes later, the courtroom was nearly empty when Eric finished packing away the remaining witness folders (Stan Norkunas was already on his way to the car with the first batch), and Eric picked up his briefcases and turned to head for the door when he nearly collided with Tom O'Reilly.

"Sorry," O'Reilly said. "Got a minute?"

"Sure," Eric said. "You want to talk about who you're putting on the stand tomorrow?"

"We'll get to that. I just want to ask: do you intend to call Bill McCabe back to testify?"

"Wasn't planning on it. Why?"

"Well…his daughter just told me he went home early. Complained of shortness of breath, nausea…" O'Reilly looked solemn. "Hopefully he's just coming down with a cold or something."

"Wow," Eric said. "Yeah. Hope a cold is all it is."

"Indeed," O'Reilly said. "Now: about those witnesses…"

The opposing attorneys were still talking fifteen minutes later when the bailiff stuck his head through the doorway to ask them to turn off the lights when they left.

EX PARTE: Trial Day 2 → Day 3

I remember, on Stan's and my ride home after that first day of testimony, us agreeing that our case hadn't taken any "body blows." (That's what I call witness testimony or pieces of evidence that, while not fatal, still hurt the defense.) I felt like we neutralized—maybe even negated—the damage from St. Peter's testimony, mainly because I think I was able to convince the jury that the "inconsistencies" in Mike Ferreira's '69 interview that St. Peter kept harping on just didn't exist. When the Commonwealth introduced the transcript of that interview during Linda Locklear's testimony, I was able to use that on St. Peter to show that Mike's simple exclusion of one detail—a detail about which he hadn't been asked during the question/answer portion of the interview—just didn't equal a true inconsistency. It was an omission, simple as that. So St. Peter's testimony had caused minimal harm to our chances for an acquittal; the other testimony on that first day had been inconsequential, for the most part.

Another good sign was that Mike's niece Danielle, my unofficial jury consultant/observer, had told me that many of the jurors were taking copious notes during witness testimony. That meant that hopefully, they were going to pay more attention to the facts than to their own feelings. That's not always a good thing, but in this trial I thought it was important, especially regarding my "bites of the apple" theory for disproving the Commonwealth's minor allegations. As for Ed Brown…well, they'd either believe him, or they wouldn't.

O'Reilly told me that his first witness the next day would be Dr. Kimberly Springer, a Massachusetts medical examiner out of Boston, who would testify as the Commonwealth's medical expert. This came as a complete surprise to me, as I'd been led to believe she would be testifying a day or two later. (It wasn't O'Reilly being tricky or unprofessional, though; it was simply a fact that that was the only day and time she was available to give testimony.) I also had very little info on Springer—and by "little," I mean none at all—because I hadn't been able to get a deposition from her before the trial started, nor did I have any reports from her stating her medical opinions about the cause of death, conditions of the body, and so forth. So during our post-trial conversation, when O'Reilly sprang the news on me about Springer's change in schedule I asked him if Springer would agree to sit down with me for a few minutes the next morning before court was in session, and he said she would. I think I got a total of two hours' sleep that night because I was at my office until about 2:00 a.m., scrambling to prepare for Springer's cross-examination.

After I was done with Springer, the plan was to finish my cross of Gerry St. Peter. The other witnesses to testify that next day, O'Reilly said, were numerous: David Beek (who would testify that he saw John McCabe outside The Oaks after the dance), Barry Moran (who'd said he'd spotted a car similar to Walter Shelley's in the area the night of the murder; Stan Norkunas would cross-examine him), Carol Ann (McFrederies) Roberts (who would simply testify that she'd danced with John at the K of C—a collateral witness, really, and Stan would do her cross also), Mary Ann (Richard) LaCourciere (the "last-minute" witness who would recount the 1969 incident with Mike and the scarf; I thought it was interesting—dare I say even fishy—that she just happened to come forth with that info so late in the game, when she'd never reported it back when it happened), Elaine (Callahan) Sutton (whom I speculated would testify about, among other things, Mike's "joke" confession during the 1969 beer run to Pelham), and Jack Ward (who would describe the incident at the pig roast; I was actually looking forward to cross-examining him).

Compared to critical ones like Ed Brown and Linda Coughlin, the witnesses for that next day were going to be minor. So I had to force myself to not jump ahead to Brown and Coughlin and overlook the relatively unimportant testimony. Because even a small bite of the apple is still a bite.

3. Thursday, January 17: Ferreira Trial, Day Three

Eric and Stan arrived at the courthouse in Woburn even earlier than usual, as Eric wanted to have a quick conversation with Dr. Kim Springer, the Commonwealth's medical expert who was unexpectedly scheduled to testify first that morning. Luckily Dr. Springer had been cordial and had arrived early as well, so at 8:30—trial was scheduled to begin at 9:00—she and Eric sat down in an anteroom down the hall from the courtroom. Their twenty-minute conversation, during which Eric told Dr. Springer what the main points of his cross-examination would be, covered all aspects of the medical evidence. Eric was professional, but careful; he didn't want to reveal *too* much about his cross and have Springer sway her answers because of it. Eric considered the pathologist to be bright and agreeable, and he didn't concern himself with the possibility of Springer modifying her answers because of their chat.

They were just wrapping up when Stan stuck his head in and said that court was in session. As Eric was hurrying up the aisle to the defense table, he glanced at some of the spectators, and he noticed a surprising attendee in the gallery: Walter Shelley's wife, who was sitting by herself in the back row. (Though Eric didn't know her name, he recognized her from previous newspaper and TV stories about the case.) He couldn't remember seeing her in the gallery on the previous two days of trial, but he simply didn't have time to speculate on exactly why she was there; as Eric neared his table, Judge Ricciardone was already entering the courtroom. As he passed the first row of spectators, Eric noticed that Bill McCabe was back in his usual spot. Eric thought he looked a bit peaked, but at least he was present.

Once the jurors were in place, Ricciardone alerted them to the fact that Dr. Springer would be testifying out of order ("We'll start today with this new witness, then when she's done we'll revert back to Mr. St. Peter and finish Mr. Wilson's cross-examination of him," the judge told them). And O'Reilly's direct examination of Springer was, at least in Eric's eyes, surprisingly brief.

Springer first listed her credentials—four years of med school, four years as a clinical pathologist at a Boston hospital, then five years at the ME's office in Boston—then O'Reilly opened his questioning with queries about the ligature marks on John's neck. When O'Reilly hypothesized about the mark being made by a rope tied from the neck to the ankles—hogtying, in other words—Dr. Springer said it was "certainly possible, if the rope is tied tightly around the neck." Later, when O'Reilly asked her to explain the lividity (the postmortem settling of blood) the coroner had identified on both sides of John's body— meaning he'd spent some amount of time after his death on both his back and his belly—Springer had quite a simple answer: that the lividity on his back had developed when the body was removed from the scene, while he was on his back being transported to the funeral home.

When he started his cross, Eric wasted no time getting right to the hogtying issue.

"Dr. Springer, you talked on direct examination just now about what appeared to be an upward slope, angle, whatever you want to call it, to the ligature mark on John's neck, correct?"

"Well…" She looked down (and to the right, Detective St. Peter would've been happy to observe) while she thought about it. "In the autopsy photographs, it's difficult to interpret. The mark appears either flat or gently rising. So…my answer would be either it's flat, or it's going upward, yes."

"Okay. And wouldn't you expect, if there were a rope to my ankles from my neck"—he turned sideways and leaned against the podium, then lifted one foot so that his lower leg was parallel to the ground—"and my feet were back like this, the rope tied to my ankles, the ligature mark would be angled toward my ankles?" He used one hand to delineate a line from his neck to his foot. "It would be lower on the back of my neck because the rope was angled toward my feet, wouldn't it?"

"Yes, I agree. If the ligature is very tight, it may not. But in textbooks where they show a person hogtied, you'll see a downward ligature furrow. It doesn't *have* to happen that way, but…yes."

"Okay. Mr. O'Reilly asked you whether it was possible that John McCabe was hogtied, did he not?"

"Yes."

"And there's a difference between something being possible and something being *probable*, fair to say?"

"Yes."

"Okay. Now: you're aware that when those two little boys found John, they said he was lying on his belly, feet on the ground. There was no rope tied from his neck to his ankles. Correct?"

"Correct."

They then discussed rigor mortis—the postmortem stiffening of the muscles—and Eric had Springer explain that if John had been killed at approximately midnight, as the medical experts believed, his muscles would have been approaching full rigor, meaning his body (including his legs) would be stiff and unmovable, at 9:00 a.m. Saturday.

"So, using that logic," Eric said, "if John had been hogtied, someone would've had to come along and cut that rope before the rigor started setting in. Correct?"

"Yes, I agree with that. For the most part."

"It is possible he was hogtied, right?"

"Yes. It's possible."

"But, given everything we just talked about, it is not *probable* he was hogtied, is it?"

"Well…" She sighed. She seemed to realize that, though Eric had backed her into a corner, his logic was simply irrefutable. "Not probable, in my opinion."

"Thank you." Eric smiled—because that was probably his biggest apple bite yet. His last line of questioning involved the lividity in John's body; though Eric didn't score any points on that issue, he sat down after his cross knowing that some damage had been done.

The rest of the day virtually flew by, O'Reilly calling witnesses to the stand with a frequency similar to that of a yearbook photo session. Eric finished his cross of Detective St. Peter, during which Eric made a preemptive strike by having the detective acknowledge that he'd confirmed during the original investigation that Walter Shelley was still employed stripping floors at the time of the murder. (The issue of Walter's place of employment, Eric knew, would come up during his questioning of Marla Shiner.) And once St. Peter left the stand, the witness parade was on.

First, David Beek testified that he'd seen John outside The Oaks a few minutes after the K of C dance had ended; on cross, Eric had Beek admit that John had been pacing back and forth on the roadside as if he were waiting for someone, and he *hadn't* been hitchhiking. Next was Barry Moran, who claimed he'd seen a "1965 Chevy Impala, two-door" vehicle in the vacant lot around the alleged time of the murder. O'Reilly asked for details of how and why he happened to be in that location at that time—"Me and the guys I was with went in there to relieve ourselves," Moran said—and, interestingly, during the direct examination Moran repeatedly referred to the prosecutor as "Tom," which suggested a conspicuous amount of coziness between the witness and the A.D.A. Stan Norkunas performed Moran's cross-examination, and Stan pressed him into admitting that his entire memory of the night—the color of the car, its location, even the license plate number—had been a collective one, consisting of different memories pieced together by Moran and the two friends he'd been with.

Carol Ann (McFrederies) Roberts testified that she'd danced with John at the K of C, during which he'd expressed a desire to go to New York City; after lunch, O'Reilly called Mary Ann (Richard) LaCourciere to recall the 1969 incident with Mike Ferreira, during which he jokingly choked her with a scarf. She also testified that on the night of the murder, Walter, Mike, and a third male (whose name she couldn't recall) came to visit her at the house at which she was babysitting. On cross, Eric had her concede that though Mike's scarf joke had made her uncomfortable, she knew even then what it was—simply a joke. Eric also pointed out that during her direct testimony, she hadn't been able to remember who the third male had been that night, but Detective Coughlin's report from December 2012 detailing LaCourciere's interview stated that "Mary Ann thought it may have been Ed Brown."

"I honestly don't remember who it was," LaCourciere said during the cross-examination. "That must've been suggested to me, that it was Ed Brown."

Eric let that statement sit with the jury, and finished his cross right there.

O'Reilly then questioned Elaine (Callahan) Sutton. In her direct testimony she recalled sitting next to Mike at John's funeral, and him grabbing her hand at one point and squeezing so tight it hurt her; she said she had looked over at Mike at that point and noticed him crying. Sutton also answered questions about the fabled beer run to Pelham, during which she'd wondered aloud who John's killer was; she said Mike had answered, "I did it." Mike said a little later he'd been kidding, Sutton testified, but his demeanor was "totally serious" when he said he'd committed the murder. Eric noticed many of the jurors writing feverishly in their notebooks during this line of questioning. And when it was his turn, Eric had Sutton acknowledge that crying at funerals is entirely commonplace ("In fact, one of the functions of a funeral is to give people who are sad that the person died a place and time to express their grief, right?" he asked her, and she agreed). And similar to his previous questioning of Mary Ann LaCourciere, Eric got Callahan to agree that when Mike had confessed to the murder during the beer run, she—along with everybody else in the car—had known he was joking.

At about 3:30, O'Reilly called his last witness of the day. As Jack Ward strutted to the stand, Eric gave him a quick appraisal: neatly fashioned pompadour, precisely manicured mustache and goatee, an orangish spray tan that was inordinately out-of-place for January in New England, and the affectation of a laid-back ladies' man (self-described, though it may be). Eric knew Ward had a diploma from an online Private Investigation course he'd completed through some unknown "career college" in California and had done a bit of his own detective work on the McCabe case. Regardless of his self-important attitude, though, Eric knew Ward was simply being loyal to Bill McCabe—whom he'd known since he was a little boy—and he was doing his best to help solve the case, even if he had to exaggerate some events and details in order to do it. And Eric knew he could put Ward's embellishments to good use.

The clerk swore him in, then Ward took his seat and gave O'Reilly a businesslike scowl.

"Good afternoon, Mr. Ward."

"Good afternoon to you, Counselor."

O'Reilly started by asking Ward about goings-on in their neighborhood—Ward said he'd lived a short distance from the McCabes—when he and John were young. Ward, through his answers, explained that Marla Shiner also lived in the vicinity. O'Reilly took the opportunity to expand on that.

"Did John have a girlfriend?"

"No…but I know he liked a few of them."

"Did you know back then what the term 'crush' meant?"

"Yes I did."

"Did you know whether or not John had a crush on anybody?"

"Objection," Eric said before Ward could answer. "It's hearsay. May we approach, Your Honor?"

The attorneys huddled with the judge, discussing whether or not Ward's knowledge (or lack thereof) of John's having a crush on someone constituted hearsay. Since hearsay is technically defined as "information received from other people that one cannot adequately substantiate"—in other words, "rumor" all dressed up—the argument was whether an answer Ward gave (which, of course, would've been "Marla Shiner") could be verified. If Ward answered the question but had no way to physically corroborate it, Eric argued, the answer would be wholly prejudicial.

The attorneys were still debating the point ten minutes later when Judge Ricciardone glanced at the clock and saw that it was already past 4:00, so he released the jurors for the day after giving them the standard warning about not discussing the case. The parties argued the hearsay objection for another fifteen minutes before the judge reserved his ruling for first thing the next morning.

So it would have to wait—and so would Eric's cross-examination of Jack Ward. That, he knew, was going to actually be fun.

EX PARTE: Trial Day 3 → Day 4

On our ride home that night (with a quick detour, which I'll explain in a minute), I again felt pretty positive about our day in court. There were a few bumps in the road—obviously, Mike's joke on the beer run about committing the murder, and his joke with Mary Ann and the scarf, didn't help our case much—but I'd anticipated these, and I think we made it through with minimal damage. And during O'Reilly's "witness parade," I couldn't help but think about the forty-three years these people had had since the murder to tailor their memories—and to forget—about the events of that night. I also found myself wondering what these witnesses, all of whom were now middle-aged, were like as teenagers back in '69.

O'Reilly told me that after I was done with Jack Ward, he would call Brian Gath, who'd hosted the '97 pig roast, to testify about what he remembered. And then…Ed Brown would take the stand.

I was lucky to have cross-examined Brown at Mike's juvenile transfer hearing in July 2011, so I'd already been able to size him up as a witness. But overall my plan with him was to deal him—and I think I've said this before—a "death of a thousand cuts." There wouldn't be one particular fact or statement he could make that would be his "death blow"; I had to try and methodically show, through various lines of questioning and statements he'd make that would contradict other evidence (including his own prior testimony), that he was completely full of shit. (Pardon my French.) I'd nearly memorized his entire witness folder, and I was prepared to notice *anything* he said during his direct testimony with O'Reilly that differed from what he'd said before, whether it was in a statement to police, grand jury testimony, what have you. Then during my cross, I wanted to first remind him that he'd taken an oath before the jury to tell the truth, then compare his contradicting statements and ask him which one was a lie.

There was no doubt that my cross-examination of Ed Brown would be the most crucial in the entire trial, and perhaps of my entire career as an attorney. And it was litigation like this that gave immeasurable value to all those years in law school. This was the case I'd always remember.

At some point during Brown's testimony, O'Reilly and I knew we'd have to interrupt him with another witness: Marla Shiner. It was an unusual circumstance, as she was a defense witness, and had flown in from California at my request. When she originally scheduled her flight, we anticipated that the Commonwealth would rest its case by Thursday afternoon, but it took them longer than they'd planned. That next day of trial would be a Friday, and we didn't want her to have to wait all weekend to testify on Tuesday—that Monday the 21st was Martin Luther King, Jr. Day, so there was no court—if Brown's testimony went long (which O'Reilly and I both anticipated it would). Having a defense witness testify in the midst of the prosecution presenting its case was obviously not normal, but luckily O'Reilly accommodated us. So after trial that Thursday Stan and I sat down to dinner with Marla, and we went over her testimony once more before she took the stand the next day.

I got home later than usual, so I gave my wife a kiss and my kids a hug, then I went straight to bed. Because the next day was going to be a big one.

4. Friday, January 18: Ferreira Trial, Day Four

The first matter at hand once court got underway was
Judge Ricciardone's ruling on Eric's objection the previous
afternoon, concerning whether Jack Ward should be
allowed to answer a question about his knowledge of any
"crushes" John had had on girls. Ricciardone ultimately
ruled in favor of the prosecution. But he explained to the
jury the basis for the argument, and advised them to
determine its importance. "The fact that I let you hear a
particular piece of evidence," he told the jurors, "does not
mean that you are required to give it any particular weight."
(The judge's subtext in that instruction, Eric thought, was
Just because Jack Ward says it doesn't mean it's true.)

"Good morning, Mr. Ward," O'Reilly said after his
witness was in place. "How are you today?"

"I'm good, Counselor, thanks."

"Now, yesterday we stopped after determining that you
and John McCabe were close friends, correct?"

"That's right."

"Did you confide in each other?"

"Yes we did."

"Did John indicate to you at any time that he had a
crush on any young ladies in the neighborhood?"

"Yes."

"Who did he say he had a crush on?"

"Marla. Marla Shiner."

"Did he say he liked anyone else?"

"I'm pretty sure he had the hots for Carol Ann
McFrederies too."

O'Reilly continued his direct, and of course it wasn't
long before he got to the subject of the '97 pig roast. Ward

described details of his alleged conversation with Mike, during which Ward said Mike told him that he (Mike) knew who had killed John. Ward said Mike repeated his statement twice, and the third time Ward responded.

"I said, 'Who did it?'"

"Did Michael answer?" O'Reilly asked quietly.

"Yes." Ward leaned toward the microphone and spoke his next few words slowly. "He said…'Walter. Walter…Shelley.'"

"What was your response to that?"

"I said, 'What would be Walter's motive to do something like that?' And he said"—Ward leaned into the mike again—"'Marla. Because of Marla.'"

"What was your reaction when you heard that?"

"My reaction was, *Bingo.* I was numb. It all made sense to me—it all came together."

"All right." O'Reilly paused to let the statement hang in the air for a moment. Then: "Was anyone else present, within earshot?"

"Yes. Three or four people."

"Where was Brian Gath?"

"Brian was standing to the left of us, and walking around. I can't speak for Brian—not sure if he heard the conversation—but he was there."

O'Reilly asked questions about Ward's response to what he said he heard from Mike that day, and Ward explained that he "thought about it for a few months. I had all kinds of emotions going through my mind: speculation, hearsay, he said/she said…but the more I thought about it, the more it made sense to me."

"Did you end up telling anyone about what Mike said?"

"I did, yes."

"Who did you tell?"

Ward puffed up a bit and looked over O'Reilly's shoulder to the first row of the gallery. Proudly, he said: "Mr. Bill McCabe." Bill, who because of his hearing loss was using an omnidirectional listening device attached to a pair of headphones he wore, either hadn't heard Ward's proclamation or just didn't care about it; either way, he didn't respond at all.

O'Reilly ended his direct after a few more secondary questions. As Eric stood to begin his cross, he glanced at Mike Ferreira. Mike smiled. Eric returned the grin, then walked to the podium.

"Mr. Ward, we met yesterday. Eric Wilson."

"We did. Good morning, sir." He was smiling broadly.

Eric got right to it. "You told us yesterday that you work for the Town of Tewksbury, right?"

"Yes, I did. The Water Department." (With Ward's thick New England accent, it came out as *Waatah Depaatment.*)

"You also have a side business, right? You do some private detective work, do you?"

"I…" Ward's smile faltered a bit. "Yeah, I do some work in that."

"So you're a licensed P.I.?"

"Uh…I have a diploma."

"Oh. A diploma. Where's it from?"

"From Foster Institute, in California."

"Did you go to California for training?"

"Uh…no. It was an online course."

Eric looked surprised. "Oh. You received your detective training online?"

271

"Uh…" Ward's face reddened. O'Reilly stood, preparing to object to the relevance of the line of questioning, but Eric waved him off. "Withdrawn," he said. "Let's move on. Mr. Ward, you told this jury that Mike Ferreira said—well, according to your memory—that Mike said Walter killed John over jealousy. Correct?"

"Yes."

"And after your conversation at the pig roast in 1997, you waited—and I quote—'a few months' before you told anyone about it, right?"

"I'm not exactly sure of the time frame, but it was sometime after that, yes." At that, Eric used a pen to make a mark on his notes.

"You said you thought about it and it bothered you, right?"

"Right."

"And after a few months, you told Mr. McCabe about it, right?"

"Correct."

"And then a little later, you talked to Lieutenant Sullivan and Detective Wayne, told them about what Mike said?"

"Again, not sure of the time frame, but it was a little while after I talked to Mr. McCabe." Eric marked his notes again.

After a brief pause while he read over his outline, Eric said, "Okay, Mr. Ward, I'd like to set the time frame, according to your memory. You seem to have a pretty good memory—you talk about dates and times and such. That kind of thing is important in your, uh…detective work, right?"

"Yes sir, it is."

"Okay. May I approach the witness, Your Honor?" The judge said he could, but Eric remained behind the podium. "At this pig roast-slash-cookout in '97, Michael makes these statements to you, right?" Now he inched around from behind the podium and began slowly walking toward Ward on the stand. He had some paper in his hand.

"Yes."

"A 'few months later,' according to you, you told Mr. McCabe about it. Right so far?" A little closer to Ward now.

"R…right." Ward was looking a little alarmed.

"And shortly thereafter, the police came to you to talk to you about it." Closer. "You assumed Bill McCabe went to the police with what you told him, correct?"

"Ye…well, I don't remember who called who, but…yes." Eric was three feet from him.

"Do you remember how much time elapsed between you telling Mr. McCabe and you talking to the police?"

"I…uh…not exactly." Sweat was glistening on his brow. "It wasn't long."

"Not long, you say?" Eric held out the paper in his hand. "Mr. Ward, would you read the date at the top of the page there? I've highlighted it for you."

Ward looked sick to his stomach. With a shaky hand he took the paper and looked at the top of the page.

"What does that date say, sir?"

"Uh…" Ward was pale. He looked again: "August 14, 2002."

"Thank you." Eric snatched the paper back and began walking back to the podium. "August of '02. This"—he held up the paper—"is the report Lieutenant Sullivan wrote immediately after interviewing you. *Five…years* after that pig roast." He was at the podium now. "Is five years your definition of—how'd you put it?—'not long,' Mr. Ward?"

"Objection," O'Reilly said. "Badgering the witness."

"Withdrawn," Eric said, but it didn't matter; his point was made. And for the next half-hour, Eric slowly and systematically sent Jack Ward's credibility into total ruin. Eric first asked him about the interview with Sullivan and Wayne, and if Ward had told them that Mike had said that Walter killed John because of jealousy over Marla. When Ward said he had, Eric had him read another highlighted portion of Sullivan's report. Ward looked it over, then handed it back to Eric with a beet-red face.

"According to this report," Eric said, "*you* said it was jealousy over Marla. That was *your* theory, not what Mike said, right?"

"Somewhat, I guess. I…yes."

"You told us that when Mike said it was Walter, you went, 'Bingo!' You had an epiphany. You thought—and you told the police—'It all made sense. It was because of Marla.' Right?"

"Right." Somehow Ward resembled a five-year-old being scolded for eating too much candy.

And Eric kept the onslaught coming. He had Ward admit that John had never verbally expressed his interest in Marla, like he had about Carol Ann; when Eric asked him about his explanation to Sullivan and Wayne during the 2002 interview that John had been "tied neck to feet like in the movie," Ward explained that it was common knowledge that John had been hogtied.

"Oh, it was common knowledge? Mr. Ward, were you at the crime scene that morning?"

"No."

"Then how do you know he was hogtied?"

"Like I said, it was common knowledge. Everybody was talking about it from 1969 on."

"Mr. Ward, do you know the difference between rumor and fact?"

"Yes I do. Everybody knew he was hogtied."

"Mr. Ward: is it possible that the matter of John being hogtied was actually a rumor? A rumor that spread so much that some people—including you—accepted it as fact? Is that possible?"

"He was hogtied," Ward said again. "Everybody knew—"

"It's a yes or no question, sir. Is it possible that a rumor can be accepted as fact?"

"Yes. It's possible."

"Thank you." *Another bite of the apple,* Eric thought, then moved on. His next line of questioning was about movies.

"You told the detectives in your 2002 interview that a week before John died you had seen the movie *The French Connection*, right, sir?"

Ward drew himself up with indignance. "I never said that."

"You—did you ever go to…" He referenced his notes. "I'm probably going to pronounce it wrong, but you can correct me—did you go to the Wamesit?" (He said it as *WAHM-e-sit,* and his pronunciation turned out to be correct.)

"The Wamesit Drive-In, yes."

"That drive-in was in Tewksbury, right?"

"Yes."

"You told the detectives that a week before John died you saw Walter Shelley, Mike Ferreira, and some other guys—their names are all listed right here—you saw them at the Wamesit, right?"

No sir, I did not say that."

Eric could scarcely believe what Ward had just said. "Approach the witness, Your Honor?" He was already walking to the stand when the judge said he could. "Why don't you read this section that begins with 'Ward said...' This is Lieutenant Sullivan's report."

Ward read the report to himself, then handed it back. He somehow managed to look smug. "That's not what I said."

Eric was stunned. "This...Mr. Ward, where do you think Lieutenant Sullivan would've gotten these names, if not from you?"

"Objection," O'Reilly said.

"Overruled," Judge Ricciardone said. "Witness may answer."

Ward knew he was trapped. "I....he...obviously, he had some names, yes. I must've given him those names. But that's not what I meant. The part about *The French Connection* was...I didn't see that movie till after it came out in '71."

"Okay, let's talk about that then. Did you tell Sullivan and Wayne that John was tied up like the guy in *The French Connection*?

"I...I told—they must've—"

"Yes or no, sir. Did you say he was tied up like in *The French Connection*?"

"I—" Ward paused, frustrated. "No. They must've misunderstood."

"Oh." Eric paused himself now. He put down the report, looked at Ward, and smiled. "Mr. Ward, do you remember the detectives taking notes of what you said during this interview?"

"Yes."

"You saw them with legal pads, pens, writing down the things you said. Correct?"

"I…" Ward slumped. "Yes."

"That's consistent with what you'd do if you were interviewing a witness in your own investigative work, right?"

"Yes."

"So Mr. Ward: are you telling me that Lieutenant Tom Sullivan, a detective with the state police, wrote down something you didn't say?"

"I….I don't know."

"You said *The French Connection* didn't come out till 1971—two years after John McCabe died, right?"

"That's right."

"Not only that, nobody—you said you've seen that movie, right?"

"Yes." He said it quietly, as if he were five again.

"So you know, as I do, that"—he spoke the words slowly—"*nobody is tied up in that movie.* No hogtying, no tying up of any kind. Right, Mr. Ward?"

Ward was staring at his lap. "Right."

"Let me postulate something to you, sir: Is it possible—just *possible*—that after your interview with detectives in 2002, you realized you may have been mistaken, that you might've confused that night at the drive-in with some other events from around that time? Is that possible, sir?"

Ward stared at Eric for a moment, then: "Yes, it's possible. It's hard to remember something like that after so many years."

Eric smiled at him. "Thank you. It's hard to remember things after so long. Right?"

"Yes it is."

The cross-examination went on, but there was almost no need for it to; the damage had been done. Eric asked Ward a few questions about a party that he and John supposedly had planned for the night of September 26 at Sullivan Parkway ("I went, but John never showed," Ward said), then Eric tied it all together brilliantly at the finish.

"You've done some private detective work on this case, haven't you?"

"Yes." He beamed at Bill McCabe. "I've been asking a lot of questions, asking around about it for a couple years since I got my P.I. diploma."

"The police are relying on Jack Ward to solve this murder, right?"

"No, not exa—"

"Objection."

"Counsel, it's cross-examination," the judge told O'Reilly. "Go ahead, Mr. Ward."

Ward looked relieved. "Thank you, Your Honor." To Eric: "It's not just me. They're getting information from a bunch of people."

"You realize, Mr. Ward, that no one from 1969 till 2002 mentions hogtying until you?"

But Ward was sticking to his guns. "It was no secret. Everybody talked about it for years."

"But you're just the first one to mention it to police, right?"

"I…I don't know that."

When Ward left the witness stand, Eric sat down at the defense table smiling to himself. The apple, he realized, was slowly disappearing. And hopefully, when Ed Brown testified it would vanish even further.

* * * *

Having Brian Gath testify at all, Eric thought later, was a mistake on the Commonwealth's part. His direct examination, which was brief, consisted of O'Reilly having Gath corroborate that he'd hosted the '97 pig roast, and that Mike Ferreira and Jack Ward had both attended it. And that was about it. During his cross, Eric asked Gath if he'd heard any of the conversation between Mike and Jack that day, and Gath said the same thing he'd told Sullivan and Wayne in 2003: "I didn't hear anything." And Eric even added a stinger at the end:

"Mr. Gath, you've heard rumors over the years about John McCabe's death, right?"

"Yes."

"And you work with Jack Ward at the Tewksbury Water Department. Most of those rumors you've heard have come from Jack Ward, haven't they?"

"Yes."

"No further questions."

* * * *

"Would you raise your right hand, please?"

Ed Brown—short, stocky, mostly bald, bespectacled, with an acne-scarred complexion and an already sweaty brow—lifted his palm to his shoulder and stood facing the court clerk.

"Do you solemnly affirm that the testimony you shall give in this matter shall be the truth, the whole truth, and nothing but the truth?"

"I do."

"Please be seated."

Ed stepped up onto the witness stand and sat down while A.D.A. Elisha Willis arranged her notes at the podium. Willis was tall and thin, attractive but severe-looking, with long, smooth blonde hair and a mind as sharp as a straight razor. In addition to her dexterous knowledge of Massachusetts law and her nearly picture-perfect memory, Willis had a gentle rapport with witnesses—which made her, in O'Reilly's eyes, a perfect fit for the Commonwealth's most crucial effort: the direct examination of their star witness.

"Good morning, Mr. Brown," Willis said. She gave him a reassuring smile.

"Good morning." Willis's comforting presence seemed to have little effect on Ed; he was a bundle of nerves, and his voice quivered as he spoke the greeting.

"Your full name is Edward Allen Brown, correct, sir?"

"Correct."

"Do you go by the name Edward?"

"Edward, Ed…Eddie…any of those." He relaxed some.

"When you were younger, did you go by another name?"

"Yes. I went by Allen."

"Your middle name?"

"Yes." Willis asked Ed these easy questions at the beginning, it seemed, to loosen him up; the later lines of questioning (and Eric Wilson's cross-examination), she knew, would not be easy. Not at all. Members of the jury, particularly a stocky, bespectacled, middle-aged juror in the front row, were focusing even more intently than usual on Ed's testimony.

"Is there a reason you, at some point in your life, started using the name Edward?"

"Yes. My father's name was Edward also, so when I was living at home I was Allen. But when I joined the service I used Edward. So I've been Edward—Ed—ever since."

Through her questions, Willis had Ed give a brief bio of his early life: Ed was born in Somerville, Mass., and lived there with his ever-growing family until they moved to Tewksbury when Ed was fifteen. Ed, his parents, and his five siblings, Ed told the jury, lived in a two-story house on Marshall Street.

"And in that house," Willis asked, "where was your bedroom in relation to your parents' room?"

"My room was downstairs in the back of the house— the back right-hand side."

"And where was your parents' bedroom?"

"Upstairs in the front, above the living room."

Ed continued the bio, testifying that he joined the Air Force in 1970, and was on active duty until 1974; during that time, he spent eighteen months in Guam. He joined the Reserves in 1985, he said, and over the next twenty years he served overseas in Qatar, Kuwait, Iraq, and Afghanistan before returning to the States in the mid-2000s. Over at the defense table, all three men—Eric, Stan, even Mike Ferreira—were busy writing on legal pads.

Slowly but surely, Willis brought her line of questioning back to 1969. Ed said that back then he was friends with both Mike Ferreira and Walter Shelley, that they lived in the same neighborhood, and that he'd often wait until his mother was asleep—his father worked the night shift at a local factory—then sneak out to meet up with Mike and Walter. They'd usually hang out and party in one of two places: with friends in a South Lowell neighborhood, or at the Tewksbury home of Nancy Williams, one of their midsize circle of friends.

"Did you also know somebody named Marla Shiner?"

"Yes. That was Walter's girlfriend."

"How did you know they were dating?"

"Well…they were together a lot. They were always close to each other, hugging, kissing, things like that."

Willis asked Ed about Walter's car—"a '65 Chevy Impala two-door coupe, maroon," Ed said—then she arrived at the heart of the matter.

"I'm going to bring you now to a specific night," she said. "Do you recall the night of September 26, 1969?"

"Yes." Ed—along with every other person in the room, it seemed—scooted forward in his chair. This was the Commonwealth's big play.

"What do you remember doing that evening?"

"I was at home watching television." Ed seemed very natural in his answers—a result, Eric guessed, of having been through this entire line of questioning more than once with Willis prior to his testimony.

"Did anyone come by your house at any point?"

"Walter and Michael. They came by at about 10:30 to pick me up to go out."

"Was your mother awake or asleep?"

"Asleep."

"What happened next?"

"Well, I saw the car pull up…I went out to see what they wanted, and they said they wanted me to go with them. To help them."

"Help them do what?"

"I didn't know at the time. I didn't find out till later."

Willis paused briefly to reference her notes, then: "What happened next?"

"I got in the car. We started driving…they said they wanted to go find this kid that had been flirting and, you know, messing around with Marla, and teach him a lesson."

"Then what happened?"

"We went down to the dance at the K of C, driving around looking for John McCabe."

"The K of C is also known as the Knights of Columbus?"

"Yes."

"What road was the K of C on?"

"Route 38—Main Street." Willis and Ed were in a total groove now.

"Who drove?"

"Walter."

"Where were you in the car?"

"In the back seat. Walter and Michael were in the front."

"Okay. You said you were on Route 38 by the K of C. What happened next?"

"We came down Shawsheen Street and took a right on 38 and drove down, then we turned around and came back. The dance had just let out."

"What did you see?"

"Well…kids were walking down the street in different directions. We drove on up to the stoplight, and Michael noticed John McCabe up ahead, thumbing. He said, 'There he is.'"

"What happened next?"

"We pulled up next to John…Michael got out and grabbed him and pushed him into the car."

"Can you describe exactly how Michael grabbed him? Did he grab John's arm, or—"

"He grabbed him in a bear hug. Mike t—Michael took him over to the car and pushed him in the back seat."

"What do you mean by a bear hug?"

"He…he put his arms around him." Ed extended his own arms into a circle in front of him and clasped his hands together, demonstrating. "You know, a bear hug."

"Front to front, front to back?"

"It was front to side."

"Like perpendicular to each other?"

"Yes."

"Then what happened?"

"Michael brought him over to the car. I pushed the passenger seat forward and Michael pushed him into the back seat."

"And then?"

"Michael jumped in the front seat, and we took off."

As the easy, obviously rehearsed examination progressed, Eric glanced up from his legal pad and noticed that every single juror was absolutely fixated on Ed Brown. Aside from the voices of Ed and Willis, the courtroom was perfectly silent—no creaks of chairs or muted rustles of clothing could be heard. Willis led Ed through his version of events that night, stopping often to ask him questions about even microscopic details.

Ed said Walter took back roads to South Lowell, John crying to be let out while Mike was leaning over his seat punching and slapping him. The three older teens, Ed recalled, were drinking cans of Budweiser; Ed wasn't sure how much the other two had consumed prior to his joining them. In South Lowell, he said, Walter drove under the Spaghettiville Bridge on Gorham Street, made a right on Maple, then another immediate right into a vacant lot. Walter drove to the back of the lot and turned left off the dirt road, drove forward a bit and stopped. He killed the engine and the headlights, Ed said, but left the parking lights on. At that point, Walter and Mike got out, and Mike pulled his seat forward; Ed said he pushed John out of the car, then exited the car himself.

"Why did you push John out of the car?"

"Um…to get him out. Obviously, they wanted him out. I thought they were just gonna slap him around or something."

"Was there talk about Marla at this point?"

"Yeah. They said they didn't like that he was messing around with Marla, and they were going to teach him a lesson."

"Okay." Willis looked at her notes. "What happened next?"

Ed took a deep breath and exhaled it. "Michael and Walter wrestled with John…they tripped him up, got him on the ground."

"Where were you in relation to them?"

"Standing next to the car."

"Were you involved at this point?"

"Not yet. They were holding him down and one of them said, 'Get over here and help us.' So I went over and sat on John's legs."

"Why did you do that?"

"Michael was trying to tie his feet together, and he couldn't hold him down." A soft moan from the gallery. Eric turned and saw all four members of the McCabe family with their eyes closed. Evelyn had her head down, and she was holding hands with her daughters as she sat between them. Willis pressed on.

"What happened next?"

"Michael tied his ankles together, then he went up and tied his wrists. I got off. Michael took another piece of rope and cut it with a pocketknife."

"And what did he do with that piece?"

"He tied it around his ankles and attached it up to his neck."

"What, if anything, is John doing?"

"He's squirming around, wiggling, trying to move…he couldn't because he was tied up."

"Could you hear him saying anything?"

"Not really. At some point his voice got muffled because somebody put tape on his mouth."

"Do you remember exactly when his voice became muffled?"

"I think it was when I was sitting on his legs."

"What, if anything, was John saying before his voice became muffled?"

"Saying, 'Get off me. What are you doing? Leave me alone.' Like that."

"When you got off John, what was his body doing— what was the condition of his body?"

"He was lying on his belly with his legs up in the air and his head turned to the side."

"Was he making any noise?"

"Yeah…but you couldn't understand what he was saying." A quiet sob from the spectators. Eric knew without turning around it had been Evelyn McCabe.

"What happened next?"

"They said, 'This will teach you not to mess with Marla anymore.' Then we got in the car and left."

Ed, A.D.A. Willis, and everyone else in the room paused to breathe. The three men at the defense table—along with the two men across the aisle on the prosecution side, and a number of jurors—were busy writing. The jurors not bent over their notebooks were still focused on Ed Brown. He said that they'd left the vacant lot and driven around for a while drinking beer, then at some point, he explained, he'd told the others they needed to go back and let John go.

"We went back to where John was," Ed went on. "Michael and Walter got out of the car and went over to him…they were there about thirty to forty-five seconds…they came quickly back to the car and got in, and we started to drive off. One of them said he wasn't breathing."

"Do you remember who said that?"

"No. I don't remember who it was."

"As you drove off, what happened next?"

"We said, 'We can't talk about this to anybody. We have to keep this amongst ourselves.'"

"Did Michael say anything at that point?"

"Yeah. He said: 'If anybody talks to anybody about this, I'll kill him.'" Willis paused to let that statement sit with the jurors. Many of them looked over at Mike Ferreira to gauge his reaction to Ed's claim, but Mike had none; he simply stared at Ed, his face blank.

"What happened next?"

"They took me home."

"What did you do?"

"I remember I think I cried."

"At some point, did you go to bed?"

"Yes."

Willis then directed Ed's attention to Exhibit 42—the detailed topographical map, which was on an easel a few feet from the witness stand. The A.D.A. had him stand next to it and point out some landmarks he'd mentioned (the Spaghettiville Bridge, Maple Street, the vacant lot), then asked him to return to the stand; Ed used a wooden pointer to easily identify the requested areas, suggesting he'd practiced with the map as well.

Now Willis tied up some loose ends, asking more questions about the manner in which John had been tied. Ed said again that Mike had tied a rope between John's ankles and his neck; when Willis displayed a photo on the Elmo of John's body as it had been found the next morning, she asked him what was different about its position.

"His legs are down on the ground."

"How were they when you last saw him?"

"Bent backwards at the knees, at ninety degrees."

Willis offered a potential explanation to this—subtle though it might have been: "When you returned to the lot after you rode around, when Michael and Walter went over to John's body lying on the ground, could you see what they were doing, if anything?"

"No. Their backs were to me. I couldn't see."

The questioning began to move forward chronologically. Ed recalled that at some point in '69 he'd given Walter a ride to the police station for questioning, but he'd been too scared to offer any info himself; detectives questioned him at his home in 2007, he said, but he claimed to remember nothing about a murder in Tewksbury in 1969.

"And now I'm going to draw your attention to February of 2011. Did you meet with a Detective Linda Coughlin and a Detective Fenlon up in New Hampshire?"

"Yes."

"Did you tell them what you've told this jury today about what happened to John McCabe, or did you tell them something different?"

"Something different."

"And why is that?"

"I was afraid of being associated with it. Afraid of going to jail."

"Now I want to bring you to March 9th of 2011. Did you talk to detectives about John McCabe?"

"Yes."

"And at that time, did you tell them what happened to John?"

"I…eventually, I did tell them. Yes." Eric noticed Ed starting to squirm the tiniest bit, as if he were leaving his comfort zone, and not happy to be doing so.

"What did you say you and Michael and Walter did to John?"

"We…I told them what I told you just now."

"Why did you tell them on that date—what changed?"

"A couple of things." Ed paused. "I…I knew this wasn't gonna be going away like it did in 2007. I was…they told me they just wanted to know the truth about what happened. They said the D.A. would help me if I told them the truth. And so…I figured it was time to just give it up." He paused again, and caught Bill McCabe's eye for a moment before he continued. "You know…I'm a parent. If something happened to one of my children, I'd wanna know what it was. *How* it happened. I just…I knew this wasn't going away. And if I finally confessed to what they were saying I did, maybe things would go easier on me."

Willis stood silently, letting the weight of Ed's words settle in with the jurors. After a beat, she asked: "At the end of that meeting, what did you expect to happen?"

"I expected to go to jail."

"And you mentioned that things would go easier on you. Did anybody promise you anything in that meeting?"

"No."

"Did you have any kind of deal with respect to prosecution or leniency?"

"No."

"You thought things would go easier on you. Was that in your own mind, or did somebody tell you that would happen?"

"Well…" Ed seemed to mull this over. "I…it was based on what they said about the D.A. helping me if I just fessed up. I thought…I didn't know what that meant, but I assumed that if I listened to—if I did something then, things would be easier for me than if I just kept hiding it."

Willis began wrapping up her questioning by asking if Ed was provided an attorney (he was—Daniel Callahan, a Lowell public defender) and the details of his plea bargain (he pled guilty to manslaughter, received probation, and served no jail time). The direct examination slowly came to a close, Willis asking about his current relationships with

Mike and Walter—he had none with either—then she posed one final question.

"Mr. Brown, did you go to the funeral of John McCabe?"

"No, I did not."

"Your Honor, at this time I have no further questions."

"Okay, thank you," the judge said, then looked at Eric. Ed Brown was looking at him too, and a miniscule amount of uncertainty and fear flickered across his ruddy face; his eyes moved over to Willis at the prosecution table, and when she gave him an affable smile, he set his jaw and returned a grin of his own. *I'm ready*, his expression said.

"Mr. Wilson?"

"Thank you, Your Honor." Eric looked at Mike and gave him a single, brief nod, then stood and walked to the podium. Eric's brain was full nearly to bursting with info: Ed's prior testimony (from the direct examination he'd just finished, yes, but also from his 2011 grand jury and transfer hearing statements), statements to police, and a wealth of miscellaneous facts. Eric had a general idea of how his cross would ensue, but he knew that depending on Ed's answers, Eric might need to explore new lines of questioning with no forewarning; in other words, he needed to think on his feet. But above all else, Eric wanted to find out—for himself *and* for the jury—if Ed was capable of honoring the oath to which he'd just sworn, or if "nothing but the truth" would be another broken promise.

"Mr. Brown, my name is Eric Wilson. We've met before, haven't we?"

"Yes sir." Ed's face was pinched—with determination, it seemed, not from fear.

"Back in 2011, at a preliminary hearing in this matter, I had an opportunity to ask you a number of questions, right?"

"Yes sir."

"When I asked you those questions back then, you provided me with answers, about the same topics you've talked about with this jury today. True?"

"That's correct."

"Okay. Before I get into what I've prepared to ask you about, I want to talk to you about some other issues." He walked out from behind the podium and took a step or two toward Ed. "What did you do to prepare for your testimony? You met with the prosecutors, right?"

"Yes."

"Did you meet with detectives? Or just prosecutors?"

"Ah…both."

"That was over at the D.A.'s office in Lowell?"

"Yes."

"And they went through all the questions, told you what they'd be asking you for, and they told you what answers they'd be looking for, right?"

"No." Ed then began making a familiar gesture: he scratched the side of his face with one hand. He scraped for a moment before he seemed to become aware of what he was doing, and put his hand back in his lap. "They said they just want me to tell the truth."

"Oh. The truth," Eric said, adding an infinitesimal touch of irony to the statement. He pointed to the topographical map on the easel next to the stand. "When did you see that exhibit before—Exhibit 42? Today's not the first time, right?"

"No. I saw it about a week ago."

"Okay. Because you seemed to be pretty familiar with it when you were describing th—"

"Objection," Willis said. Eric looked at Judge Ricciardone with his eyebrows raised and his hands up. He started to say, "But it's cross-examination…" when the judge interrupted him.

"Overruled. I'll allow it."

Eric repeated his query. "Mr. Brown, it didn't take you long to identify a number of things on that exhibit, true?"

"Correct."

"You and the prosecutors and the detectives went over it in detail, didn't you?"

"We did."

Eric asked a few questions about Ed's high school days, pointing out that Mike had been two grades behind him (and thus younger). Then he had Ed acknowledge that Willis had asked him about sneaking out at night as a teenager—and Eric pointed out the reason for Willis's questions.

"You've had discussions in recent years with your mother regarding your whereabouts on the evening of September 26, 1969, haven't you?"

"Yes."

"And she said you weren't with Walter and Mike, you were home. That was your mother's memory, right?"

"Yes."

"That's why you were asked about sneaking out without her knowledge, right?"

"I think so."

"So: you just told this jury during your direct testimony that you were home watching TV at 10:30 p.m. on September 26th of '69, right?"

"Right, yes."

"Do you have a memory of that, Mr. Brown?"

"Well…" He gave his head a single scratch. "That's what I'd be doing if I was home alone. I don't have an exact memory of it, but…I'm sure that's what I was doing. That's what I always did."

"When Miss Willis asked you what you were doing that night, you told this jury you were home watching TV. Right?"

"Yes."

"You don't really remember that, do you?"

"I…" Ed's eyes flicked momentarily to Willis over at her table. "If I wasn't out with Wally and Mike, that's what I'd be doing—home watching TV."

"So you're just assuming today that's what you were doing. You don't actually have a present-day memory of doing that, though, do you?"

"I…no."

"Okay." Eric briefly looked at his notes. The first bullet point in his cross-examination outline read *Grand jury*. "Mr. Brown, you told this jury that you were picked up at 10:30 at night, right?"

"Yes."

"That's your sworn testimony?"

"Yes."

"But that hasn't always been your sworn testimony, has it?"

"As…as far I know it has been, yes. 10:30 at night."

"Did you testify before a grand jury in 2011 that Walter Shelley and Michael Ferreira picked you up around *7:00* p.m. that evening?"

"I don't remember saying that."

"You told the grand jury a different story, right?"

"Objection," Willis said, but Ed either didn't hear it or ignored her.

"I've told different stories."

The judge interjected: "I'll allow it. He's answered anyway."

Eric barely heard the objection; his focus was on Ed Brown. "You've told different stories, Mr. Brown?"

"Yes."

"You took an oath before this jury today, yes?"

"Yes." Another head scratch.

"And you took the same oath before the grand jury in 2011, didn't you?"

"Yes."

"Okay. They have you raise your hand and swear to tell the truth. And that's how the jury relies on what you say. Because you take that oath. Right?"

"Uh…right."

"Okay. Mr. Brown, didn't you tell that grand jury you were with Mike and Walter at 7:00 p.m. on that Friday night, riding around?"

Ed's eyes flicked to Willis again, then back to Eric. "I don't remember saying that, no."

"It's in the…I'll show you the transcript in a bit, if you like. If you said seven o'clock to that grand jury, you must have misled them, right?"

"Objection."

"I'll allow it." Judge Ricciardone seemed as interested as anyone to see where the questioning was headed.

"Did you mislead that grand jury, sir?"

"No." Much as he didn't want it to, Ed's brow was starting to bead with sweat droplets.

"Then you must have misled *this* jury." Eric acknowledged the jurors with a simple head nod. "Because earlier today, you said you were home till 10:30. Right?"

"I don't remember exactly what I told the grand jury."

"Didn't you swear to that grand jury you would tell them the truth?"

"I did."

"Then Mr. Brown: shouldn't it be the same time? Not 7:00 to them, and 10:30 today?"

Ed scratched his face again. "I'm just…I'm telling what I remember."

"Your memory is different now than it was two years ago, isn't it?"

"Could be."

"Okay. Let's talk about Marla Shiner. You didn't tell this jury that you, Walter, and Mike dropped Marla off at the K of C dance. Did you?"

"No, I did not."

"That didn't happen?"

"I don't remember it happening like that, no."

"Do you remember telling the grand jury that not only did you drop her off at the dance, but you picked her up afterward and took her home?"

"I…I don't remember saying that."

Eric just gave the jurors a confused look. He noticed that many of them had similar expressions: confusion, doubt, or simple uncertainty. He knew he'd made his point: either Ed had lied to the grand jury, or he'd lied to them.

The morning wore on, and Eric's cross-examination became like a boxing match—one he was winning. Eric would attack with questions about the differences between Ed's current testimony and his prior statements, and Ed would dodge them by giving variations of what had become his go-to answer: "I don't remember." Eric would often counter with facts—usually ones Ed himself had confirmed in his own testimony—that repeatedly demonstrated to the jury that Ed Brown just didn't have his facts straight.

First, Eric asked about Ed's testimony concerning Mike's "bear hug" of John; when Eric asked Ed if he was aware that Mike and Nancy had given John a ride earlier that night (a fact Ed hadn't known about), Eric wondered why a "forcible" bear hug had even been necessary, when Mike and John had been on good terms a mere three hours earlier. Then Eric pointed out that in his direct testimony that morning, Ed had said that he, Walter, and Mike had told John they were "teaching him a lesson for messing around with Marla." But in Ed's 2011 grand jury testimony, Eric indicated, Ed had said that nothing was mentioned about Marla at any time—and in fact, Ed had told the grand jury, none of the three boys had ever told John exactly why they were abducting him. Ed also acknowledged that when Walter and Mike had gone to John's body upon their return trip to the vacant lot, he hadn't been able to see what they were doing, and from Ed's vantage point neither of them appeared to be holding a knife. (Eric anticipated that in his closing statement, O'Reilly would speculate that that was when they'd cut the "hogtie" rope, so Eric wanted to dispel that idea even before it was suggested.)

As the questioning progressed, Ed started showing visible signs of defeat. He repeatedly scratched the side of his face, which Eric now recognized as Ed's unconscious sign of his uncertainty. He often cut his eyes to Willis at the prosecution table, either as a need for approval or a simple plea for help. Willis objected to Eric's lines of questioning multiple times, but Judge Ricciardone overruled her on every occasion. And as Eric made his way through his notes, it became apparent to everyone in the courtroom—most of all to the attorneys sitting helplessly at the prosecution table—that Eric was making Ed Brown look ridiculous.

Just before the lunch recess, Eric dealt his biggest blow yet. They were exploring a line of questioning about the ropes used to tie John up, and Eric was using the transcript from Ed's grand jury testimony to continue punching holes in Ed's statements to A.D.A. Willis earlier that morning.

"You told Mr. O'Reilly in front of the 2011 grand jury that you tied ropes around his ankles and his wrists, right?"

"Yes."

"Mr. O'Reilly asked you"—he looked down to read from the transcript—"'Was there rope tied anywhere else?' And your answer was, 'That's all I remember, tying his wrists and his ankles.'" He looked up at Ed. "Right?"

"Yes." Scratch, scratch.

"Mr. O'Reilly asked you a question: 'Not his neck?' Do you remember your response?"

"No, I do not."

"You said, 'No, it was not.' Right?"

"I don't remember saying that."

"Approach the witness, Your Honor?" When the judge nodded his approval, Eric went to the stand and held the grand jury transcript so that he and Ed could both read it. "Question: 'Where did Michael tie the rope?' And your answer was?"

Ed looked closely at the transcript. "'Around his ankles.'"

"Next question: 'And where else?'"

"'Around his wrists.'"

"'And then where else?' was the question. And your response: 'That's what I remember, tying his wrists and his ankles.' Then O'Reilly says—down here—he asks, 'Not his neck?' And your response was?"

"'No.'"

"Then Mr. O'Reilly says, 'Do you remember what you told the police a couple of weeks ago?' Your answer: 'I just remember his ankles and his wrists. I don't know why they would tie a rope around his neck.' Right?"

"Yes."

Eric walked back to the podium. "And it was then that Mr. O'Reilly suggested that you take a recess, right?"

"Yes."

"You went and had a conference. And you reviewed a police report. Correct?"

"Correct."

"The report was something Detective Linda Coughlin typed up, wasn't it?"

"Yes."

"*Not* something you drafted, but what Detective Coughlin drafted. Right?"

"Right."

"And once you reviewed the report Detective Coughlin wrote about what happened in that field that night, you came back in front of the grand jury?"

"Yes."

"And it was then, sir, that you said there was a rope from his ankles to his neck?"

"Yes."

Then the knockout punch: "You didn't have your facts straight, did you?"

"No sir."

"It was Mr. O'Reilly's suggestion, and Detective Coughlin's report, that helped you get your facts straight, true?"

"Correct." Ed's answer was equivalent to the sound of his back hitting the canvas.

Barely two minutes later, though, Eric waded in for more. He began a line of questioning about *The French Connection*, and when he asked how Ed remembered that that movie was where they'd learned how to tie John up, Ed admitted he'd been fed that memory.

"When you took that deal and told Detective Coughlin and Mr. O'Reilly the same thing you've told this jury, you said, 'We tied him up just like in the movie.' Right?"

Ed looked genuinely surprised. "I never said that."

"Oh no?" Eric searched through Ed's witness folder and quickly found what he needed. "Detective Coughlin's report from March 9, 2011, says: 'Brown told us that they decided they would tie him up'—and this part is in quotes—'like in the movie.' You're telling this jury you never said those words?"

"I never said that, no."

"But the tying-up reference from *The French Connection*—that came from Mr. O'Reilly, right?"

"Yes."

"He fed you that information, didn't he?"

"He told me that, yes."

When Judge Ricciardone took the lunch recess shortly afterward, the prosecution team—and most of all, Ed Brown—breathed a sigh of relief. And as Eric went to lunch at the café next door with Stan, Mike, and some of the Ferreira clan, he did his best not to grin from ear to ear.

* * * *

After the lunch break, Eric picked up where he'd left off with Ed—but he knew he'd have less than an hour for cross-examination before Marla Shiner took the stand, so he decided to save his more crucial lines of questioning for Monday morning, when Ed returned. (Prior to bringing the jury in after lunch, Judge Ricciardone, O'Reilly, and Eric had agreed to take a short recess at 2:45 in order to switch witnesses, and Marla's testimony would finish out the day.)

There were inconsistencies between Ed's current trial testimony and his statements at the 2011 transfer hearing, Eric noted, about how far Shelley had driven into the dirt lot. After exploring that for a few minutes, Eric asked about Ed's March 2011 interrogations (which Eric indicated had been disguised as "interviews," essentially meaning detectives felt they didn't need to be recorded); Ed testified that he was not aware of any recording devices present. Eric also asked about exactly when during the March 9 meeting Detective Coughlin had shown Ed the photo of John McCabe after he'd died.

"At this meeting, you're maintaining your innocence," Eric said, "and Linda Coughlin starts showing you crime scene photos, right?"

"Yes."

"Those photos clearly show John McCabe tied at his ankles, tied at his wrists, tied at his neck, right?"

"Correct."

"The photos show tape on his mouth and eyes, right?"

"Yes."

"So: you're maintaining your innocence, and Detective Coughlin is telling you how that boy died in that field, right?"

"Yes."

"So in essence, they showed you the manner and method of this murder, didn't they?"

"Yes they did."

"And in your mind, Mr. Brown, long before you told them you were involved, you basically knew what happened just by looking at those photos, didn't you?"

"That's correct." During this entire line of questioning, Ed was showing none of his usual signs of unease; he hadn't scratched the side of his face for a number of minutes, and the sweat on his brow was minimal.

"And they told you—before you said you were involved—that you were with Mike and Walter that night, right?"

"Yes."

"And it was after all that that you began to change your story, right?"

"That's right."

Eric started questioning Ed about the various versions of what had happened—five in all—that he'd told the detectives before he gave the "final" one, but Ricciardone stopped Eric before he could get anywhere with it.

"Sorry, Counsel, I'm going to interrupt you there." He looked at the jurors. "Ladies and gentlemen, I'm going to give you a short recess, then by prior arrangement we're going to interrupt Mr. Brown's testimony and call another witness out of order. This other witness has traveled a long way to be here, so both parties have agreed to let her testify now so she can return home. We'll hear the remainder of Mr. Brown's testimony once we're finished with the other witness. I'm telling you this because I want to avoid any confusion on your part.

"Now, this other witness is being called by the defendant. Keep in mind that the prosecution is still presenting its case, which makes this an unusual circumstance; normally the defense presents its witnesses— if it chooses to present any—after the prosecution has rested. But like I've said, the parties have agreed to accommodate the witness so her testimony can be heard. During your deliberations, try to keep that in mind, and try to give her testimony the same weight as if she had testified in a 'normal' fashion. Okay? Any questions?" When the jurors indicated they had none, the judge recessed for about ten minutes.

Once the jury was back in place precisely at 3:00, Stan stood. "Marla Shiner, Your Honor."

Marla entered from the rear of the courtroom and made her way down the aisle and past the bar separating the gallery from the litigation well. As she passed the McCabe family in the first row, she offered them a gentle (if somewhat forced) smile; her acknowledgment was not returned. The court clerk swore her in and asked her to have a seat. Once she was on the stand, the clerk asked her to state her name and spell her surname.

"My name is Marla Shiner—S-H-I-N-E-R," she said, leaning forward so that her mouth practically touched the microphone. Marla was a schoolteacher and a single mother, and time and a stressful life had aged her; she had bleached-blonde, mid-length hair, and a hardened appearance. Her personality was equally abrupt; she spoke in harsh bursts, and exuded an almost confrontational vibe. But as callous as she appeared, Marla's heart, as it was discovered during her testimony, was bursting with love and sympathy.

"Good afternoon, Miss Shiner," Stan said. He was a solid, skilled attorney, but his style was more laid-back than was Eric's; Stan remained behind the podium during the questioning to make frequent references to his prepared notes.

Marla leaned forward to the microphone. "Good afternoon," she said, then collapsed back in her chair. Her curious habit of speaking directly into the mike assured Eric (and everyone else in the room) that, for better or worse, they would have no problem hearing her answers.

"What state do you now live in?"

"I live in California."

"And who do you live there with?"

"A family member." When she sat back after giving her answer, the look on her face told Stan not to ask who the family member was.

Stan guided her through the prerequisite establishing questions: Marla had been a teacher for ten years; she'd moved to Tewksbury in grade school; she was the second of four siblings; she'd lived on Grasshopper Lane in

Tewksbury, in the same neighborhood as John McCabe and Jack Ward. With the informational matters out of the way, Stan moved into the relevant lines of questioning.

"In September of 1969, how old were you?"

"Um...thirteen?"

"Your date of birth is May of '56, correct?"

"Uh huh."

"So if my math is right, that would've made you thirteen and a couple of months, right?"

"Correct."

"And during that period of time—fall of '69—did you attend any Knights of Columbus dances in Tewksbury?"

"Fall of '69?" She stared upward for a moment to think, then leaned in to the mike: "No. I was too young."

Stan glanced at his notes. "Miss Shiner, on September 26, 1969, did Michael Ferreira, a man named Walter Shelley, and a man named Edward Allen Brown drive you to the Knights of Columbus hall?"

Emphatically: "No."

"At some later point in time, did you encounter Walter Shelley?"

"At some point in time, yes." At that Marla gave an ironic smile.

"And at some point, did you and Mr. Shelley enter into a dating relationship?"

"Yes we did."

"Do you know when that relationship would have begun?"

She stared upward again. "Hm...to my recollection, that would be when he—he worked at Astro Circuits. And I have no recollection before that at all."

"So he was working at Astro Circuits when you started dating him?"

"Yes, he was."

"To your knowledge, was Walter still in school when you started dating him?"

"No, he was not."

"Okay." Another glance at his notes, then: "Now, you indicated that you knew John McCabe."

"Yes."

"Were the two of you friends in September of '69?"

"Well…just in passing, like, 'Hi, how are you,' you know. We weren't close. More like acquaintances, I guess."

"But you would've known each other from the—"

"From passing," she interrupted. "As kids do. That's all."

"Okay. In August or September of 1969, did you ever go to a dance with John?"

"Never." She was so close to the mike on that answer that her lips actually touched it; her one-word reply was simultaneously amplified and muffled.

"Did you ever attend a dance during that time period that John also attended?"

"No."

"In August or September of '69, was it ever conveyed to you that John had a crush on you?"

"*No.*" She leaned so far in that her answer was preceded by a soft *thump* from the P.A. system when her mouth struck the mike.

"Were you ever aware of any romantic interest John had in you?"

"Never."

"All right. When did you become aware of the death of John McCabe?"

"Right after it happened."

"Would it have been the next day—Saturday, the 27th?"

"Probably. I think it was in the newspapers, on the news on TV…it was everywhere. It was very sad." Marla's eyes misted a bit.

"Do you have any memory of when the last time was that you saw John?"

"None."

Stan asked a few questions about her interviews with police—the first one by telephone in 2003, the second in 2011 at her home—then he posed one last question.

"Miss Shiner, are you testifying today from the best memory you have of these events?"

"Yes. It was a very long time ago."

"Nothing further, Your Honor." Stan took his seat, and Judge Ricciardone inquired of A.D.A. O'Reilly, who took Stan's place at the podium.

"Good afternoon, Miss Shiner."

"Good afternoon, sir."

O'Reilly began his cross by asking more questions about Marla's 2003 telephone interview with Sullivan and Wayne. And an interesting thing happened: O'Reilly's demeanor during his cross-examination of Marla Shiner was quite different. He exhibited none of the same energy and interest he'd displayed while questioning the previous prosecution witnesses; he just stood at the podium and read most of his questions, almost in a monotone, directly from his notes. To those watching from the gallery, O'Reilly seemed to be simply going through the motions of questioning Marla, like it was a waste of his valuable time. In essence, it was as if he were mailing it in.

O'Reilly asked Marla about the 2003 interview, then followed up with questions about her talk with Escondido police at her home in 2011. Marla acknowledged that she told the Escondido detectives as much as she remembered about the events in 1969, and that she'd been completely honest with them. But O'Reilly opened a line of questioning in an attempt (if only a half-hearted one) to refute that honesty.

"Miss Shiner, did you know a man named Joey Richard?"

"Yes I did, sir."

"He came out to visit you a couple of years ago, just before he passed away, didn't he?"

"Yes, he did."

"Did you have a conversation with Joey Richard about—"

"Objection," Stan cut in. "Hearsay."

"Do you want to be heard?" the judge asked.

"Yes, briefly." The five attorneys huddled with Ricciardone at the bench. Stan argued that O'Reilly was trying to introduce statements made to Jack Ward by Joey Richard—classic hearsay—that during Joey's visit to California, Marla had told him that she and John had had a relationship, and they'd kept it a secret. (Jack Ward had testified at a previous grand jury hearing, during which hearsay rules are less strict, that Joey had told him about Marla's revelation.) O'Reilly pointed out that he planned to simply ask Marla if she ever made such a statement, and Jack Ward's name would never be mentioned. Ricciardone overruled Stan's objection, warning O'Reilly that he should ask Marla only about her own statements to others. The attorneys returned to their seats, and O'Reilly to the podium.

"Miss Shiner, did you ever tell Jocy Richard that you were in a relationship at any point in time with John McCabe?"

"*Never.*" Her face sizzled with underlying anger.

"Did you tell Joey that Walter had a mean streak?"

"Yes."

"And that he was a jealous person?"

"I didn't have to, he already knew. But the answer is yes."

O'Reilly further explored Marla's relationship with Walter, trying to pinpoint whether or not they'd begun dating at the time of the murder; though Marla said she couldn't remember exactly when it was, she recalled that it was definitely after John's death. But O'Reilly refused to move on. He circled around the topic before finally asking her his most crucial question yet.

"Did you at any time blame yourself for being in the middle of John McCabe's murder?"

Marla's eyes narrowed. "Wha…? *No.*"

"Did you not tell people that?"

In her distress, Marla either ignored his question or didn't hear it. "When I heard that might be the reason why, I was devastated. But blame myself? No. I was not to blame."

O'Reilly seemed completely ignorant of her anguish. "You're aware, of course, that people have said you may have been the cause?"

"I…" She stopped and pursed her lips, and a tear rolled down her heavily rouged cheek. "The detectives in 2003 hinted at it, but they never came out and said it. When the Escondido cops came to my house, they said that's what the Massachusetts cops believed. So…yeah. I'd heard that."

O'Reilly continued down the same path, asking about her later relationship with Walter; when he began asking about their marriage (and divorce), Stan objected, arguing that the line of questioning was irrelevant since the marriage occurred five years after the crime. Judge Ricciardone sustained Stan's objection, and O'Reilly said he had nothing else.

"Redirect, gentlemen?"

"Thank you, Your Honor," Stan said as he popped up. "Miss Shiner, in response to one of Mr. O'Reilly's questions, you indicated that you had felt bad when you heard what was being reported as the reason for the death of John McCabe. Is that correct?"

"Yes."

"And you had heard that for the first time when you were out in California, right?"

"The reason? Yes. I was devastated."

"And the reason for your devastation was because your name was being associated years later with John's death, right?"

"I…" She took a deep breath. "I felt bad for the family. It just…brought the whole thing out in the front again. I was…" Tears were falling now. "I was really devastated for the family. And I still am!" She broke down and sobbed. After a moment, she said through a flood of tears: "But I knew I wasn't the cause. *I* wasn't the reason why." She dug in her jacket pocket for a tissue.

"Thank you, Miss Shiner," Stan said. Instinct told him to end his questioning right there. "Thank you very much. Nothing further, Your Honor."

When Ricciardone released the jurors several minutes later, several of them were silently crying too.

EX PARTE: Trial Day 4 → Day 5

Normally in a trial of this magnitude, there's not much time to reflect back on a previous day of testimony. I'm usually thinking ahead to upcoming witnesses, how to structure my closing argument, that type of thing. If anything, I'll contemplate how a previous day went and try to figure out how it'll help me moving forward. And a later witness's questioning may change a little—or a lot—from what I've already prepared, depending on what was revealed by previous testimony. In essence, I like to keep things fluid, if that makes sense.

But I will say that after I'd started my cross-examination of Ed Brown that Friday, I was very pleased with how things were going. I think at that point I was making a lot of headway in convincing the jury that he wasn't believable—and the jurors had the whole weekend to think about that. And then, when Marla Shiner testified right in the middle of it, she added to the doubt by saying, "No, I wasn't dating Shelley at the time. There was no romantic involvement between me and John." In retrospect, I think having Marla testify out of order helped our case.

Tom O'Reilly told me Friday evening that on Tuesday, after I finished up with Brown, he planned to call only two witnesses: Father Tom Walsh, one of the two priests who'd received an anonymous phone call from a man claiming to be the killer, and Detective Linda Coughlin. The priest was a relatively minor witness, but an important one, as I wanted to present third-party culprit evidence about the caller to priests. Then later, when I cross-examined Linda Coughlin, I wanted to tie in the idea that Richard Santos (the man who'd been arrested in '74 for abducting a woman, and later admitted he'd done it before) *was* the caller to the priests. And I wanted to have Coughlin admit that she'd never given these suspects a second thought, that her focus was only on Shelley/Ferreira/Brown. (In fact, I'd show that Coughlin *didn't even know who Richard Santos was* until a couple of months before the trial, when I just happened to find that forgotten box of discovery materials at our meeting at LPD.)

A word or two about Linda Coughlin: she is one of the better detectives I've dealt with. In court, she was…a formidable adversary, I'll just say that. I knew she would fight me at every turn, so I had to be ready for that. And I was.

But her manner and method of "solving" this case just didn't sit well with me. This murder had been investigated—thoroughly—for forty years. Hundreds of people interviewed, dozens of leads followed…nothing. Then Coughlin takes up the case, and cracks it in *three months*? Something wasn't right. So I wanted to show that she went to lengths to make arrests for the murder that just didn't add up. And here's why: One, she basically fed Ed Brown the story of how the murder happened. And two, the story she fed him didn't match the evidence. The story she fabricated and fed Brown—the hogtying, the *French Connection* theory, the motive of jealousy over Marla Shiner—was all speculation by Jack Ward, and Coughlin just ran with that, for better or worse. What I hoped to impress upon the jury was that because of her eagerness to solve this, she ignored everything else and focused on having Brown roll over and admit to her version of what happened.

After Ed Brown, Linda Coughlin would be the most critical witness in the entire trial. So to prepare, rather than spend the long weekend at my office reviewing discovery info, I went home and spent it with my family. Even so, I found time to sneak down to the basement and work on it from time to time.

5. Tuesday, January 22: Ferreira Trial, Day Five

At 8:55 a.m., the spectators, along with members of the prosecution and defense teams, were huddled in loose knots around the courtroom, conversing quietly amongst themselves. Stan, Mike's wife Nancy, and his niece Danielle were bemoaning the previous Sunday's AFC Championship game (which, to New Englanders' surprise and horror, the Patriots had lost to the Baltimore Ravens). And mere feet away, O'Reilly and Willis were talking with Bill McCabe about the very same subject.

But Mike Ferreira and Eric Wilson, attorney and client, were seated at the defense table conferring about Ed Brown's testimony. Eric told Mike that he wanted to start his cross-examination of Ed, which would continue from Friday, with questions about Ed's whereabouts earlier in the evening on the night of the murder. As Eric continued asking Mike about it, what he'd previously suspected became clear: after forty-three years, Mike just didn't remember. So how could Ed Brown be expected to? That is, unless he'd been "told" what those memories were?

Once Judge Ricciardone was seated, the jurors were brought in. "I hope and trust everyone had an enjoyable long weekend," the judge told them once they were all in place. (The previous day had been Martin Luther King, Jr. Day, a federal holiday, so court hadn't been in session.) Ed Brown was sworn in again, and Eric went to the podium.

"Good morning, sir. We stopped Friday afternoon, and I want to ask you some questions to follow up." As he'd told Mike, Eric started with a line of questioning about the evening of September 26. Ed maintained that without a doubt, Walter and Mike had picked him up at 10:30, but

Eric again pointed out the fact that in both his grand jury and transfer hearing testimonies, he'd told different stories: that he'd been with them starting at 7:00 p.m. Eric continued identifying the differences between Ed's direct testimony in the current trial and his previous statements, in hopes of revealing to the jury that, like Mike, Ed just didn't remember. And Eric indicated that during Ed's transfer hearing testimony, A.D.A. O'Reilly had "suggested" info about the crime when Ed had said he didn't remember details like the name of the street that bordered the vacant lot, or the exact location of John's body. The matter of Marla Shiner, too, came into question.

"In your story Friday, there was no mention of Marla Shiner being with you, was there?"

"No."

"She wasn't with you, was she?"

"No, she was not."

"But you've testified under oath before that Marla was with you—that you dropped her off at the dance, right?"

"Yes."

"So before you said she was, and Friday you said she wasn't. One is a lie, one is the truth, right? Or are they both lies?"

Scratch scratch scratch. "I—no. They're not lies. I was just telling what I remembered."

"I understand, sir. It's hard to remember details of something after forty-three years, isn't it?"

"Yes it is."

Eric went over other alleged aspects of the crime—the *French Connection* angle, the hogtying, the presence of tape over John's eyes and mouth—and in every instance, when Eric pointed out the differences in his various testimonies, Ed attributed that to a repressed memory. With that, Eric finally arrived at his objective.

"So: in your March 9 interrogation, Detective Coughlin told you that Shelley and Ferreira were also suspects, right?"

"Yes."

"And she told you that Walter Shelley was jealous over Marla, right?"

"Correct."

"She told you that John McCabe was hogtied, right?"

"Yes."

"They got you to adopt their beliefs, didn't they? Weren't you confronted with their beliefs of what happened out in that field?"

"They were questioning me, and…yes. I was."

"And then—*then*—they told you they had evidence against you, and that you were going to jail unless you told them what happened, right?"

"Yes." Upon Ed's answer, Eric stopped and slowly turned his head to look at the jury, his eyebrows raised. Then he looked back at his witness.

"So you told them a similar story to the one you've told this jury, true?"

"Yes."

"You connected the dots, Mr. Brown. You knew what you needed to say, right?"

"I knew what I needed to say because I was th—"

"They told you everything about it. After they threatened you with jail, you connected the dots for them, didn't you?"

"I…if you want to call it that, yes."

The last bullet point in Eric's outline was *Kids*.

"Now: as you told the jury on Friday, part of the reason you told the police your last version of what happened was because you're a parent, and you'd want to know, right?"

"Yes."

"When the detectives questioned you in 2007, and they questioned you again earlier in 2011, you had the same children, right?"

"Yes."

"And according to your statements, you lied to them on those occasions, right?"

"I did."

"On March 9, you expected to go in front of a grand jury and tell them what you knew, right?"

"Yes."

"And on that day—same children, same reasons—you were prepared to lie to that grand jury, weren't you?"

"Yes."

"Mr. Brown, you've lied under oath when you've been scared and nervous, right?"

"Yes."

"You were scared and nervous on the 9th of March, when you told all those versions of what happened, weren't you?"

"I was."

"And you were scared and nervous when you told Detective Coughlin a similar story to what you've told this jury, right?"

"Yes."

It was time for the finish that the jurors would remember. "During my cross-examination, Mr. Brown, I've shown you numerous instances of your prior testimony being different from what you've told this jury, haven't I?"

"Yes."

"Despite everything—all the various versions of events, the grand jury testimony, transfer hearing testimony, multiple sessions with the prosecutors prepping you for your testimony in this trial—despite all that, you *still* can't get your facts straight, can you?"

"No, I can't."

"No further questions, Your Honor." Eric hadn't even sat down when Willis popped up for a redirect. Her questions, a feeble attempt to repair the damage Eric had caused, were about whether anyone had fed him details about the crime (they hadn't, he of course answered), and whether he'd been too busy committing the crime to notice many details (of course he had been). But Willis's damage control was for naught; Ed Brown left the stand, head down, and plodded through the courtroom to the door like he'd just been whipped. Which, metaphorically speaking, he had been.

* * * *

Father Tom Walsh was in his late seventies, silver-haired, rheumy-eyed, and in possession of an excellent Boston brogue.

"What is your current assignment, Father?" O'Reilly asked to begin his direct examination.

"St. Christine's, down in Marshfield." It came out as *MAASH-field*.

"And how long have you been in the priesthood?"

"Forty…" He thought for a moment. "Forty-six years."

"And back in 1969, do you recall where you were assigned at that time?"

"Yes—St. Margaret's in Lowell."

"Okay. Now, were you aware around September 26 or 27 of the death of a young man found in Lowell?"

"Yes I was."

"Do you recall receiving a phone call at the St. Margaret's rectory shortly after that?"

"Yes."

"Do you have a memory of how long after the boy's death that you got that call?"

"Hm. I think…probably a day or two afterward. I'm not sure on that."

"Do you recall the contents of the call?"

"Well…I remember parts of it, yes. Not the whole thing."

"All right. If you could tell us what you remember, please?"

"Certainly." He took a quick breath. "The person who called said something about reading an article in the paper, and it had disturbed them, or they were distraught by it, something along those lines. They said they wanted to go to the police but they were afraid they were going to get beaten up. I told them if they came to the rectory, I'd, you know, take them to the police so they wouldn't get beaten up. And…that's all. That's all I remember."

Eric noticed that at no time during his recollection of the call did Walsh say that the caller claimed to have killed John McCabe. Eric grabbed Walsh's witness folder—which was thankfully thin—and found the corresponding police report from '69. He scanned it until he found what he was looking for: according to the report, Walsh had said back then that "the caller told him he had killed John McCabe, and he wanted to talk to a priest about it." Eric gave the report to Stan, who was doing Walsh's cross-examination, and whispered to Stan his reason for doing so.

Meanwhile, O'Reilly was already finishing up. "Father, do you have a memory as to whether the voice of the caller was male or female?"

"It was a male."

"And sometime after that, maybe several months later, did the police come to the rectory again?"

"They did."

"And did you listen to a tape recording of a male voice that they provided?"

"Yes, I did."

"Did you recognize the voice as compared to the person who called you?"

"No, I didn't recognize the voice."

"Thank you. Nothing further." O'Reilly sat down, and Stan took his place at the podium.

"Good morning, Father Walsh."

"Morning." *Moah-nin'.*

"I'm Stan Norkunas. I, along with Eric Wilson, represent Mr. Ferreira in these proceedings. You and I have spoken previously, correct?"

"That's correct."

"You were very gracious to allow me to come down to your rectory in Marshfield and speak with you a couple of months back, correct, sir?"

"That's correct," Walsh said again.

"You also brought in one of the archdiocesan attorneys to be present at that meeting, right?"

"Yes sir." Walsh was extremely forthcoming, Eric noted, and exhibited no hostility at all in his answers; he was just telling the truth, and nothing but the truth.

Stan asked Walsh about the regularity of which he received "distress calls" from parishioners—people who'd recently lost loved ones, were having marital problems, or suffered from various addictions. Walsh said he had calls of that nature often; when Stan asked him if a particular call from 1969 stood out as "different" from the others, Walsh was noncommittal. In essence, he said, the caller told him he'd read something in the paper that disturbed him, and he wanted to talk to a priest about it. No mention of the caller confessing to a murder—even though the police report expressly described a direct confession. (*Either he doesn't remember, or the police report is fictitious…or Coughlin got to him*, Eric thought.) Stan made a few more attempts at having Walsh acknowledge the caller's confession, but the priest stood firm. As Walsh left the stand, Eric thought his testimony had been a wash.

* * * *

Detective Linda Coughlin walked purposefully down the courtroom aisle, and when she stopped to be sworn in in front of the clerk, she did so with equal resolve. She took her seat on the stand, and surveyed the room with intelligent, seeking eyes that peered through her long blonde bangs. Whatever transpired during her testimony, her expression declared, she was ready for it.

"Detective Coughlin," O'Reilly said from the podium, "what is your current employment?"

"I'm a police officer with the City of Lowell."

"Your current assignment?"

"I'm a detective in the Criminal Investigations Division." She said with no pride or arrogance—just a simple, factual statement.

"Now, how long have you been a police officer?"

"Nineteen years."

"And did you know a former detective by the name of Gerald Wayne?"

"I did."

"He was a Lowell detective who is now deceased, correct?"

"That's correct."

"Thank you." O'Reilly paused to reference his notes, then looked up at his witness. "Now, in January of 2011, did you take on an assignment as directed by the captain of the criminal bureau?"

"I did."

"And what was that assignment?"

"He asked me to pick up the McCabe homicide investigation."

"Prior to your involvement, who had handled that investigation, if you know?"

Whether it was calculated or not, Coughlin let the tiniest bit of remorse peek through her iron countenance. "Detective Wayne had."

"Had anyone else worked the McCabe case with him?"

"Yes—Lieutenant Tom Sullivan with the Mass State Police."

"And Lieutenant Sullivan continued working the case with you, correct?"

"He did."

"Okay. Now, what were the steps you took when you picked up the investigation?"

"The first thing I did was read the case file, which was quite extensive."

"And when you read through the file, a majority of the reports were from 1969, correct?"

"That's right. Most of them were from the original investigation—from before it became a cold case."

"And during your review of those files, and in your investigation, you were basically trying to analyze those old reports and the thoughts of the detectives—many of whom are dead, correct?"

"Yes, many are deceased."

"Did any names jump out at you when you were going through the files?"

"A lot of names, yes."

Then O'Reilly took Eric—and everyone else, it seemed—by surprise. "Specifically, did you read about an individual by the name of Robert Morley?"

"I saw that, yes." *It's a cautionary move, questioning her about Morley,* Eric thought from the defense table. *O'Reilly knows I'll accuse her of ignoring other suspects, so he's trying to get in front of it.* Eric paid extra-close attention, curious to see where the line of questioning went.

And it didn't go far. Coughlin revealed that Robert Morley's brother had approached police in November of '69 with the belief that Robert may have been involved in the McCabe murder, but the brother had no specific evidence; Robert was brought in for an interview, Coughlin said, but walked out shortly after the questioning began. In essence, she explained, the detectives dismissed Robert Morley as a suspect because there was nothing that directly linked him to the crime.

Then O'Reilly entered into a similarly short line of questioning about Father Cahill, the second priest who'd received an anonymous phone call in the days following the murder. Coughlin said she'd interviewed Cahill in late 2012, and learned that he'd resigned from the priesthood,

323

and that he'd had no memory of receiving an anonymous call in 1969.

O'Reilly then got to the meat of the matter.

"Detective, did you participate in any interviews of Michael Ferreira?"

"No."

"Did you participate in any interviews of Edward Allen Brown?"

"Yes." Everyone in the courtroom, it seemed like, scooted forward in his chair.

"When was the first time you had contact with him?"

"That was in February of 2011."

"And there was a succession of interviews after that?"

"Yes."

"Culminating in him appearing in front of a grand jury?"

"Yes."

"Where did you speak to him the first time?"

They were locked in now. Eric guessed that O'Reilly and Coughlin had rehearsed this line of questioning at least once. "Detective Fenlon and I met him at a Park n' Ride in Salem, New Hampshire."

"How long did that interview last?"

"About forty-five minutes."

"Okay." O'Reilly glanced briefly at his notes. "And your next interview with him was not long after that, on March the 2nd, correct?"

"Yes."

"How long did the interview portion of that day take?" (Though Ed had taken a polygraph on March 2, O'Reilly knew that any mention of lie detector tests was expressly forbidden, and thus he framed his question accordingly.)

"Hm…I'm going to say an hour and a half, maybe."
Eric noticed that Coughlin's answer was the first one she'd
given with any sign of indecision.

"And then there was another interview on March 9. Do
you recall that one?"

"Yes. At the district attorney's office, yes."

"And how long did that one take?"

"Hm…" Coughlin looked away—to the left. *A chink in
the armor,* Eric thought as he looked on. "It was…a few
hours, I'd say."

O'Reilly now came from behind the podium. Either he
felt confident enough to ignore his notes, or he'd
memorized this part. "Detective, at any time during your
interviews with Mr. Brown, were promises made to him?"

"No, there were not."

"Did Mr. Brown inquire of you as to what was going
to happen?"

"Well, at one point, yes—he assumed he was being
arrested."

"At any point during your interviews did you threaten
him with arrest?"

'No. Well—on March 2, when I gave him a subpoena
for the grand jury, I told him that if he failed to appear, a
warrant would be issued for his arrest for failure to appear.
That's the only time."

"Other than that concerning the subpoena, was he ever
threatened with arrest?"

She smiled slightly. "He was never threatened,
period."

"At any point—you showed him photographs,
correct?"

"I showed him *a* photograph."

"At any point did you feed him information about the investigation?"

"Never."

"At one point, did you tell Mr. Brown how his name came into the investigation?"

"Yes."

"What did you say to him about that?"

"I told him that Michael Ferreira had said they were together on September 26th of 1969."

"At any point did you tell Mr. Brown that Michael Ferreira had implicated him in the death of John McCabe?"

"Absolutely not. I did not."

"At any point did you tell Mr. Brown that Walter Shelley had said he was with Ed Brown on the night of the 26th?"

"I did not say that."

"At any time did you tell Mr. Brown that Walter Shelley had implicated him in the death of John McCabe?"

"I did not."

"One moment please, Your Honor," O'Reilly said as he walked back to the podium. Once there, he looked at his notes for a moment, then: "Nothing further at this time, Your Honor."

"Okay," Judge Ricciardone said, and looked at Eric. "Counsel?"

Eric shot out of his chair. He knew Detective Coughlin would antagonize him at every turn, so he wanted to meet her head-on. And throughout his cross, he wanted to show the jury that during her investigation, she didn't play fairly—that she'd "solved" the crime according to what she believed happened. So with no prelude, no mannered greeting, he went after her right out of the gate.

"Detective, these interviews with Ed Brown on March 2 and March 9: you chose not to record those, didn't you?"

Coughlin seemed as stunned as anyone. "Ah—" Her mouth hung open for a moment, then snapped shut. Her face set in indignation: "That's not true."

"There's a policy of the Lowell Police Department wherein all interviews, whether with suspects or witnesses, will be recorded unless the subject doesn't want it recorded. True?"

"That's from the—no. That's not my und—"

"Is it the policy of the Lowell Police Department to record all interviews so that there's a record of the discussion?"

"You're taking a form out of context." She paused briefly to gather herself. "You're referring to the *Miranda* form; on the bottom of that form there's a section that asks whether or not a suspect chooses to have the interview recorded."

"And in fact, the suspect has to say, 'No, I don't want this recorded,' for you not to record it, true?"

"That's true, they say yes or no."

Eric stood motionless. Softly, he said: "You never asked Ed Brown if he refused to be recorded, did you?"

"I didn't know he was a suspect until after he confessed."

"Wha…" Eric's mouth literally hung open for an instant. "You—you didn't know he was a *suspect*?"

"That's right."

"I…" Eric was standing in front of the podium, and now he took a step back to grab Coughlin's witness folder off it as he talked. "Detective: on March 2nd of 2011 you began interviewing Mr. Brown"—he rifled through the

327

folder's contents until he found the relevant report—"at 10:00 a.m., right?"

"Yes."

"And what time did he leave that day?"

"Um…I'm not exactly sure, but it was sometime in the afternoon."

"Okay. And are you suggesting that during that interrogation, you never made accusations that Mr. Brown had information, or that he was involved in John McCabe's death?"

And here it was: Coughlin could again paint the picture she wanted others to see. She said: "I thought he was not being truthful with me. Did I know what he knew at that time? No. I—"

"That's not my question, Detective. My question to you is: didn't you tell Ed Brown that *you* believed he was involved in the homicide of John McCabe?"

"I told him I believed he was lying to me."

"And what you thought he was lying about was when he said, 'I have no involvement.' Right?"

"No, that's not exactly what happened. He—"

"Well, we'll never know—it wasn't recorded, was it?"

"No, it wasn't."

"You told him on March 2, 'You're lying. You do know about the murder of John McCabe.' Right?" Eric was trying to control himself, and keep the cross-examination from turning into a full-blown argument. And it was difficult.

"He denied even knowing that a murder took place." Coughlin was having her own difficulty staying in control. "I didn't believe that."

"No, that's—" Eric almost groaned aloud. "Not 2007, when Detective Wayne and Lieutenant Sullivan questioned him. Let's focus on March 2, okay?"

"Okay."

"On March the 2nd, Detective…" Eric took a deep breath. "You talked to Mr. Brown at length about his knowledge of the murder. Right, Detective?"

"I didn't—I asked him—" Coughlin's agitation grew. "I don't understand what you're asking me, or what you're trying to get me to say, but—"

"I want you to tell me the truth, Detec—"

"That's *all* I'll tell you, sir." Eric and Coughlin stared each other down, each of their faces set. After a moment, her eyes never leaving Eric's, Coughlin said: "I had a discussion with Mr. Brown. And I didn't believe him."

"And so he wasn't a suspect, is that what you're honestly telling us?"

"He *became* a suspect, yes."

"And you never read him *Miranda*, did you?"

"He was advised of *Miranda*, yes."

"When? When was he advised?"

"He—" Coughlin paused. "He was advised of *Miranda* at our meeting at the district attorney's office."

"It's the policy of your department to record interviews when *Miranda* is given, right?"

"That form is read to the individual, yes."

Eric froze again, and smiled. "So with Mr. Brown, did you just skip over the part on the *Miranda* form where it asks about recording the interview?"

"I—" Coughlin wilted slightly. "No."

"You never verbally asked Mr. Brown if he didn't want to be recorded, did you?"

"Correct."

"Thank you." *Another bite of the apple.* Eric looked down at the notes he'd scrawled during O'Reilly's direct examination of her. "I want to cover some things you talked about on direct, then I'll get to my prepared stuff." He looked back up. "You indicated to this jury that Ed Brown's name was mentioned by Michael Ferreira, right?"

"Yes."

And for the next two hours, Eric and Detective Coughlin verbally sparred over a variety of seemingly infinitesimal matters—but as was Eric's style, he made sure to cover each and every detail. And in this bout, Linda Coughlin was a much more formidable foe than Ed Brown; each time Eric revealed that Coughlin had pursued the case according to her own beliefs, the detective countered with seemingly logical, "truthful" reasons why she'd done so.

Eric first expanded on the issue of Mike's mention of being with Ed the night of the murder—which Mike had done during his 2008 grand jury testimony—and Eric contrasted that with Mike's original statement in 1969, during which Mike had never mentioned Ed's name. Eric asked Coughlin whether Mike had been allowed to review his 1969 statement prior to his '08 grand jury testimony; when Coughlin said Mike hadn't, Eric suggested that since Mike and Ed were friends at that time (meaning they spent a good bit of time together, particularly on Friday nights), during Mike's 2008 statement he might have confused the night of September 26 with numerous other evenings from 1969. To this, Coughlin was basically nonresponsive.

Then Eric accused Coughlin of investigating the case with blinders on.

"You began this investigation with the presumption that Walter Shelley and Michael Ferreira were the primary suspects, didn't you?"

"I knew they were suspects, yes."

"There were a number of investigative reports and materials that you either overlooked or didn't even know about, true?"

"I don't know what you're referring to."

"How about Richard Santos?"

Coughlin pursed her lips. "Okay."

"You didn't even know about Richard Santos till well over a year after Michael was arrested. In fact, three months ago is the first time you ever heard Richard Santos's name, right?"

"True."

"And information on Richard Santos was right there in your office the whole time, wasn't it?"

"I don't…what information are you referring to?"

"Do you recall late September of 2012 when you, me, Mr. O'Reilly, and Lieutenant Sullivan were going through discovery materials in your office?"

"Yes."

"And you permitted me to look through boxes of Gerry Wayne's material?"

"Yes."

"Do you remember the document I found in one box regarding Richard Santos?"

"I—" Her mouth snapped shut. "Do I remember that specifically? No."

"Prior to that, you hadn't even heard the name, had you?"

"I may have read it, I don't know. There is a Santos mentioned in the case file, but I'm not sure."

"The Santos mentioned in the file is in the document you hadn't seen before I showed it to you, right?"

"I…I don't really know." *Another bite.*

"Well, in your decision to identify Mike and Walter Shelley as the suspects, you hadn't evaluated Richard Santos at that point, had you?"

"I would say I picked up where Detective Wayne left off." This led to a line of questioning during which Eric had Coughlin admit—begrudgingly—that she'd not looked into suspects like Santos, Robert Morley, or the caller to the priests until late 2012, most likely in preparation for the Ferreira trial.

As Eric's cross progressed, it became a battle of wills. Eric asked about John's belt (and the fact that the caller to the priests said he had it), and Coughlin countered with the knowledge that the caller's statement may have been coincidence, and it had never been proved that John had even worn a belt that night. Next Eric revisited the Richard Santos evidence, and pointed out that Coughlin had only recently reviewed the Santos case file from 1974; though Coughlin agreed that she hadn't looked at the file until just before the trial, she said it didn't contain enough similarities to the McCabe homicide to warrant further review.

Eric had just finished having Coughlin acknowledge that no physical evidence existed connecting Mike to the murder, when Judge Ricciardone stopped the proceedings for the lunch break. Eric—along with Coughlin and the entire prosecution team—took a deep breath. Because the fight was still in the early rounds.

* * * *

Before the jurors were brought in after lunch, Judge Ricciardone had an on-the-record discussion with both the prosecution and defense concerning a single piece of physical evidence: the insurance card belonging to Robert Morley, which had been found in an evidence box with no explanation of why it was there. (The judge's discussion was a continuation of a pre-trial hearing about third-party culprit evidence, during which O'Reilly and Eric had argued at length over what evidence should be presented to the jury.) In essence, Ricciardone said, he would not allow the insurance card (or any mention of it) to be introduced, because its origin could not be confirmed. Though Eric was disappointed, it was a ruling he'd expected, and was a minor detail (even by Eric's standards).

Once Detective Coughlin was back on the witness stand, Eric continued his cross—and the more he explored the flaws in her investigation, the harder Coughlin dug in her heels. He asked about the cars the 1969 railroad tower employees had owned, and mentioned that one of the employees' cars had been a dark-colored mid-'60s Chevy sedan similar to the one Barry Moran had testified to seeing (and similar to Walter Shelley's vehicle); Coughlin acknowledged that she'd seen the report with that detail, but again questioned its relevance. Then Eric inquired as to why, after Mike's "joke" confession during the 1969 Pelham beer run, he'd never been asked about it again—not in the original investigation, nor during the 2003 interview with Sullivan and Wayne, nor at his 2008 grand jury hearing. Coughlin simply said she didn't know why.

Then at last, Eric arrived at perhaps his most crucial line of questioning: Coughlin's interrogation of Ed Brown on March 9, 2011. He skirted around the subject first, asking her about interview techniques (and her training in them); when he asked if it was important not to impose beliefs upon a suspect, meaning the suspect might adopt those beliefs, Coughlin wholeheartedly agreed. At that, Eric pounced.

"But on March 9 with Mr. Brown, that's exactly what you did, isn't it?" And the battle intensified.

"Absolutely not, sir."

"Mr. Brown told five or six versions of what happened that night, right?"

"He told some different versions in which he minimized his involvement, yes."

"Okay. Then after he told you all those versions, you told him he was lying. And you confronted him with your beliefs, didn't you?"

"No." And here, Coughlin seemed to shape her story even more. "What I told him was that I didn't believe what he was telling me."

"Then why—" Eric grabbed a report off the podium and walked hurriedly over to the stand, asking, "Approach the witness, Your Honor?" almost as an afterthought. Once there, he showed Coughlin the report she'd written— mainly from memory, nearly seven weeks later—detailing the March 9 interrogation. "Detective, this is what you wrote in your report regarding this unrecorded interrogation on March 9. Your words: 'He was confronted with our beliefs.' Right?"

She examined it briefly, then: "He was confronted with the belief that I thought he was lying. That's exactly what that says."

"I'll read the entire sentence: 'He was told he was lying. He was confronted with our beliefs, and he eventually admitted that he was in fact lying.' Detective, when you used the words 'He was confronted with our beliefs' in this report, you're not talking about what you thought happened out in that field?"

"I'm talking about the fact that he was lying. *That's* what I confronted him with."

"Detective." He said it as if he were talking to an eight-year-old girl with a dirty bedroom who'd just said she'd cleaned it. "When I read this report—well, when *anybody* reads it, the inference is that you told him what you thought happened. Do you understand why that assumption is made?"

"Yes. And you can assume whatever you want, sir. But again, what I confronted him with was his dishonesty."

"If you thought he was lying, and confronted him about it, why didn't you specify that in the report?"

"I...I believe I did. What someone infers from what I wrote, that's their business. But I stand by what I said."

"It's hard to be exact when you wait two months to write a report from memory, isn't it?"

"Objection," O'Reilly said as he started to stand, but Eric waved him off. "Withdrawn," Eric said.

Figuring he'd hopefully made his point with the jury, Eric moved on. Eric asked about the March 9 interrogation report itself, and Coughlin said she'd written it using her memory and using notes she and Sullivan had made that day; when Eric asked where those notes were, she said that like she usually did after writing an official report, she'd destroyed them. (*Convenient*, Eric thought but did not say.) When Eric asked about how she'd developed her theory of

motive—again, Walter's jealousy over Marla Shiner—
Coughlin explained that she'd gotten it from reading the
case files. To that, Eric wondered aloud if she remembered
reading Marla's name in any report prior to Jack Ward's
2002 interview, during which *he'd* postulated the "jealousy
over Marla" theory; Coughlin agreed that the 2002 report
was the first time.

"Yet in one report, you wrote that Marla Shiner and
jealousy—and I quote—'were always considered the
motive.' Right?"

She faltered a bit. "I…I may have written that, yes."

"Can you point out any report before Jack Ward is
interviewed where jealousy over Marla is mentioned?"

"I don't know if I can."

"Then why would you write in your report that Shiner
and jealousy was always considered the motive?"

Coughlin took a slow, deep breath. "I'm not exactly
sure." *Crunch—another bite.* Eric was on a roll now, so he
revealed the same scenario—that Coughlin had advanced
Jack Ward's theories as facts—as it related to *The French
Connection* and to the rumor that John had been hogtied.
And here, Coughlin had nowhere to hide, so she, in
essence, agreed that she'd done so. Eric decided that he'd
finish on a winning note, so he ended his cross there. As
Detective Coughlin left the stand, Eric followed her with
his eyes, thinking: *I'd call that a drawn match.*

The rest of the afternoon consisted of a reading of
portions of Mike Ferreira's 2008 grand jury testimony,
during which he'd told a different version of his
movements on September 26, 1969, than what he'd told
detectives in his interview immediately after the murder.
The transcript of the 1969 interview had been read

verbatim by Linda (King) Locklear during her direct testimony on the second day of trial, so Eric figured the Commonwealth's strategy was to show the contrast between Mike's 1969 statements and his 2008 grand jury testimony.

So with O'Reilly reading his own questions from the grand jury hearing, and A.D.A. John Mulcahy reading Mike's answers, the Commonwealth recounted Mike's statements: he and Nancy Williams had picked up John shortly before 8:00 p.m. and given him a ride to Chandler and Main; Mike had then gone home for a bit, but went to the K of C dance at about 9:30 to "see what was going on." He met up with Nancy, who *had* attended the dance, and they went back to Nancy's house in her car. After being at Nancy's for about fifteen minutes, Mike had testified, Walter Shelley and Ed Brown had arrived in Ed's car. The three boys had gotten in Walter's car, which was parked at Nancy's house; they'd gone to pick up Marla at the K of C dance, then headed over to South Lowell to get cigarettes, then dropped Marla off at her home. The boys had made a trip to Waltham to get beer, then Walter had dropped Mike off at his house, where he'd gone to bed.

The Commonwealth was successful in showing that Mike's 2008 version of events differed drastically from his 1969 statement (or anyone else's version, for that matter). But Eric had anticipated this. So his plan—some of which he'd already put into effect with previous witnesses—was to show that after so many years had passed, nobody could be expected to remember details of a given night without confusing their own memories.

Everyone involved with the Ferreira trial—Eric, Stan, Mike, the prosecution team, the jurors, even Judge

Ricciardone—was glad when court adjourned that day, as it had been a long one. The Commonwealth was nearly finished presenting its case; now Eric had to decide who he should call as defense witnesses. And the biggest question of all: should Mike Ferreira testify or not?

EX PARTE: Trial Day 5 → Day 6

"So far, so good." I remember that being the sort of "theme" for Stan's and my ride home after trial that Tuesday. What was most pressing on my mind at that point was how to explain the departure in Mike's memory from his 1969 statement to police when he testified in the 2008 grand jury. Listen: I don't know about you, but I can't remember details of a particular day from *one* year ago, much less four decades. So my plan was to cross Lieutenant Sullivan (whom O'Reilly said would testify the next day) about not allowing Mike to review his 1969 statement prior to the 2008 hearing. I'd point out that he, Coughlin, and other detectives reviewed all the old statements available when preparing for court—mainly to refresh their memory. And in 2008, when Mike wasn't allowed to do that, he confused that night with other nights. Simple as that.

O'Reilly told me that prior to calling Sullivan, who would be the last witness before the Commonwealth rested, we'd hear from retired Deputy Chief Walter Jamieson. He was the man who, back when he'd been a patrolman, had driven Bill McCabe around looking for John the night of the murder. But more importantly, he'd worked extensively on the Richard Santos case in 1974, so I wanted to question him about that, hopefully to have him reveal that Santos had been a suspect in the McCabe homicide.

Then it would be our turn. Since Marla Shiner had already testified, I planned to first call Nancy (Williams) Ferreira. My main objective with Nancy was to have her reveal that, without reviewing her prior statements, her only independent memory of that night was that she, her sister, and Mike—who'd only been a friend at the time—had given John a ride from the novitiate to Main Street. So I hoped to show that, like Mike's, her memory was simply exhausted. I also wanted to portray to the jury that when she'd given her original statement in 1969, she'd told police that Walter and Mike had been with her and some other kids—meaning they couldn't have picked up Ed Brown and done the things to which he'd testified.

Then we'd call Mike Richard. Stan would examine him, and though it wouldn't be lengthy testimony, it would be tricky: he'd recently reneged on what he'd told me he remembered about that night—basically, that he'd seen Mike and Walter in Tewksbury around 11:30, making him the perfect alibi witness—and we figured he'd follow suit on the stand. But our hope was to somehow introduce his original 1969 statement, then give the jury a clue as to why he "couldn't" remember it.

Then, our last witness would be Dr. Thomas Andrew. But before I explain about him, let me tell you about our decision to not have Mike Ferreira testify. After numerous discussions about it, we decided he would not take the stand. In essence, we thought, it might do more harm than good. Mike was prepared to testify, and he and I had spent a lot of time prepping for his testimony, but by the time the Commonwealth rested, I figured I'd done a pretty good job explaining Mike's disparity between his various statements about the events of that night. Simply put, he just didn't remember. So the benefit of him testifying in his own defense was outweighed by the prospect of O'Reilly grilling him about his exhausted memory in open court.

My hope for Dr. Andrew was to let his credibility speak for itself. Our greatest asset in having him testify last was that he didn't have a dog in the fight—he would testify only to his knowledge of the medical evidence. So when the jurors started their deliberations after closing arguments, I wanted his testimony to be one they'd be remembering most.

6. Wednesday, January 23: Ferreira Trial, Day Six

Last day of testimony.

At least, that's what the Commonwealth and the defense both hoped. The last witness to testify would be Dr. Andrew, the defense's medical expert, and he wouldn't be available to continue the next day. So Eric and O'Reilly (and Stan, who would perform the cross of Walter Jamieson and the direct of Mike Richard) had agreed to keep things moving, and had alerted Judge Ricciardone of their plan to do so. As a disciplinarian regarding scheduling, the judge had been happy to accommodate them; likewise, he told them he would, if needed, ask the jurors to stay for a few extra minutes. In the end, though, the overtime wasn't necessary.

Walter Jamieson was first up, and he took the stand wearing a powder blue shirt, a maroon tie, and a shiny brown leather jacket; he had neatly combed silver hair parted on the side and an easy-going, affable personality. (Essentially, he resembled a seventy-year-old Fonzie.) O'Reilly got right to it. Jamieson had retired in 2002, he said, after a thirty-five-year career with Tewksbury PD; he'd started as a patrolman in '68, became a detective in '73, and was named deputy chief in '89. As a patrolman, he recalled, he'd driven Bill McCabe around in his cruiser looking for John the night of the murder; when O'Reilly asked if he remembered what the weather had been like that night, Jamieson said that it had been misty.

"No rain, if you recall?" O'Reilly asked him.

"No rain, best of my recollection," Jamieson responded.

The majority of O'Reilly's questioning, though, was about the 1974 abduction/rape case involving Richard Santos, on which Jamieson had worked as a detective. After he gave some details of the crime, O'Reilly asked if Jamieson and other detectives from nearby jurisdictions had found any connection between the '74 case and the McCabe murder. Jamieson said there had been no link between the two.

On cross, Stan had Jamieson acknowledge that even though it had only been misting in the early morning hours of September 27, there was enough moisture present for Jamieson to turn on the windshield wipers in his cruiser. Then Stan asked about specific details of the McCabe case, like the color of the adhesive tape over John's eyes and mouth, and the possibility that John had been hitchhiking, and Jamieson's answers to those questions were shaky at best. This was a smart bit of strategy on Stan's part: next he asked Jamieson if he'd met with O'Reilly any time *after* Ed Brown's March 2011 "confession" to discuss the details Stan had just asked him about—and Jamieson said he had, "several times." Stan finished by having Jamieson concede that, though they'd originally found no link between John's murder and Santos's abduction/rape, numerous similarities—rope, adhesive tape, the dumping of the victim near railroad tracks—had in fact existed.

* * * *

As Lieutenant Tom Sullivan was being sworn in, an uninformed spectator might think that Mr. Clean was taking the stand. The thirty-one-year Massachusetts State Police veteran was burly and bald...but it was his keen mind and his steadfast sense of logic that made him such a first-rate detective. And it was Sullivan's rational sensibility upon which the Commonwealth hoped to capitalize as its last witness.

Sullivan began his testimony by saying that he was a twelve-year-old living in Tewksbury at the time of the murder, and that he knew about the crime, but didn't personally know John McCabe. O'Reilly asked him about how he'd first gotten involved in the McCabe homicide case, and Sullivan said it had been in 2000 at the request of Detective Wayne.

O'Reilly: "Now, when you and Detective Wayne were reviewing the material, did you decide to interview anyone?"

"Yes."

"Do you recall, in the early 2000s, any of the names of people you interviewed?"

"Yes." Sullivan paused briefly to think, and looked down and to the right before looking back at the attorney to answer—a tendency he would exhibit throughout his testimony. This mannerism was lost on no one, particularly Eric. *Credible guy,* Eric thought. *Let's see what happens when I confront him with the truth.* "We interviewed Jack Ward," Sullivan said, "Brian Gath, Marla Shiner, and Michael Ferreira back in the early 2000s."

"Do you recall the date you interviewed Mr. Ferreira?"

"Yes—October 30th of 2003."

"Do you see that man in court today?"

"I do."

"Could you point him out and describe what he's wearing, please?"

Sullivan pointed at Mike, who simply stared stone-faced back at the lieutenant. "He's seated at the defense table with a yellow shirt and a beige-colored jacket."

"May the record reflect the witness pointing to and describing the defendant, Your Honor?"

"Yes," the judge said.

"Where did you speak with Mr. Ferreira?"

"At his home in Salem, New Hampshire." O'Reilly continued the line of questioning, asking about specifics of the interview. When he inquired of Sullivan about what Mike recalled concerning the night of the murder, Sullivan gave a detailed answer.

"He said it was a Friday night—he was with Walter. They went to Waltham to clean a restaurant. The other guy with them was Ed Brown." At that, over at the defense table Mike quickly leaned over and started whispering to Eric, who stopped him with an *I know* gesture. Meanwhile, Sullivan continued. "He believed that someone else was with them. They went to Cunningham's to buy cigarettes…he thinks it was Walter and someone else. He was not sure of the time that they were out, only saying it was late at night."

"Did Nancy say anything at this point?"

"I believe she said she was home all night." O'Reilly asked about other parts of the 2003 interview, and Sullivan said Mike had told him and Wayne that he'd been interviewed multiple times immediately following the murder, that Marla had been Walter's girlfriend, and that Walter had beat her. Then O'Reilly asked if Sullivan and Mike had discussed the '97 pig roast (they had), and whether he'd interviewed Marla Shiner (yes to that too, in 2003).

Then O'Reilly asked: "Did you participate in any interviews of Ed Brown?"

"I spoke with Ed Brown, yes."

"How many times, if you recall?"

"Twice, I believe."

"When was the first time?"

Sullivan paused, looked down, then back up. "That was in the fall of 2007."

"And the second time?"

"That was in March of 2011."

"Lieutenant," O'Reilly said as he came from behind the podium to stand in front of it, "in any of the conversations you were involved in, or observed, was Ed Brown ever threatened?"

His eyes were locked on O'Reilly. "No."

"Was he ever promised anything?"

"No."

"Was he ever fed evidence as to what happened?"

"No."

O'Reilly paused to reference his notes, then: "Nothing further at this time, Your Honor."

"Okay," the judge said. To Eric: "Would you like to inquire?"

Eric stood. "Yes, Your Honor." He walked to the podium. "Good morning, Lieutenant."

"Good morning, sir." Sullivan's face was totally blank.

Eric addressed the discrepancies in Sullivan's (and by extension, Detective Coughlin's) investigation right away. "You were asked a question just a minute ago by Mr. O'Reilly regarding whether Ed Brown was ever fed any information, right?"

"That's correct."

"Do you remember writing a report regarding the interview with Jack Ward in 2003?"

"Yes."

"In that report, Lieutenant, you wrote that Jack Ward told you about the movie *The French Connection*, and being at the Wamesit Drive-In in 1969, correct?"

Pause to look down. "I believe he told me he was at the Wamesit in 1969 and he believed the movie was *The French Connection*. Yes."

"And he told you he knew John McCabe was tied up just like what happened in that movie, right?"

"Did you tell anybody about *The French Connection* and the tie-up of John McCabe?"

Pause. "I'm not sure."

"Okay. You…you were assigned at that time, as you are now, to the Middlesex District Attorney's office, right?"

"That's correct."

"You knew Mr. O'Reilly, right?" Eric pointed to the prosecutor.

"Yes."

"Thank you." Eric simply looked at the jurors momentarily, allowing the mere suggestion to do its work, then he moved on. He asked if, when Sullivan joined the McCabe case in 2000, he'd reviewed all the case information (including the crime scene photos); when Sullivan said he had, Eric explored that further.

"There was nothing—no police report, no crime scene evidence, forensic evidence, no autopsy report—that ever suggested John was hogtied, true?"

Pause, downward look. "You're asking prior to my involvement?"

"Yes. You reviewed all the information from 1969 to 2000, which included the crime scene photographs, didn't you?"

"Yes."

"There was no suggestion from those photos, or from any other report, that establish anything about John being hogtied, is there?"

"Correct, there is not."

"Lieutenant, do you know when the first time the word 'hogtied' was ever used in this investigation?"

"I believe it was in newspaper articles back when the murder ha—"

"I'm not talking about those. I'm talking about reliable, credible sources. Police reports, photos…*official* sources. Do you know the first time hogtying was ever mentioned in an official capacity?"

Longer pause this time. One could practically hear the cogs spinning in Sullivan's brain as he looked down to think. After he raised his head again: "I do not."

"Could it have been by Mr. O'Reilly when he was questioning you in front of the grand jury in 2008?"

"That's possible, yes."

Eric walked quickly to the witness stand with a file, asking, "Approach the witness, Your Honor?" as he went. When he got there: "Page 32 of your grand jury testimony transcript." He showed Sullivan the page. "Mr. O'Reilly asked you, 'In other words, the rope had been around his neck, *hogtied* to his ankles, correct?'" Eric looked at Sullivan. "Do you remember that question?"

"I do."

"And your response, sir"—he pointed at the page— "was: 'I believe so at the time he was found.' Right?"

"Correct."

Eric started back to the podium. "Lieutenant, why would you say that when you knew from the scene photos, from all the documentation, that nobody ever proved—why would you say 'I believe so' when Mr. O'Reilly asked if John was hogtied?"

Sullivan was unfazed. "I cleared up that error right afterwards."

"You did, in the next line of questions. You backtracked and said, 'I'm not sure if he was hogtied.' But—"

"Correct. I'm not certain he was hogtied, sir."

At that, Eric sneaked a glance at the jury. Then: "But…you were asked if any information was ever fed to Ed Brown. And when Mr. O'Reilly suggested that John was hogtied, your first response was to agree with him, right?"

"It appears that way, yes."

Eric paused, then softened a bit. "It was almost as if Mr. O'Reilly was feeding *you* information. Right?"

"I don't agree with that, sir."

"Hm. Okay," Eric said dismissively, and moved on. He asked more questions about the 2002 interview with Jack Ward, and Sullivan conceded that prior to that interview, no "official" mention had ever been made of hogtying. Nor, Sullivan admitted, had anyone ever offered the "Walter's jealousy over Marla" theory of motive until Jack Ward had. *Crunch.*

Then Eric circled back to the subject of Mike's 2003 interview; Eric's focus this time, though, was exhausted memory. He had Sullivan acknowledge that at that interview, Mike hadn't discussed the night of September 26, 1969, in thirty-four years. And, Eric pointed out, Sullivan and other detectives had reviewed Mike's prior statements—as they often did with their own—but Mike hadn't been allowed to refresh his own memory.

In the midst of this line of questioning, Eric inquired about an interesting item.

"Lieutenant, you took notes at that meeting, right?"

"Yes."

"Four pages of notes, correct?"

"Yes."

"Again: that meeting with Mr. Ferreira took place in October of 2003, right?"

"Yes."

"Lieutenant, you waited eight years to write the report regarding that meeting, didn't you?"

"Yes, I did."

"Okay. And it's no coincidence that the date of that report is March the 9th, 2011, right?"

"That's the date of it, yes."

"That's the same day that Ed Brown told you…a story about what happened that night, isn't it?"

"It is."

"Lieutenant, why would you wait so long to write that report?"

Downward look, then: "I'm not sure. It may be because Detective Wayne and I were confused about who would write them."

Eric was prepared for exactly that answer. "Possibly. Or—*or*—could it have been because you, sir, didn't think there was anything there?"

"That's not the case."

"You figured writing a report about the Mike Ferreira interview was a waste of time, didn't you?"

Another quick look down to think. "I don't have a plausible answer for that, sir."

"Thank you, Lieutenant." *Cruuunch.*

The cross-examination went on, Eric and Sullivan discussing even the barest minutiae of Sullivan's (and again by extension, Wayne's and Coughlin's) investigation. One point of interest was in Sullivan's report on the 2003 Mike Ferreira interview: in Sullivan's notes, Eric pointed out, he'd written the words "Allen Brown, Londonderry or Derry, first name Edward"—but Sullivan had written that in the margin of the page, not amongst the actual notes, which suggested that the words in the margin were possibly written at a later date.

"There is no suggestion in your notes—at least, the ones taken contemporaneously with the Mike Ferreira interview—that he and Ed Brown were together that night, is there?"

"No."

"In fact, in those contemporaneous notes, there's no mention of Ed Brown at all—only his name and location written off in the margin, right?"

"Correct."

Eric also repeatedly established the fact that Mike's original 1969 statement about the events of September 26 differed from those of his 2003 interview and his 2008 grand jury testimony (which were actually different themselves). This was not due to any grand cover-up by Mike and others, Eric revealed through his questions, only to a confused memory. One glaring example of this lack of recall was that when Sullivan interviewed him, Mike didn't remember his mother being present when he gave his statement in '69, even though it had been previously established that she was there. Mike didn't remember details of the night of September 26, Eric declared, because there was nothing memorable about it.

Then, finally, Eric arrived at his last line of questioning.

"Lieutenant, you've taken part in hundreds, if not thousands of interviews, right?"

"Yes, sir."

You've had extensive training in the do's and don'ts of interview techniques, correct?"

"I have."

"If you're interviewing—or interrogating—a suspect in a crime, there are some things you don't want to do, right?"

"Correct."

"You would not, for example, want to confront a suspect with your beliefs about how a crime happened, would you?"

"No."

"Okay. Because, if you do that, you may be transferring facts to that witness or suspect, and they may just adopt your theory, right?"

"That's possible, yes."

"Lieutenant, did you participate in the March 9, 2011 interrogation of Ed Brown?"

Sullivan looked down for a moment. "Well, I was there. I wouldn't say I really participated, but I was present, yes."

"Did you ask Ed any questions?"

"Yes…but only one or two."

"Who asked most of the questions?"

"Detective Coughlin. It was her investigation at that point, so she controlled the interview."

Eric couldn't have given a better answer himself. "No further questions, Your Honor," he said, and took his seat.

The judge asked O'Reilly if he wanted a redirect, and the prosecutor said he did. He simply stood at his table during the exchange.

"Lieutenant, Mr. Wilson suggested that there was no indication of the word 'hogtied' being used prior to it being mentioned by me in 2008, is that right?"

"Correct."

"Had someone else besides Jack Ward mentioned it to you prior to 2008?"

"Yes."

"And who was that?"

"Marla Shiner."

"When you interviewed her by telephone in 2003, correct?"

"Correct."

"Do you recall exactly what she said?"

"She said: 'I heard he'—meaning John—'had been hogtied.'"

"Nothing further." O'Reilly sat down. Eric popped up an instant later, not waiting for Judge Ricciardone's prompting.

"Marla Shiner said she *heard* John had been hogtied, correct?"

"That's correct."

"What she heard was based on a rumor, wasn't it?"

"I don't know what it was based on."

"But prior to that, no reports or evidence—*official* reports, I mean—had ever suggested that John had been hogtied. Correct, sir?"

"Correct."

"Thank you, Your Honor." Eric sat again. O'Reilly said he had no rebuttal, so Lieutenant Sullivan left the witness stand and exited through the gallery. As he passed by the attorneys' tables, Eric noticed Sullivan slow a bit and give him a single nod, his face blank as he did so. (The prosecution team he ignored completely.) The gesture bewildered Eric; whether it was out of respect, or a sign of neutrality, or something else entirely, Eric wasn't sure…but he interpreted it as a positive thing. As Eric watched, Sullivan exited the rear door without another look.

After he was gone, O'Reilly stood. He announced regally: "The Commonwealth rests, Your Honor."

"Thank you," Judge Ricciardone said, then addressed the jurors. "The Commonwealth rests. That may be something you've heard before…what it means is that the prosecution has finished presenting the evidence they want you to see and hear in support of the indictment. I'm going to hear from the attorneys on a matter; it should take no more than fifteen minutes, so you'll have a brief recess, then we'll all resume again after we're done. Thank you." At that, a bailiff showed the jurors out.

"All right," Ricciardone said after the last alternate juror was through the door. "Upon the conclusion of the Commonwealth's case, it's my understanding the defendant moves for a required finding." He looked at the defense table. "Do you want to be heard?"

"Yes, Your Honor," Stan said as he stood. And for the next several minutes, he and O'Reilly debated whether the Commonwealth had presented sufficient evidence to support the murder indictment. It was a routine motion filed by the defense in criminal trials in Massachusetts (and some other states) asking a judge to render a not guilty verdict after the prosecution finished presenting its case; only in extremely rare instances did a judge actually announce a "required finding" of not guilty, but the defense went through the motions of asking for it nonetheless.

And as everyone expected, Judge Ricciardone announced that the trial would continue. After Stan and O'Reilly (the latter assisted by young A.D.A. Mulcahy, who'd apparently been tasked with researching the "required finding" statutes) discussed the merits of the possible jury findings—murder in the first degree, murder in the second degree, or felony murder in the second degree—Ricciardone kept things moving.

"It's now 12:30. Do you have witnesses you want to present, Mr. Wilson?"

"Yes, Your Honor," Eric said. "We have three. Like we talked about, we should be able to finish up with them today."

"Okay," the judge said. "Why don't you bring your first witness in, and we'll get started on them before the lunch break?"

Once the jurors were back in place, Ricciardone nodded to Eric, who stood and said, "The defense calls Nancy Ferreira."

Nancy entered through the gallery door and made her way to the stand, stopping to take the oath from the clerk; she was visibly nervous, but the two hours she'd spent with Eric prepping for her testimony the previous evening had steeled her countenance. Still, she boosted herself onto the witness stand with a hand that shook slightly, and her expression was one of mild nausea.

"Good morning, Mrs. Ferreira," Eric said, a gentle smile on his face. (Nancy simply answered with a brief, forced smile of her own.) "Could you please introduce yourself to the jury?"

"Hi, everyone," Nancy said in the general direction of the jury box. "I'm Nancy Ferreira. I'm the defendant's wife."

"Where do you reside, Mrs. Ferreira?"

"Salem, New Hampshire."

"What is your maiden name?"

"Williams."

"How long have you lived in Salem?"

"Thirteen years."

"And how long have you been married to Mike?"

She smiled over at her husband. "It'll be thirty years this year."

"And when did you two start dating?"

"I think it was in 1975."

Eric went on, asking her about growing up in Tewksbury. Hers was a close-knit neighborhood, she said, with all the families—the Richards, the Wards, the McFrederies—spending plenty of time together. She knew John McCabe, she added, but they weren't close. Then Eric quickly arrived at the subject of September 26, 1969.

"Do you have a general memory of any events from that day, or that evening?"

"That evening I picked up John McCabe by the novitiate and gave him a ride to the corner of Chandler Street and Main."

"Was anybody with you at that time?"

"Yes."

"Who was with you?"

"My sister Sandy, and Michael Ferreira."

"Do you remember where you were going?"

"To Sandy's house, to take her home."

"And where did she live?"

"On Pond Street, in Lowell."

"Okay." He came from behind the podium. "Mrs. Ferreira, do you have any other memory of that night, independent from what you've just told us?"

"I do not."

Eric then inquired of Nancy's memory of the statement she gave police in the days following the murder; the line of questioning was repeatedly interrupted by objections from O'Reilly about whether Nancy should be allowed to review the report on the stand, since she said she'd looked at it with Eric the night before to refresh her memory. In the end, the objections didn't matter, as Nancy remembered the contents of the report just fine.

Nancy's account of her movements on the night of the murder: after dropping her sister off in Lowell, she and Mike went back to her house, where they met up with Jane Thompson and Bobby Brown. About 9:30 p.m., Bob Ryan (Nancy's then-boyfriend) and Walter Shelley arrived in separate vehicles; Bob Ryan, Mike, and Walter left shortly thereafter in a search for beer. They came back an hour or so later, and Mike and Walter left again immediately after that. Nancy said she didn't know where they went, but when her boyfriend left at 11:00, she got in her car to go see Mary Ann Richard, and Mike and Walter pulled up right behind her as she was leaving. (This was precisely the time that Ed Brown had said he was with Mike and Walter when they were abducting John McCabe outside the K of C dance—halfway across town.) The three visited with Mary Ann until about 11:45, she said, then parted company when

Nancy went to see Carol Ann McFrederies. She said she didn't see them again that night.

"Thank you, Mrs. Ferreira," Eric said when they were finished with the line of questioning. "One more thing: do you remember ever going to the dances at the Knights of Columbus?"

"I think I did a couple of times, yes."

"On that particular night, the 26th of September, did you attend the dance at the K of C?"

"I did not." (This line of questioning was more strategy; Eric wanted to again reveal that Mike's 2008 grand jury testimony was simply the result of a faulty memory.)

"Did you ever give Michael Ferreira a ride home from a K of C dance?"

"Not that I remember, no."

"Mrs. Ferreira, I have no further questions. Thank you. Mr. O'Reilly may have some questions for you. Okay?" Eric gave her his most reassuring smile, then sat. Nancy smiled in return, but she looked a tad bit closer to vomiting.

"Thank you, Mr. Wilson," the judge said. "Cross-examination, Mr. O'Reilly?"

The A.D.A. stood with a scowl. "Miss Ferreira, which reports did you review prior to testifying?" He crossed to the podium, attempting (mostly unsuccessfully) to look menacing.

"I saw my report and Bobby Ryan's report."

"Your report from when?"

"From 1969."

"When did you review that report?"

"Last night."

"Did you memorize it?"

"No, I didn't."

O'Reilly kept at it. Though his objective seemed to be to throw Nancy off-balance (which he actually did, to a point), it looked to everyone else like he was simply picking on her. And, Eric was glad to notice, Nancy was standing her ground. O'Reilly asked why she had trouble remembering the events from that night, and Nancy replied by saying there'd been nothing to remember, other than giving John a ride from the novitiate to Main Street. When he tried to have her reveal info from Mike's 2003 interview with Sullivan and Wayne (of which she'd been an indirect participant), Nancy likewise had little memory of it. He then returned to the subject of Nancy's memory of the events of September 26, and began a rapid-fire succession of questions, seemingly in an attempt to catch her in a lie. But his volleys were fruitless; Nancy was telling the truth. Frustrated, O'Reilly ended that line of questioning.

"Did reviewing your '69 report help your memory, Miss Ferreira?"

"Yes. I don't have an independent memory of it otherwise."

"Well, when you say 'independently,' are you assuming that what's in a police report written forty years ago has to be the truth?"

Nancy stood firm. "I stated it back then, and it was the truth. I didn't lie then, and I'm not lying now."

Judge Ricciardone called for a lunch recess shortly after that exchange. When the jurors were back in place an hour later, O'Reilly was back at it.

"You were interviewed in 2011 by Detective Coughlin, correct?"

"Yes."

"And at that point your husband had already been charged, right?"

"I—" Nancy looked confused. "When they interviewed me in 2011?"

"When Detective Coughlin interviewed you, correct."

"No. The detective interviewed me in…February, I think? Mike wasn't charged till April." At the defense table, Eric was surprised at O'Reilly's confusion, minor though it may have been. Whether it was a lack of understanding or a lack of preparation, Eric knew he'd never allow a mix-up like that to occur.

Meanwhile, O'Reilly seemed to take no notice. "Was it then that you realized you'd provided an alibi for your husband?"

"I didn't provide an alibi for my husband."

O'Reilly seemed genuinely shocked. "Oh. You—you didn't?"

"Not an alibi. What I provided was the truth."

When O'Reilly sat down a moment later, no amount of his regal posturing could disguise the fact that Nancy Ferreira had held her ground. And when she left the stand, Nancy couldn't hide a nervous smile.

* * * *

Mike Richard's testimony was short, but interesting. And it was what Richard *didn't* say, rather than his statements, that held the most weight. Back in 1969, he'd told police that he'd seen Ferreira and Shelley outside his home in Tewksbury—they were there visiting his sister Mary Ann—at about 11:30 the night of the murder. When Eric had read this in a police report while he was sifting through all the discovery info, he'd contacted Mike Richard right away, and Richard had confirmed what was in the report; if what Richard had said back then was true, Eric had thought, that meant Shelley, Ferreira, and Brown couldn't have killed John (at least, not in the manner Ed Brown so richly described) because they were in Tewksbury at the precise time Ed had said they were in the vacant lot in Lowell. Mike Richard had agreed to testify, giving Mike Ferreira a rock-solid alibi.

But a few weeks before the trial, Richard had abruptly changed his tune, saying he suddenly had no memory of what he'd seen. Eric had thought this bizarre…and then he and Stan had learned that Richard had met with Detective Coughlin and Lieutenant Sullivan; that meeting had occurred either just prior to Richard recanting his story, or immediately afterward. During his questioning of Richard, Stan planned to reveal the fact that that meeting took place, in hopes that the jury would somehow put those pieces together.

When Richard took the stand, Stan first gathered some establishing info—Richard had lived on Boisvert Road in Tewksbury with his family (which included his sister Mary Ann), and Mary Ann had often babysat for the McCarthys, the Richards's next-door neighbor—then Stan got to the relevant stuff.

"Do you remember when you learned about the death of John McCabe?" Richard didn't respond right away; he just stared blankly at Stan. "Would it have been the weekend they found his body?"

"Uh…probably," Richard finally said. "I believe it was in the newspaper."

"Okay. And after that, did any police officers ever come and speak to you about John McCabe's death?"

"I think so."

"To the best of your memory, did you give a truthful response to those officers?"

"Yes. I mean, I would have, yes."

"And Mr. Richard, do you have a clear memory here today of what you told those officers?"

There was no pause. "No, I don't."

It was exactly the answer Stan expected. "Okay." He picked up a file off the podium and started toward the witness. "If I show you a document—may I approach, Your Honor?" Ricciardone said he could, so Stan went to Richard with a copy of the 1969 police report containing Richard's statement. "Please read the highlighted paragraph to yourself." Richard scanned the page, then returned the file to Stan.

"Now Mr. Richard," Stan said, "having had the opportunity to read that, does it refresh your memory as to what you told those officers that day?"

"I don't recall saying that, no."

So Stan enacted his Plan B. "Can we go to sidebar, Your Honor?" Ricciardone motioned the attorneys to the bench. The attorneys debated for several minutes over whether Richard's 1969 statement should be introduced to the jury; Stan said he could either read the relevant info to Richard and ask him if it was truthful, or mark the report as an official exhibit so the jurors could read it during deliberations. The problem with admitting the report as evidence, O'Reilly argued, was that its author—a Detective Hague, a Lowell PD officer who'd helped out on the McCabe case for a short time in 1970—was deceased. That meant no one could testify as to the report's truthfulness. And with Richard claiming he didn't recall making the statements, O'Reilly said, the report was unreliable. It was a slippery legal slope, Judge Ricciardone surmised, but he ruled in favor of the Commonwealth. Mike Richard's 1969 statement—and with it, Mike Ferreira's perfect alibi—was out.

With his last question, Stan tried his best to help the jury understand Richard's sudden lack of recall. "Back in November of 2012, sir, were you interviewed by Detective Linda Coughlin and Lieutenant Thomas Sullivan?"

"Yes."

"No further questions, Your Honor." O'Reilly had no questions, so Mike Richard slinked out of the courtroom, head down, averting his eyes from everyone as he went.

* * * *

Eric's decision to have Dr. Tom Andrew testify last was a brilliant one. The pathologist was slight of build, mostly bald, with glasses and a beard. He possessed a cheerful, inviting demeanor, and when he began speaking everyone in the room was instantly convinced that he was astonishingly sharp.

Eric first asked Dr. Andrew to "go quickly" through his educational background—but *quickly* was a near-impossibility. Dr. Andrew spent a couple of minutes listing his credentials: undergrad from the University of Dayton (Ohio) in '78; med school, University of Cincinnati, '82; Chief Resident of Pediatrics, Cincinnati Children's Medical Center, '85-'86; *another* residency at CCMC, this time in anatomical pathology, in 1991; two years' training in New York City in the field of forensic pathology; several years on staff at the medical examiner's office in Manhattan; Assistant Deputy Chief Medical Examiner of the Staten Island borough; and in 1997 he was named Chief Medical Examiner for the State of New Hampshire, a position he currently held. He had academic appointments at five different colleges in New Hampshire and Massachusetts, and served as a private consultant for White Mountain Forensic Consulting Services.

"And it is under the White Mountain umbrella, if you will, that I'm testifying here today," Dr. Andrew said. "Nothing that I say today represents any opinions by the Department of Justice or the Office of Chief Medical Examiner for the State of New Hampshire. I'm here as a privately retained consultant."

Eric asked him about the autopsies he'd performed—"over 4,700," Dr. Andrew said—and how many had been homicides ("roughly five hundred"). Then Eric got to the point of Dr. Andrew's testimony.

"Doctor, were you asked to review material with respect to <u>The Commonwealth vs. Michael Ferreira</u>?"

"Yes I was."

"Could you explain to the jury what you reviewed in preparation for your testimony?"

"Sure." Dr. Andrew turned to face the jurors as he spoke, something he often did during his testimony. He said he received a "discovery packet" of police reports, interview transcripts, lab studies of scene evidence, and the original 1969 autopsy report from Dr. Luongo, along with numerous photos depicting John McCabe's body as it was found at the scene and images taken by Dr. Karbowniczak at the autopsy. When Eric asked about the autopsy itself, Dr. Andrew said that in the report he'd read, John's body was in full rigor mortis, he was bound at the neck, ankles, and wrists, and ligature marks were present in all three places. There were no indications of any injuries—no gunshot wounds, stab wounds, lacerations, or contusions—

other than a minor abrasion on the shaft of John's penis ("which is neither here nor there in this case," he said).

"Thank you," Eric said. Then: "Dr. Andrew, are you familiar with the term 'hogtying'?"

"Yes sir." Eric had him give a brief explanation of hogtying—essentially, he said, ankles tied to the neck—then asked him if he'd made any determination of whether John McCabe had been tied in such a manner.

"Well, that was the fairly narrow focus of my inquiry. I was asked to look at this material and see if there was evidence consistent with hogtying, yes."

"And did you make a determination?"

"I did. In my opinion there is no evidence that he was hogtied, neither in the scene images nor in the forensic evidence that can be gleaned from the examination of the body."

"And what is that opinion based on?"

"Well, as I said, one basis of that is the scene images." He turned to the jurors again. And Dr. Andrew exhibited none of the sliminess or superiority often seen in expert witnesses; he was simply sharing information, and he seemed happy to do so. "Those images are of the body as it was first discovered. The boy is laying prone, and his legs are perfectly straight. One of the observing officers at the scene noted at that time—early morning, 9ish, 10ish—that the boy was in full rigor mortis. That was the case at autopsy as well. If he had been hogtied—remember the attitude that the body is in after hogtying?" He bent his hands to demonstrate. "The legs are bent up, and the neck and the ankles joined by rope. But here, if rigor mortis had set in and were complete, the legs would've been bent up. They would not have been arrow-straight like they were at the scene and at the autopsy." Satisfied with his explanation, he turned to Eric with a smile.

Eric then had his expert give a complete description of rigor mortis—the postmortem stiffening of the muscles—and how it affects the body. When he finished, Eric asked: "If he were hogtied at the time of death, what would you expect to find when he was discovered?"

"If he were hogtied and no change were made to the body, when he was discovered, his rigor mortis would've had his legs bent upwards even after the ligatures are loosened, because the muscles are rigidly fixed in that position."

Next Eric asked about the ligature mark on John's neck. Dr. Andrew explained that if a rope had been attached from his neck to his ankles, the mark would've had a downward slope because, logically, the struggle from John's ankles would've pulled the rope downward. "In the autopsy images, as well as in the description of the ligature mark in the autopsy report, the ligature mark was fairly uniform circumferentially around the neck. It was relatively straight. And that's not what I would've expected in someone struggling against having been hogtied while they were alive."

Eric's next line of questioning was about livor mortis. Dr. Andrew gave another detailed description—"in short," he said, "it's the postmortem settling of blood"—and noted that livor existed, as expected, on the front portion of John's body since he'd been found lying on his stomach. But interestingly, he noted, there was also fainter evidence of livor on the posterior portion. "So at some point, the body was in a position long enough to start to develop livor mortis on the rear portion, but then the body was repositioned such that the more exaggerated livor mortis was on the front of the body."

"Was it your determination that the body was moved?"

"Well, it's not so much a determination as an opinion. And my opinion is that the boy died and was in a supine position—lying face-up—long enough for early livor mortis to develop. He was then subsequently put in this prone position, out where he was discovered, for a much longer period of time."

Eric reminded the jury: "And again, your opinion on the hogtying?"

"There's no evidence for it. It's my opinion that this boy was never hogtied."

"Thank you, Doctor. No further questions, Your Honor."

"Thank you, sir," the judge said. "Mr. O'Reilly?"

"Yes, please," the A.D.A. said as he rose. "Good afternoon, Doctor."

"Good afternoon, sir."

"What percentage of your professional life is dedicated to your private consulting service?"

"I take, oh, I'd say twelve to fifteen cases a year as a private consultant. My agreement with the New Hampshire Department of Justice is that none of my private work should negatively impact my state work. So I limit it to about twelve to fifteen cases annually."

"And none in New Hampshire, obviously?"

"Oh no, sir. That would constitute a conflict of interest."

"So…you go around testifying in other states when you're not busy in your own, right?"

"Well…I don't 'go around testifying.' I'm engaged as a consultant. Sometimes I end up testifying, sometimes I don't have much of anything helpful to offer the person who has retained my services, so I end up not testifying. Sometimes I simply provide an opinion letter. I serve various functions."

"Okay." O'Reilly smiled. "And you're financially compensated for being here, correct?"

"Oh, quite handsomely." And with Dr. Andrew's simple, open declaration, O'Reilly's subconscious accusation—that Dr. Andrew was being paid to say what the defense wanted him to say—seemed to completely backfire. But as was his style, O'Reilly moved on without noticing. And to his credit, the prosecutor scored a minor point with his next line of questioning.

"I want to pose a question: You told us earlier that rigor mortis starts with the facial muscles, then slowly works its way down the torso, with the legs being the last muscles affected, correct, sir?"

"That's correct."

"Okay. The question is: hypothetically, if a person was hogtied, and he was in that position—legs bent at the knees—for an hour, two hours tops, then someone came along and manipulated the rope so that his feet were no longer tied to his neck…would you expect the rigor to have advanced to the legs after only an hour or two?" (O'Reilly's obvious inference: Walter and Mike had cut the hogtying rope when they returned to the vacant lot to find John dead.)

"No," Dr. Andrew answered. "Rigor wouldn't have advanced that far yet."

"So if the rope was manipulated after a short time, the legs could've fallen to the ground at that point?"

"Yes."

O'Reilly inquired about whether the livor on the back of John's body could've occurred after he was rolled over when the body was discovered, and Dr. Andrew said that was "very highly unlikely." Then, in his last line of questioning, O'Reilly asked about the angle of the ligature mark on John's neck.

"Now Doctor, you explained also that you'd expect to see a downward angle on the neck from the ligature if he had been hogtied, is that correct?"

"Yes sir."

"What if the rope was tied real tight?" O'Reilly put his fists together, then moved them apart to pantomime the pulling of a rope. "Would you expect movement on the rope then?"

"Even then." To the jury: "If a person is struggling for their very life, and their neck is tied to their ankles and they're moving their ankles, they're *going* to move that ligature in a downward fashion. They may not be able to move the knot, but the ligature would be pulled in a downward fashion, such that the ligature mark it leaves behind would be more deep in the front and have a downward slope."

O'Reilly seemed confused. "You mean a downward slope in this direction, correct?" With his finger, he delineated a line running from the top of the back of his neck to the bottom of the front of it.

"No." Dr. Andrew smiled. "That's an upward slope. Pathologists describe ligature marks going from anterior"—

he pointed to the front of his neck—"to the posterior." He pointed to the back of his neck now.

"Oh. Could you just say front and back, please?" A muted titter came from the gallery.

"Sorry. Front and back. The angle you described would have an upward slope from front to back. Someone who was hogtied would have a ligature mark with a *downward* slope from fr—"

"Thank you, Doctor. I get it now." O'Reilly asked a few more questions, but he'd lost the witness—and the jury, it seemed—entirely. He finally sat down...and even Eric was relieved.

* * * *

"The defendant has exercised his right to not testify in this case, Your Honor," Stan said. He, Eric, and Mike were standing at the defense table; upon Stan's announcement, a slight murmur arose amongst the spectators. "We'd also like to disclose that the defendant rests at this time."

"Thank you, Mr. Norkunas," Judge Ricciardone said, then turned to the jury. "We've reached a good point to quit for the day as far as you're concerned. So I'm going to let you go home now...and I can tell you we're in the homestretch. It's expected at some point tomorrow that you'll begin deliberations." He gave the jurors the usual instructions not to discuss the case, then released them for the evening.

After a bit of judicial discussion, during which Judge Ricciardone had Mike confirm that it was his decision not to testify, court was adjourned. As Eric and Stan were walking to the car, they spied Dr. Andrew standing next to his own vehicle, which was parked a few feet from Eric's.

"Great work in there," Eric said when they reached him. They shook hands.

"Thanks," the pathologist said. "But...there at the end, with the D.A. I didn't—I hope I didn't make him look bad. That was never my intention."

"Haha," Stan said. "Don't worry. *You* didn't do anything." The men got in their respective cars and went home.

EX PARTE: Trial Day 6 → Day 7

I remember thinking that Dr. Andrew's testimony had gone even better than I'd hoped. Though he wasn't able to definitively prove it, I think his opinion that John hadn't been hogtied was going to carry a lot of weight with the jury. If nothing else, it further damaged the credibility of Ed Brown's story. And I was proud of Nancy Ferreira, too. She'd held her own against O'Reilly, and then some. Overall, I thought we'd presented the case we set out to present.

The next day, O'Reilly and I would give our closing arguments. The way I normally put together my closings—or the framework of them, anyway—is that I start a running list on a legal pad when I begin preparing for a trial, and I jot down ideas as I'm going through everything. (I usually do the same with my openings too.) And of course, openings and closings are often very similar. One usually dictates the other. To explain the relationship between the two, I'll use the analogy of a jigsaw puzzle: during my opening, I reveal what the puzzle pieces are. Then during witness testimony (both my cross-examination of prosecution witnesses and direct examination of my own), I try and put the puzzle pieces together. Hopefully, my closing will reveal the completed puzzle.

For Ferreira, I wanted to reveal that after the original investigation went cold, nothing new happened for about thirty years, then Jack Ward crawled out of the woodwork with his version of what he believed happened. And even though they had Ward's allegations, Sullivan and Wayne didn't do anything with them—possibly because they thought Ward's story was total BS. When Linda Coughlin took up the investigation, she ran with Ward's story. And I wanted to go point by point in my closing and show that the evidence just didn't match up. According to Dr. Andrew, there was no hogtying. According to Marla Shiner, jealousy couldn't have been the motive. And according to...time, I guess, *The French Connection* element was false because the movie hadn't even been released yet when Jack Ward said he (and the defendant) saw it—*and* there's no hogtying in the movie in the first place. Put together, those factors made Ed Brown's story a complete materialization. So my theme for the closing was that the McCabe investigation was a case not of fact-finding, but of fact-*feeding.*

I never write and memorize my closings; I think the message comes across better if I speak more extemporaneously. I use bullet points, like **Hogtying, *Jack Ward,* etcetera, but that's it. Even so, I had a pretty good idea of what I would say in the beginning of my closing for this trial. But something happened just before court convened the next day that made me change the beginning entirely.

7. Thursday, January 24: Ferreira Trial, Day Seven

Eric, Stan, and Mike were already seated at the defense table when the prosecution team arrived, O'Reilly swaggering through the gallery in the lead. But instead of taking a seat with Willis and Mulcahy, O'Reilly walked over to the court clerk's table, upon which was the stack of evidence photos. He sifted through the photos until he found the one he wanted, placed it on top of the stack, then went to his chair. Eric noticed what O'Reilly had just done, and from his vantage point a few feet away he could see the photo O'Reilly was looking for: John McCabe's smiling face. His eighth-grade yearbook photo. *He must be planning to use that in his closing, maybe to gain sympathy from the jury,* Eric thought. That gave him an idea.

Judge Ricciardone took the bench, the parties cleared up a few logistical matters, then the jury was seated—for the last time.

"All set? Okay," the judge said to the jurors. "Ladies and gentlemen, under our system of justice, the Commonwealth has the burden of proof, so they get to argue to you last and the defendant goes first. So: Mr. Wilson?"

"Thank you, Your Honor." Eric went to the podium, placed his list of bullet points there, then addressed the sixteen jurors. He'd originally planned to begin with something different, but after noticing what O'Reilly had done with John McCabe's photo, Eric decided to totally wing it at first. "Good morning. On September 27, a Saturday morning in 1969, at about 9:40 a.m., two boys, Dennis Cole, age seven, and Robert Bastine, age nine, were going down to that pond that you've heard about, and that you saw when we visited the crime scene. They were going down there to look for frogs because they knew frogs were most active after it rained. Instead, they discovered"—he stepped over to the clerk's table and grabbed John's yearbook photo, then held it up—"the body of this boy: John Joseph McCabe. Fifteen years, six months, and two weeks old. And there is no question that the death of John McCabe is a tragedy. No one can imagine the sorrow the McCabe family has felt all these years." He went and put the photo back on top of the stack (where it would remain unused by O'Reilly), then returned to stand directly in front of the middle-aged, bespectacled male juror in the front row.

"Over the next forty years, there was an investigation. It was very heavy for the first year, year and a half, but then literally decades went by and nothing happened…and then Linda Coughlin happened. From the beginning of her investigation, she excluded all other suspects except Walter Shelley and Michael Ferreira. She fabricated reasons to arrest them for murder. And in Ed Brown, she found the perfect way to make that happen."

Eric shifted his focus and continued. He explained that multiple detectives had testified that they often reviewed their notes and previous reports to refresh their memory about an old case; when Mike Ferreira was interviewed in 2003 and 2008, Eric said, he wasn't allowed to see his original 1969 statement, so his accounts differed because he just couldn't remember what happened. Then Eric named each witness individually, and added a bit of relevant info for each.

Detective St. Peter, for example, acknowledged that John's body was dry, even though the field was damp, Eric said. "He also told me, 'You're on the wrong team.' Remember that? To me, this trial isn't about whose team you're on—it's about justice." And Jack Ward, Eric continued, tried to play hero by giving police his version of what happened—and his story was simply inaccurate.

And then: "Ed Brown. Where do we even begin in our evaluation of him? His own *mother* even told him his story was wrong." Between the grand jury, Mike's transfer hearing, and Ed's multiple interrogations, Eric reminded the jury, Ed Brown told eight different stories about what happened on the night of September 26, 1969. "Whether he was involved in the murder or not, Ed figured he was going down for it," Eric said. The jurors were totally captivated by Eric's narration now. "First he finds out he'll get a great plea deal. Then he was fed information by Linda Coughlin and Mr. O'Reilly. And it was *incorrect* information. Hogtying? Wrong. Jealousy over Marla? Wrong again. *The French Connection*? We know that's wrong, because the movie hadn't even come out yet when Jack Ward said he saw it." Ed Brown adopted Detective Coughlin's beliefs, Eric said, then Ed told the jurors what Coughlin wanted them to hear.

Detective Coughlin herself, Eric continued, ignored suspects like Richard Santos ("whom she didn't even *know* about until a month or two before this trial," he said), Robert Morley, and the caller to the priests, and focused on Shelley and Ferreira. Coughlin used Jack Ward's beliefs to supply information to Ed Brown, Eric explained, and "that got her the arrests she so badly wanted."

Lieutenant Sullivan, even though he'd never seen evidence that John was hogtied, "was fed the idea of hogtying right there in front of the grand jury." Nancy

Ferreira said in 1969—a decade before she married Mike Ferreira—that Mike was with her at the time the murder was being committed. ("How could Nancy have 'provided an alibi for her husband' when Mike wouldn't be her husband for another ten years?") And Dr. Andrew, Eric said, was a definitive pathological expert who let his testimony speak for itself. "He told you there was no hogtying. He told you John McCabe spent some time after death—and before the body was discovered—lying on his back, meaning the body was moved soon after John died. That evidence alone makes Ed Brown's story simply false."

Eric neared the end now, with every juror hanging on his words. "This was not a fact-finding case…this was a fact-*feeding* case. And the information fed wasn't factual—it was speculation from Jack Ward. He had a 'bingo' moment about jealousy over Marla Shiner, and he goes to the police on that. And it wasn't for another decade that Linda Coughlin used that information to arrest Mike Ferreira—to arrest him for something the evidence just doesn't support.

"I told you in my opening that perhaps the most critical question you may have is: why is Ed Brown not telling you the truth? Well, desperate people will do desperate things. But what he's told you does not match anything else you've heard in this case. The evidence tells you that Edward Allen Brown's story doesn't make any sense.

"Mr. O'Reilly gets to go last. And he'll get up here and tell you that the death of John McCabe was a tragedy. There's no question this was indeed a tragedy. But when you deliberate, ask yourselves how John McCabe *really* died. And as we've shown you during this trial, it just wasn't in the manner the Commonwealth claims.

"On behalf of Michael Ferreira, Stanley and I thank you for your time and your consideration." Eric paused for a moment to look the jurors over one last time, then took his seat.

"Mr. O'Reilly?"

The A.D.A. stood, briefly glared at Eric (probably for one-upping him with the photo, Eric guessed), then walked to the podium, where he remained for the entirety of his closing.

"A fifteen-year-old boy, John McCabe, lying on his stomach in the middle of a deserted field. His eyes have tape on them so he can't see. His mouth is covered with tape so he can't yell. His feet are tied. His hands are tied behind his back. There's a rope around his neck, tied to his feet. And every attempt to move brings unconsciousness a little closer, death a little closer. What's he thinking? The last words he hears: 'That will teach you to not mess with Marla.' The last words. He may hear the sound of the car drive away before he loses consciousness…or maybe he's already dead.

"*That's* what this case is about. Who put John McCabe there? *Why* did they put him there? To teach him a lesson? They came back an hour or so later. Why did they come back? To untie him, of course. His lesson was learned by then. So Ferreira and Shelley go to him and undo the rope from his neck to his feet. And as Dr. Andrew—the defense's own medical expert—testified, his legs would've fallen to the ground. Then as they're driving away, Michael Ferreira says, 'If anyone talks, I'll kill them.' He didn't think that forty years later, Ed Brown would finally come forward."

O'Reilly listed numerous factors that pointed to Mike Ferreira's guilt—but each factor had been seemingly discredited by Eric and Stan. He mentioned Mike's varied accounts of September 26: Walter Shelley's jealousy over Marla; the "feeding" of Ed Brown ("He was shown the photo of John McCabe at the scene. In the photo, John's legs are on the ground. If that's how he figured out how John was killed, how would he have known he was hogtied?"). And like Eric had just done, O'Reilly named each witness and rattled off more factors about how they'd helped prove the Commonwealth's case…but again, O'Reilly seemed not to notice that every element seemed to have been disproved by the defense. The jurors were engaged, but lacked much interest as O'Reilly went on. Eric noticed multiple jurors checking their watches as the prosecutor talked…then talked some more.

At last, O'Reilly began winding down. "Ladies and gentlemen, I could go on. Because there is so much to talk about concerning this case. But I will say this: people are human. They make stupid damn mistakes when they're teenagers. They perform intentional acts, not thinking of the consequences. But this act, Michael Ferreira did do. He, along with Walter Shelley and Ed Brown, *did* kill John McCabe. They put a rope around his neck and tied it so tight he couldn't breathe. What was John McCabe thinking as he lost consciousness, and as those three boys were driving away? My guess is, he was wishing they would be more responsible. And that's putting it lightly.

"Well, ladies and gentlemen, you are now responsible for your decision. Ed Brown has taken responsibility for what he did. And I ask you to hold Michael Ferreira responsible for his actions too. Thank you." O'Reilly sauntered over and sat down.

Before the jurors retired to their holding room to begin their deliberations, Judge Ricciardone spent close to an hour issuing his formal jury instructions. A routine practice in jury trials, the instructions detailed the types of charges the jury could consider, the different forms of evidence the jurors would have at their disposal (exhibits and scene photos, for example), and how to interpret witness testimony.

First the judge explained that since Mike Ferreira had entered a plea of not guilty, the jury had to unanimously determine that the Commonwealth had proved beyond a reasonable doubt that Mike had committed the crime. If they came to an agreement of guilt, Ricciardone continued, the jurors could consider one of three charges: first-degree murder with extreme atrocity or cruelty (a premeditated act), second degree murder (*not* planned, but the result of a bodily assault), or felony second degree murder (when a murder is committed, whether intentional or not, during the commission of a felony). Manslaughter was not included as a possible charge because in Massachusetts, its statute of limitations was twenty years. Judge Ricciardone went to great lengths to describe the details of each of the three charges; the jurors, he informed them, would have a written copy of the instructions to use during deliberations.

When he finished: "Okay. So, ladies and gentlemen, for a week and a half now I've been saying to you don't start your deliberations. But now is the time for you to begin. Thank you, and good luck." With that, the jurors filed out of the courtroom one by one, and walked down the hall to the jury room. The time was 1:20 p.m.

"Counsel, if I may," the judge said, motioning for both teams of attorneys to approach the bench. Once they were before him, he said, "I thought both sides here were represented very professionally and very ably, and I want to congratulate you both. No matter how it turns out, I'm always reminded of what a pleasure and an honor it is to be a judge in such a case. Thank you for that." He stood. "So…I'll see you back in here for the verdict." The judge left through the same door the jurors had used. The five battle-weary attorneys shook hands all around, then went their separate ways.

Obviously, only the jurors themselves know what transpired in the jury room during deliberations. But according to one juror who was interviewed by *48 Hours* prior to the October 2014 airing of "The Pact," the episode of the show about the John McCabe case, most of the jurors favored one particular verdict, seemingly from the beginning. At about 3:00 p.m., the juror said in the interview, the group took a vote, and the results were 10-2. When Judge Ricciardone reconvened everyone at 4:15, he said that one juror had expressed to a court officer that, given a bit more time that day, the jurors might be able to reach a consensus. "I'm hesitant to give a finite time period for today," Ricciardone said, "because that might be giving the impression that you have to move things along in a certain direction. So I'm suspending your deliberations for today, and we'll continue in the morning." The judge adjourned for the evening, and everybody went home.

For Eric, Mike Ferreira, and people across the nation monitoring the case, the verdict would have to wait.

EX PARTE: The Waiting Game

Believe me when I tell you: there are no words to describe the emotions a trial attorney goes through while he or she is waiting around the courtroom for a verdict. (And the notoriety of this case made it that much worse.) You're nervous, you're anxious, you're wondering if you covered everything…and waiting on the Ferreira verdict, I was nearly jumping out of my skin. The one thing that kept my sanity was this: Oftentimes, while the opposing attorney is giving his or her closing argument, I'll get a mental "gut punch" when he or she talks about an aspect of the case I feel I didn't cover well. But when O'Reilly gave his closing, that never happened. Every aspect O'Reilly discussed I felt like we'd covered to the best of our ability. In short, we'd done the very best we could.

When Judge Ricciardone told us at the end of the day that one juror had asked for a little more time because they were close to a verdict, I took it as both a great and a terrible sign. In my experience, a quick verdict more often than not means an acquittal. (But in rare instances, it can also mean the jury found the defendant guilty.) Regardless, a quick verdict means it was one-sided, and that the jurors didn't have to discuss it much before coming to a unanimous decision.

I remember on the ride home that night, Stan, as an eternal optimist, was convinced we'd get the acquittal. I tend to be more pessimistic, though, and I told him I just knew those jurors thought Mike was guilty from the get-go. I got very little sleep that night, and I remember being at the gym when it opened at five the next morning so I could work off some of my nervous energy.

Stan and I arrived at the courthouse in Woburn at about 8:30, and on the way in we saw Mike and Nancy Ferreira. When the jury had begun their deliberations, I'd told Mike what to expect when the verdict was read: for the three possible charges—murder one, murder two, and felony murder two—the court would ask for the jury's verdict on each separate charge. (I'd never tried a murder case in Massachusetts, but that's what happened in New Hampshire murder trials, so I figured it would be no different in the Commonwealth.) Mike understood this, and he said he was prepared for whatever the jury decided.

Before we headed into court that morning, Nancy Ferreira pulled me aside. She hugged me so tight and for so long, I thought she'd never let go. She looked at me, tears in her eyes, and told me: "No matter what happens, we're happy with the job you and Stan have done. We don't think it could've gone any better."

Then the four of us headed into the courtroom to learn Mike Ferreira's fate.

8. Friday, January 25: Ferreira Trial, Day Eight—The Verdict

The gallery was nearly full as Eric, Stan, Mike, and Nancy entered the courtroom. Behind both the prosecution and defense tables, additional extended family members had joined the McCabe and Ferreira clans. (Bill McCabe was absent, Eric noticed, but this didn't surprise him; Bill's health, Eric knew, had been failing rapidly as the trial wore on.) The rest of the spectators were either family friends, members of the press corps, or simply curious onlookers thirsty for some drama. Though the jury could conceivably deliberate for as long as they needed to, somehow everyone knew that today would be the day.

Once Judge Ricciardone took the bench, the jurors were brought in, only to exit again a mere two minutes later to continue their deliberations. Ricciardone instructed both parties to stay close to the courtroom, and had Eric and O'Reilly leave their cell phone numbers with the court clerk so they could be contacted if/when the jury reached its verdict.

The prosecution and defense teams, family members, friends, and spectators all scattered throughout the immediate area to wait. The time was 9:13 a.m.

Eric and Stan went with Mike, Nancy, and Mike's niece Danielle to a nearby café (where Eric got a large decaf—he had plenty of energy as it was). During the five-minute walk there, Eric reminded Mike of what to expect when the jury came out to announce its verdict: the clerk would ask the foreperson (a young, pleasant-looking lady) for the verdict on each of the three charges. Then, depending on the verdicts, Mike would be formally discharged by the judge…or taken into custody by the bailiffs.

"How you holding up?" Eric asked Mike as they neared the café.

"Oh, I'm okay, I guess. Ya know, for better or worse…I'll accept whatever they decide." But like his wife during her testimony, Mike looked slightly sick to his stomach.

Eric patted him on the back, then they went in. They sat at a table and attempted small talk, but no one was in the mood. Eric himself wore out the hardwood of the café floor with his pacing. And not a minute went by without one of the five glancing at his or her watch—or at Eric's cell phone, which sat like a talisman at the center of the table.

At 10:40, the phone rang.

Everyone froze. Eric snatched it off the table and read the Caller ID—*Unknown Caller*—then pushed the Phone icon on its face. "Eric Wilson." He listened for a moment. "Okay. We'll be right there." He looked up at the other four. "The jury's ready."

It took nearly thirty minutes to gather everyone—the prosecution and defense teams, the families, and the press. Bill McCabe was not with the other members of the McCabe tribe; Eric learned later that Bill couldn't bring himself to hear the verdict first-hand, and had camped out in the prosecution's anteroom just down the hall. (Evelyn had promised to come bring him the news the first chance she had.) Judge Ricciardone had ordered that several extra court officers should be on hand amongst the spectators in case anyone reacted inappropriately to the verdict. (For his part, Eric had told every one of Mike's supporters that, no matter the verdict, they should *remain quiet* after it was read to show respect for the judicial process.) As Judge Ricciardone entered, Eric glanced over his shoulder at the gallery. Nearly every seat was occupied.

Ricciardone rapped his gavel, then ordered the jurors in. One by one, they walked stolidly to their seats. The last juror to enter was the stocky, bespectacled man to whom Eric had paid close attention during the trial; it seemed to Eric that he hadn't missed a thing. And now, though his face was expressionless, Eric noticed the man staring at him as he sat down.

"Good morning, Your Honor," the court clerk was saying. "May I proceed?"

"Yes, please."

The clerk turned to the jury. "Madam forelady, has your jury agreed upon its verdict?"

The foreperson stood. "Yes."

"May I have the verdict slip please?" A bailiff delivered the sheet of paper to the clerk. She glanced at it, her face blank, then handed it to Judge Ricciardone, who did the same. Meanwhile, Eric noticed that the bespectacled juror's eyes were still locked on him; his face, as were the faces of the other jurors, was unreadable.

"Madam forelady," the clerk said, "on Indictment 2011-793, Count 1 charging this defendant, Michael Ferreira, with murder in the first degree, what say you to this indictment, ma'am: Is the defendant guilty or not guilty?"

"Not guilty."

An intense but silent reaction from the gallery, almost as if someone had pushed the Mute button on the scene in the courtroom. Eric turned and glanced at Mike Ferreira, who looked simply overwhelmed. *One down,* Eric thought as he turned his attention back to the clerk. *Now let's see about the other two—*

But the clerk had put the verdict slip on her table. "The jurors, upon their oath, do find Michael Ferreira not guilty," she said. Stan, a huge smile on his face, was reaching around Eric to pat Mike on the back. "Wait," Eric whispered to Stan. "Aren't they gonna read the verdict for each ch—"

"No, that's it," Stan whispered back in a near-laugh. "One verdict across the board. Not guilty!" Now he patted Eric's shoulder several times.

"Oh," Eric said. It took a moment to sink in. "Oh!" To Mike, in a whisper: "That's it! Just the one verdict. Not guilty!" Eric hugged his client tightly.

The judge was thanking the jurors for their service. Just before they exited the courtroom, Eric caught the eye of the bespectacled juror; the man just raised his eyebrows, pursed his lips, and shrugged one shoulder. Eric couldn't quite read the expression's intent, but…it didn't matter.

Once the jurors were gone, the judge addressed the clerk. "Okay. You may discharge Mr. Ferreira."

"Michael Ferreira," the clerk said, "on Indictment 2011-793, Count 1 you are discharged and dismissed of this indictment." Hugs all around. As Eric hugged Nancy, he saw over his shoulder that the row behind the prosecution table where the McCabe family had sat was now empty.

"Thank you very much," the judge said and left the bench. And the trial was over.

Outside the courtroom, Nancy, Danielle, and others in the Ferreira tribe let out victory whoops. Eric and Mike gathered with numerous reporters, who, as Eric had expected, had swarmed them as soon as they exited the room.

"We are, of course, extremely pleased with the jury's verdict," Eric said as the cameras rolled. "But their verdict doesn't change the fact that John McCabe's death was a tragedy. We hope that whoever is responsible for this crime will be brought to justice...our hearts go out to the McCabe family, and our prayers and blessings go out to them as well. Thank you." The reporters shouted questions, but Eric and Mike were gone.

The entire Ferreira faction had a celebratory pizza party at a restaurant in Tewksbury, so Eric and Stan stopped off for a slice, then Eric drove by his office back in Nashua to return a few overdue phone calls and e-mails. He then went home to relax—for the first time in months—and had dinner with his family. He and his wife retired to the living room, and Eric laid on the floor in front of the fireplace, where he fell asleep within seconds.

He awoke to a darkened room. As he walked through the kitchen to go upstairs, the digital clock on the microwave told him it was nearly 3:00 a.m. He peeked in on his kids, who were sleeping soundly, then crawled in bed next to his wife. He slept until almost noon.

EX PARTE: Putting This Case to Bed

We did it.

Regardless of how you may feel about what transpired here, I firmly believe that I assisted in justice. Some people might not call it that. Because Mike Ferreira was acquitted of murder—the most serious crime that exists in our society—some people (like the McCabe family, the prosecution, and Detective Coughlin, I'm sure) probably feel like justice wasn't served. But like I said in my closing argument, the government has to convince twelve citizens that they're right. If they can't do that—in this case, because of fed and fabricated testimony—then to me, that's justice. The success of the Commonwealth's case hinged on the credibility of Ed Brown; the jury just didn't believe him. (The juror interviewed for *48 Hours* said that very thing.) My job was to show that what the Commonwealth was trying to prove was unprovable, and I did my job to the best of my ability.

Listen: in a case like this, no one is truly happy. Are Mike and Nancy Ferreira happy? No. They're relieved, sure, but…for two years, Mike was the subject of national media attention. TV crews would show up at their house looking for interviews. They were shunned by their community, and Mike was completely stigmatized for being charged with murder. Are they happy about that? My guess is no.

The impetus for this trial was John McCabe's death in 1969. Who could possibly be happy about that? I have an eleven-year-old son. If something happened to him, my whole world would collapse. For the McCabe family— most of all, Bill, may he rest in peace—to deal with that kind of anguish for forty years, then to lose the trial? I can't imagine. Though it may sound cliché for me, a defense attorney, to say this, my heart really goes out to them.

There's no question that my work on this case solidified a principle that I've always tried to adhere to: that if everybody does his or her job, and does it *correctly*, then justice will be served. (Sorry if I sound like Bill Belichick, but it's true.) If they don't, the scales of justice might be tipped in one direction. I don't want to throw stones here, but if Detective Coughlin hadn't conducted those interviews like she did, if she hadn't spoon-fed Ed Brown all that information, if she'd recorded those interviews, then this book probably wouldn't exist.

This trial also reminded me that tenacity, perseverance, and preparedness are immeasurably valuable in my job. When I became an attorney, I took an oath, just as trial witnesses take one, to defend the Constitution and assist in justice. And in this trial I did everything I could to honor that oath. It's what I'll do in every case I'll ever have.

9. Tuesday, January 29

Just four days after the Ferreira verdict, Bill McCabe died.

His passing can be attributed to a broken heart, in both the literal and figurative sense. According to a report from WCVB, a Boston TV station, Bill had suffered two heart attacks in two days during the trial and died in a hospital in Lowell the following Tuesday. In one of her numerous *48 Hours* interviews, Evelyn McCabe said that her husband died from "stress—the stress of the trial."

Bill was laid to rest next to John—for whose killer Bill had relentlessly searched for forty-three years—in a plot at the Tewksbury Cemetery. As Bill lay in his hospital bed, Evelyn said during the *48 Hours* episode, she told him, "I'll pick up and take over for you."

In the coming months, the McCabe family's desire to see someone pay for John's murder was fulfilled, if only in part. That September, Walter Shelley went on trial for the murder, and *this* trial—both in litigation and results—would be markedly different.

Epilogue

On September 13, 2013—Friday the 13th—a Middlesex Superior Court jury found Walter Shelley guilty of John McCabe's murder.

The trial, which took place in a Lowell courthouse, included the testimony of many of the same witnesses—medical experts Dr. Kimberly Springer and Dr. Thomas Andrew, Detective Coughlin, and Marla Shiner, among others—and once again, Ed Brown was the Commonwealth's star witness. A.D.A. Tom O'Reilly reprised his role as lead prosecutor, and Shelley was represented by Stephen Neyman, a criminal defense attorney from Boston. Superior Court Judge Janet Kenton-Walker presided over the week-long trial.

One difference between the Ferreira and Shelley trials was that for <u>MA vs. Shelley</u>, the Commonwealth apparently learned from the mistakes it made during <u>MA vs. Ferreira</u>. This time, O'Reilly's main question to the jury was: Why would Ed Brown lie? In his closing argument, O'Reilly asked, "Why would a sixty-one-year-old man—thirty-eight years in the Air Force—confess, thinking that once he did he would go to jail?" In the months between the two trials, the Commonwealth seemed to "clean up" Ed Brown's testimony, so to speak, tweaking his account of the events to make it more believable. And Ed was apparently much more prepared for Neyman's cross-examination (which consisted of many near-duplicate questions as those from Eric Wilson during the Ferreira trial).

Another glaring departure of the Shelley trial from Ferreira's is that defense attorney Neyman seemed to prepare for it with nowhere near the same zeal as did Eric Wilson. Neyman's cross-examination of witnesses was, on average, much shorter than Eric's, and his lines of questioning lacked the depth and substance. And unfortunately for the defense, Neyman presented Dr. Andrew's medical evidence without Dr. Andrew's actual presence. In a stipulation agreement similar to that of Robert Ryan during the Ferreira trial, Neyman read the questions (which, again, mirrored those from Eric Wilson during MA vs. Ferreira), and another member of the defense team read Dr. Andrew's answers from the witness stand. And without Dr. Andrew's compelling physical presence, his testimony must've held much less value to the jury.

On February 20, 2014, Judge Kenton-Walker sentenced Shelley to life in prison. Under Massachusetts law, anyone who is seventeen or younger at the time of the commission of a murder cannot be sentenced to life without the possibility of parole; because Shelley was seventeen in 1969, he will be eligible for parole in 2029.

At the sentencing, a family friend read an impact statement, written by the surviving McCabe family members, to a packed courtroom. "Our dad, Bill McCabe, was a great father, but he always felt like he wasn't because John was murdered," the McCabes said in the statement. "When we think of John, we think of peace…and with this guilty verdict, we are hopeful that somewhere, John and Dad are enjoying some sort of peace too."

Also in February 2014, the McCabes filed a $10 million wrongful death lawsuit in civil court against Shelley, Ferreira, and Brown. As of this writing, the civil case is still pending.

* * * *

After Shelley's conviction, the John McCabe murder case was officially closed—by the authorities, at least. But even now—nearly half a century later, as of this writing—questions still remain. And the most burning one is this: was Ed Brown telling the truth? Was he being honest, as A.D.A. O'Reilly repeatedly claimed in the Walter Shelley trial? Or, as Eric Wilson fought so hard to prove, was Ed so afraid of going to jail that he adopted Detective Coughlin's theories, even though they were false? And the validity (or lack thereof) of Ed's story brings about an unfortunate paradox: If it's true, then Mike Ferreira got away with murder. If it's false, then Walter Shelley sits in prison as an innocent man. And if only *parts* of it are true…well, the possibilities there are too numerous to name.

At the beginning of this book, the reader was asked: Who *really* killed John McCabe? And now, at the end, it seems that question may never be answered. Perhaps more questions are in order: Did Shelley, Ferreira, and Brown commit the murder? Or was it only one (or some combination of two) of them? Was it another suspect entirely, like Richard Santos, Robert Morley, or the caller to the priests? (And just who *was* the caller to the priests, anyway? One of the named suspects, or someone else entirely?) Along those same lines, could John's killer have been a person no one ever knew about?

What *is* known is this: six feet below the ground in a plot at Tewksbury Cemetery, John McCabe's bones are slowly turning to dust. And even after his body has become part of the soil, the true identity of his killer may never be known.

Acknowledgments

Eric Wilson wishes to thank:

My wife Kristin—thank you for listening to me and for all you do.

John Turner—thank you for your tremendous ability to create this story.

Stan, Tim, and Cara…thanks!

John Turner wishes to thank:

My beautiful wife Kari, for listening to my boring explanations of trial testimony, offering advice on story lines, and supporting me every step of the way. I love you, sweetness!

My dearly departed mother Jane, for cultivating my love of language. I miss you, Mama.

Cara Hatch and the staff at Wilson, Bush, Durkin & Keefe Law Offices, for scheduling interviews, copying hundreds of files, and for their unflinching assistance and grace. This book wouldn't exist without you!

Peter Thomas, narrator of *Forensic Files*, for being the voice in my head when I struggled to find the right narration.

The inimitable Eric Wilson, for your openness, honesty, and understanding. It's your astonishing skill as an attorney that made this book possible in the first place.

Author Bio

Eric Wilson was born and raised in Nashua, New Hampshire. After first serving in the United States Marine Corps, Eric began his legal career in 1992 as a trial associate working for a Nashua law firm. He focused and excelled in his new career as a criminal defense and litigation attorney. During that time he tried many cases for clients being charged with an array of crimes from murder, negligent homicide to other major felony matters. In 1998, he became partner in his own law firm, Wilson, Bush, Durkin & Keefe. Through the years, Eric has represented thousands of clients after they have been arrested for a variety of offenses. He has also successfully obtained precedent-setting decisions in the New Hampshire Supreme Court. Eric is a prominent attorney in the area and due to his expertise he has lectured other attorneys on aspects of criminal defense litigation.

When he is not busy with work, Eric enjoys spending time with his wife and two children. He is also an avid New England sports fan, enjoys coaching baseball, and relaxing at the beach.